GRACE UNDER FIRE

GRACE UNDER FIRE

THE STATE
OF OUR SWEET
AND SAVAGE GAME

LAWRENCE SCANLAN

PENGUIN
CANADA

PENGUIN CANADA

Published by the Penguin Group

Penguin Books, a division of Pearson Canada, 10 Alcorn Avenue, Toronto, Ontario,
Canada M4V 3B2
Penguin Books Ltd, 80 Strand, London WC2R 0RL, England
Penguin Putnam Inc., 375 Hudson Street, New York, New York 10014, U.S.A.
Penguin Books Australia Ltd, 250 Camberwell Road, Camberwell, Victoria 3124,
Australia
Penguin Books India (P) Ltd, 11, Community Centre, Panchsheel Park,
New Delhi – 110 017, India
Penguin Books (NZ) Ltd, cnr Rosedale and Airborne Roads, Albany,
Auckland 1310, New Zealand
Penguin Books (South Africa) (Pty) Ltd, 24 Sturdee Avenue, Rosebank 2196,
South Africa

Penguin Books Ltd, Registered Offices: 80 Strand, London WC2R 0RL, England

First published 2002

1 2 3 4 5 6 7 8 9 10

Printed and bound in Canada on acid free paper ∞

NATIONAL LIBRARY OF CANADA CATALOGUING IN PUBLICATION DATA

Scanlan, Lawrence
Grace under fire : the state of our sweet and savage game / Lawrence Scanlan.

ISBN 0-14-301343-2

1. Hockey. 2. Hockey—Canada. I. Title.

GV847.S32 2002   796.962   C2002-901940-0

Visit Penguin Books' website at **www.penguin.ca**

For Bill Fitsell

CONTENTS

INTRODUCTION

TWO IMAGES TO SET THE TABLE.

One is a tinted photograph of Lionel Conacher taken in the 1930s after a game. His skate blades are still thickly white with ice; he has doffed his sweater to reveal his soggy, long underwear—the left suspender bloodstained, it appears—and he looks utterly spent as he smiles gamely into the camera. Conacher's nose is undeniably, almost comically, broken. You can see the deep horizontal crease in the bridge where the stick did its work, leaving the end of the nose unduly bulbous. A clown's nose, with a grin to go with it. The hockey player happy in his role as warrior.

The second image, more familiar and more contemporary, is a colour shot of Bobby Clarke in his old Philadelphia Flyers uniform— the "C" for "captain" near his heart. There is a hole in his mouth where his front teeth should be, yet Clarke's smile is exuberantly wide, even gleeful. What's understood is that hockey made that hole: The puck or fist, elbow or stick that performed the rude extraction is not to be dwelt upon, for look how the boy-man smiles.

I read into both images a pure joy, an appetite for the game so powerful that a cracked beak or a few teeth scattered on the ice like Chiclets, hardly warrant a pause in the action. In *Grace Under Fire*, I wanted to investigate two things: the reasons for those smiles, and the violence that can make a hockey player's smile so distinctive. The yin and yang of hockey.

I would ask the hard questions but also the obvious questions, hoping to park my own long-held personal opinions, striving for an open mind. The history of the game, I felt sure, contained at least some of the answers to my essential questions: Why do hockey players sometimes fight and resort to violence? Why is fighting condoned as part of this game and virtually no other? Hockey is the only team sport in the world (other than lacrosse, another Canadian invention) that blesses war. And why, on the other hand, does passion for the game in this country run so deep? Why do I still dream hockey? Why does the game sustain me, grip me, reward me like no other?

I went to where I thought the answers might lie. I spent time with former enforcers—including "Red" Horner, a hard-rock Leafs defenceman in the '30s who, at ninety-three, is among the oldest living players of his era, and Marty McSorley, a latter-day tough guy whose career ended in court with his infamous hit on Donald Brashear. I pored over books and articles trying to understand the thinking of current and former NHL players. I watched films and videos. With the help of a radio documentary, I went back in time to hockey's first homicide, in 1905, and then examined the many cases since that have landed hockey players in court. I travelled to Minnesota to watch women contest the world championship, wondering if elite female players had answers to hockey's old conundrum. For a year, I kept a hockey diary and recorded some of my own experience as a player (old and middling), coach (prone to high seriousness), and fan (now despairing, now hopeful, ever a Leaf). I also plumbed almost five decades of my own hockey past, calling on my sprawling family for cameos.

I invited scientists and doctors and professors, poets and writers of fiction to weigh in. I consulted hockey scribes, hockey historians, and hockey-mad friends—one a stick boy at Maple Leaf Gardens in the 1960s with vivid memories of a stick-swinging duel. I took notes at an unprecedented five-day conference in Halifax on the future of hockey, and at another in Toronto on hockey violence. I did what I always do while writing a book: I listened, I read, I slipped into the project as I would a deep, warm bath. But no bath, no book project, ever managed to relax and invigorate me as this one has.

The research process brought home to me how much the game courses in my veins, for it seemed the most natural thing in the world to delve into this sport, to probe its lore and literature, its pranksters and storytellers, its code of honour, its elaborate system of justice. I set out to write a book on violence in hockey, but along the way I discovered many things about the game I had either forgotten or had not known. I was a fan trying to achieve a deeper understanding of the game, one that I was sure required more and more courage the closer you got to professional ranks.

Though history very much informs this narrative, *Grace Under Fire* became a more personal book than I imagined it would be. That's fitting, because hockey is such a profoundly tribal game, marked by allegiance and retribution. The game is also mesmerizing in its speed and intensity, and you may feel—as I did when I considered the physics of the game—an even deeper respect for those who play at the highest level.

Still, I hope I do not blithely celebrate the professional game, or criticize it lightly or thoughtlessly. I have tried to paint the game's two polarities, the grace and the fire. What I came to believe is that the genius—and, sometimes, the bane—of hockey lies in the grace and the fire being so tightly interwoven.

1

A KID'S GAME

I WAS BORN IN A CATHOLIC HOSPITAL, not a hockey cathedral, but it could have gone the other way. Several weeks before I took my first breath, on March 11, 1949, my father took my mother to watch a Saturday night game at Maple Leaf Gardens. During a fight on the ice, a sports reporter—Jim Vipond of the *Globe and Mail*—fell over the press-box railing in the Greens and landed on my mother ten feet below in the standing room that then existed behind the Blues. Vipond had leapt up on a desktop to get a better view of the fracas when he was shoved from behind. No one was seriously hurt, and I emerged later in Toronto's St. Michael's Hospital maternity ward, where stern nuns with clacking rosaries held sway. I was under four pounds and one month premature. That spring, the Leafs would go on to win the Stanley Cup.

A year later we were living in the small (my mother might say "godforsaken") railway town of Nakina, nearly 1,000 kilometres to the northwest. As the family of a man who worked with the Canadian National Railways' telecommunications side, we lived in an apartment in the telegraph-repeater station, alongside the tracks. My father, Bernie Scanlan, played goal for the town team (he also played Santa Claus at the Hudson's Bay store every Christmas). The outdoor rink, like something out of Roch Carrier's *The Hockey Sweater*, featured a change room with rough pine floors, a pot-bellied stove, and a caretaker named Hank Côté, whose name would live on in Scanlan family lore for years, long after we had left Nakina and gone back to Toronto when I was six.

Hank Côté was a simple man but he wanted the world to know he was not a stupid man. In the face of some remark meant to test his gullibility, he would scoff knowingly and say, "Hank Côté wasn't born yesterday, you know." Or on the dance floor, lost in his own high-stepping solo, he would be heard to exclaim, "You think Hank Côté can't *dance*?!"

My father would leave my younger brother, then a toddler, in the rink's dressing room. Tommy remembers looking out through the wide expanse of thick glass as the team practised. Hank Côté kept an eye on him, made sure he stayed clear of the stove. My father would come in after practice and invariably find Tommy asleep. I remember, vaguely, tooling around on the ice with the players, who occasionally humoured me, passing me the puck. Winters were long, and it was not so unusual that I was skating well by the age of four. Temperatures would hover at minus-forty degrees for weeks on end, or so my mother told me, and years later I would brandish that number as a badge of toughness in the sultry south. My memories of that rink in Nakina are fuzzy, but in another way as clear as a cherished dream: The rink is alabaster white and I am deep in one corner, arcing right leg over left, right over left, and again, as I cut and head up the ice, trying to muster more and more speed and get those eyes to watering. The rink is all about freedom; I do not remember cold.

Nakina would play exhibition games against teams from Hearst, Hornepayne, Sioux Lookout. Some of these men had played junior hockey, a few were former pros—such as "Boomer" Doran, who skated in the 1930s with the New York Americans.

"Were the games ever nasty? Any fights?" I once asked my father.

"Not in the games," he replied. "But the night before. . . ." And then he laughed, recalling the rough-and-tumble Kibzey boys and how the ginger got up when Nakina and the opposing team found themselves in the same hotel bar. "One night," my father recalled, "some of the Sioux Lookout players made fun of Mike Kibzey's rolled-rim Stetson hat—his pride and joy—and there was nearly a full-scale riot. Cooler heads finally prevailed and the teams went off to bed."

My father remembers one game in particular against Sioux Lookout, which Nakina would win handily 7–2. His own defencemen egging him on, Bernie Scanlan left his net near the end of the game, took the puck and embarked on a solo rush, finally passing off at the other team's blue line as all five Sioux skaters, their stupefaction now hardened to fury, had him in their sights.

What is true of my earliest hockey memories still holds true today: the pure rush of delight that often comes with the game, how much it knit the fabric of every Canadian village, town or city I ever lived in, how easily a flying fist enters the picture.

Ernest Hemingway once defined "guts" as "grace under pressure." This book, in part, is about what that writer had in mind. It's the Stanley Cup playoffs of spring 2001; my Leafs are in tough against the previous year's champions, the New Jersey Devils. The Leafs have dispatched the favoured Ottawa Senators in four games during round one, and in round two taken the first game against Jersey. But in game two, Toronto looks flat, the usually stalwart Curtis Joseph lets in some soft goals, and the third period starts with the score 5–1. Miraculously, the Leafs come back to tie it, the last goal coming only three seconds from the end.

Right winger Steve Thomas, who would score that fifth goal, is driving for the net, heading fearlessly for that no man's land where defencemen feel free in the dying seconds of playoff games to slam-dunk the enemy, to wrestle and cross-check. In such mêlées, more players may be down than up. It takes courage to swarm the net, and anyone on the ice in the dying seconds of a playoff game has already displayed his finesse and grit; those lacking look on from the bench.

The darting Leafs winger Sergei Berezin has come in from the left side and aimed a pass through the throng. The puck hits a stick, rises six feet in the air, and dances like a knuckleball right to Thomas, who, all in one motion, cradles it with his left hand, sets it down on the ice, and rips the puck into the top right-hand corner of the net past Martin Brodeur, one of the best goalies in the world. Thomas does all this with the Jersey crowd in a frenzy, with his heart beating like a kettle drum, does it all in a second or two. Some inner calm guides him, some happenstance gives him the puck in a free space, some gift of mind and body lets him execute that exquisite unleashing of power. This is grace under fire.

The Leafs would then lose in overtime, but that moment stayed with me and I would offer it as a counter to any who dismiss modern hockey as a thug's game.

But the phrase "grace under fire" can be taken another way. In hockey, and especially in the playoffs, grace comes under siege. Even someone watching a playoff game, let alone someone playing in one, can be taken to emotional territory he or she would prefer to avoid. Not long after Thomas's goal, on the night of May 3, 2001, I happened to miss the first two periods of the third playoff game between New Jersey and Toronto. I felt a certain apprehensive joy when I got home in time for the third period, flicked on the television, and found the score 3–1 in favour of the team I have backed since I was a boy old enough to know one team from another.

My younger brother Stephen, when he was five, one day confided to a family friend that "*This* is the worst day of my life." And then he listed, in a grim monotone, his sorrows: His football had blown up, his toy guitar had broken, and the Leafs had lost. It was the last item that had put Stephen into the black and the bleak. Billy Harris, in *The Glory Years,* had thoughtfully included in his memoir a dressing-room seating plan for the 1961–62 Leafs. So I know that were wee Stephen to have been airlifted into that room and had he looked west, he would have seen inscribed on the wall, over the heads of Stewart, Stanley, Hillman, Nevin, Brewer, Kelly, and Horton, these words in bold caps: "TORONTO MAPLE LEAFS—DEFEAT DOES NOT REST LIGHTLY ON THEIR SHOULDERS." Nor on Stephen's.

The joke in my sprawling Irish-blooded family—I am the eldest of eight children—is that when the Leafs score, my brother Stephen's cry of joy in his home in west Toronto can be heard at our old homestead in east Toronto, and that Stephen's heart will surely stop one spring when his Leafs take him to some great hockey height and then drop him. His worst déjà vu.

I am my brother's brother. We live and die by our team and are almost beyond feeling embarrassed by it all.

The Leafs would win the game that damp May night in 2001, but the victory would be tainted. In the dying seconds Tie Domi, the rugged Leafs winger and one I had always counted an honest pugilist (though there was that time he sucker-punched Ulf Samuelsson), caught Devils defenceman Scott Niedermayer with an errant elbow and laid him out cold. The puck was miles away, the game miles past doubt. This looked to be an act of casual violence.

Scott Stevens, the Devils defenceman and a savage in his own right, saw the foul hit from the penalty box and was beside himself with rage. I knew that the next time Domi faced the Devils he would be hunted like an animal, and somewhere in my psyche I wanted him hunted.

No grace here. No fire. Don Cherry was later asked by fellow broadcaster Ron MacLean about the incident, and Cherry fumbled and shrugged, claimed that Domi never meant the result. But as I watched my little black-and-white TV in the room above the porch, what I saw was shame all around. MacLean, Cherry, me at home: We were all profoundly embarrassed. The game had ended on a disparaging, sour note.

Domi was suspended immediately, and an NHL hearing the next day yanked him from what remained of the playoffs and, should the Leafs lose the series (which they did), the first eight games of the following season. Colin Campbell, the NHL's vice-president, who conducted that hearing, had coached Domi in New York and knows him well. He believed Domi had no intention of hurting Niedermayer. But "he crossed the proverbial line," Campbell told MacLean on national television the night after the incident. "Ken Dryden said during the hearing," Campbell went on, "that he had never heard the Air Canada Centre so loud as it was in the last minutes of that game. But Tie's excitement took him to a place he shouldn't have gone."

Domi, in his own defence, cited a dangerously high stick from Niedermayer earlier in the series, and said he worried about another one coming as he passed him in the dying seconds of the game. Tie

Domi himself cannot be sure what compelled him to deliver such a cheap shot. Marty McSorley, whom I would interview at length for this book, had called Domi an honest broker. McSorley himself will be remembered all his remaining days, and beyond, for his clubbing of Donald Brashear; McSorley, too, in my books anyway, had been an honest broker. In the space of less than a year, two honest brokers had lost it.

Why?

Don Cherry uttered a terrible truth in his "Coach's Corner" commentary during the game that followed the Domi hit. "This has been going on since 1918," he said. For most of its history, Canadian hockey has been war.

Domi would issue a heartfelt and emotional apology for his assault, but he must have been as heartbroken on his own account as he was sorry for the hurt he had inflicted on both Niedermayer and his fellow Leafs. Many in the broadcast booth had picked Domi as the game's first star, and there was a feeling of euphoria in that building, something I could feel in Kingston, 200 kilometres away. All that good feeling had vanished. The Leafs would lose the series and never recover that spring from Domi's wild indiscretion.

No game stirs what hockey does. Many, even on the Leafs side, were actually glad to see the eight-game suspension. The game, they said, needs a lid, some restraint. For a long, long time, there has been none.

Yet there is no denying the powerful, almost ancestral tug of hockey in this country. An estimated eleven million Canadians—a CBC-TV record—watched the gold medal game in hockey at Salt Lake City in February 2002.

To fathom hockey's grip on me, you should know something of my youth. My neighborhood in Scarborough felt connected to the highest levels of the game we all played most days of our lives. Mr. Walsh, two doors up on Sherwood Avenue, worked at Maple Leaf Gardens, repairing nets and equipment and acting as chauffeur to Conn Smythe, the old Leafs' general.

"Conn Smythe's limo," my younger brother Wayne remembers, "was routinely parked in their driveway, and Mr. Walsh would take us for rides, including to Conn's other love—the racetrack. Mr. Walsh would bring home all kinds of broken or cracked hockey sticks, which looked pretty good to Brian Walsh and me. Ed Litzenberger, Andy Bathgate, Doug Acomb: These were the names on sticks I can recall acquiring from Mr. Walsh."

Rick Kessell, who pumped gas at a local Esso station, had star quality and would one day play in the NHL. (Pittsburgh made him their first-round draft choice, fifteenth overall, in 1969. But his stay in the big league was of the cuppa-coffee kind; he would score four goals over parts of five seasons.) Tam O'Shanter, the curling-and-hockey complex where our church league played, was where the Leafs practised when rock stars and rodeos took over the Gardens. We skated in the wake of the gods.

Hockey was not just another sport for us. It hung in the air, in defiance of the seasons. When each of our backyard rinks—the Scanlans', the Zambris', the Kellys'—melted in March or early April, we pulled the plywood off the basement windows (protection against flying pucks) and got out the road hockey sticks. Asphalt whittled away at the blades, which eventually grew thin and needle sharp at the ends. Spring and fall were dedicated to road hockey, summer only marginally less so. Droxford Avenue was a rink, Courton Drive was a rink, Precious Blood schoolyard was a rink. Hockey alchemy turned rubber boots into goalposts, tennis balls into pucks, us into stars. "Skinny Scan" became, on those asphalt playing fields, a smaller version of "Red" Kelly—I had his freckles and red hair and loved the number four. Joe Zambri, who lived across the road, used to play goal in our road hockey games and call them, as Foster Hewitt did, the real thing. Joe, a Wings fan, was Sawchuk when he played goal, Howe when he played out; his brother "Yiffie" was "Fats" Delvecchio. Always, I was Kelly.

Hockey was a torch passed from one generation to another, even from one hemisphere to another. When my youngest brother, David, and his wife, Patti, moved to São Paulo a few years back, my wife

Ulrike, our son, Kurt, and I went for a visit at Christmas. My brother-in-law Donny McClean, who had played university hockey at Waterloo and pro hockey in Europe, insisted I take with us an imposing package for Dylan, David's four-year-old son. Only in Brazil did the contents of the cardboard box from Canadian Tire become clear: a hockey net.

Road hockey memories are light and restorative; small wonder they've been applied as balm to frazzled pros. My cousin Lorne Flynn, an elementary school teacher in Toronto, once taught Brendan Shanahan, the Detroit Red Wing who can play it smooth and play it tough. Shanahan and Lorne went out for a beer one time after a school reunion, and the player recounted the story of a shootout in international competition. On the bench one of the players picked for the shootout was expressing doubts about his chances. Shanahan and the others were telling him, "Just imagine it's a road hockey game and you're Mario Lemieux." Just be that boy, they were saying, be a boy. And in Shanahan's telling, the player swallows the advice as he would a timely pill and approaches centre ice confidently. But as he heads towards the goal, the medicine is unmasked as placebo. A voice in his head is saying, "This is *not* road hockey, it's the Olympics; I'm *not* Mario, I'm . . ." who does not score.

My brother Tommy remembers, as a boy, giving up watching the first period of Leafs games for Lent—a forty-day period of penance and prayer; for the same period his saintly grandmother Gertrude Flynn would forsake meat *and* dessert. No doubt my brother saw her sacrifice and his as equal in merit. My sister Theresa remembers another ritual: me collecting twenty-five cents from each of my siblings on hockey nights in Canada so I could bike to the store and buy cheese popcorn and pop. Sometimes I would prepare supplementary fare—rice pudding. Food for the frantic. Theresa remembers praying at playoff time for the boys in celestial blue.

Sometimes, as a child grows up, the love for hockey becomes a passion, even an obsession. Witness John Lynch. He would drive down

Sherwood Avenue, past our house in his gold Cadillac convertible—top-of-the-line model, brand new, 1966. Stories swirled about him, stories about his obsession with the Leafs and, in particular, Frank Mahovlich. But though the stories painted him as wildly eccentric, I don't remember him being dismissed as mad. My father loved to tell John Lynch stories, for he could not tell them without smiling throughout and laughing at the end. And like all my father's stories, there was no short version.

"He was a big man," my father would tell people who hadn't known John Lynch. "He may have touched six feet. He had sandy-coloured hair, was balding, and had a fair-sized paunch. I remember him sitting with a tray on his belly watching sports on TV at home. 'Georgie, my lunch!' he would yell. His wife was very pretty and crazy in love with him. He was loud and he loved to hold court."

He sold us a car once, a canary-yellow 1967 Pontiac, the classiest car we had ever owned. But selling cars and houses were minor pursuits for John Lynch—hockey, and Frank Mahovlich, had him by the throat.

Today we have a name for people like John Lynch. We call them stalkers. But the telling part of Mr. Lynch's obsession is how the object of that pursuit, Frank Mahovlich, handled it—with the patience of a kindly old priest whose altar boy can't stop sipping the wine. There was something approaching affection between them, and nothing made that clearer to John's daughter Judy than when Frank Mahovlich showed up at the funeral home after her father died in 1991, to express his condolences, and, further, to ask if he might be a pallbearer.

John Lynch had been coaching a men's hockey team, a particularly affluent and well-educated one, and all the players turned up for the wake. One of them approached Mahovlich. "If John had known you were coming to his funeral," the player told the "Big M," "he would have died a long time ago." Mahovlich thought that was pretty funny. "Before they closed the coffin," Mahovlich would say later, "I threw in a couple of autographed pictures. I thought he'd like that."

Years later, Judy Lynch, now Judy Spring, a community college teacher and municipal politician in Oshawa, decided to attend a

$100-a-plate fundraiser at which the speaker was her father's hero. Judy and Frank ended up sitting beside each other and he fell to reminiscing about John—who wanted more than anything in the world to coach the Maple Leafs, for he alone knew how to tease genius out of the impenetrable Big M. As my brother Tommy remembers it, Mr. Lynch said the key was to play him more—on the power play, killing penalties, taking a regular shift. Mr. Lynch wrote Punch Imlach often, suggesting that the foul-tongued, military-minded coach pursue other lines of work and yield the reins to him.

For those of us who dreamed of playing for the Leafs, his was a strange ambition. Players played, sometimes heroically, got traded, retired. The pro's life was short but surely sweet. Coaches, on the other hand, got blamed, got fired, worked in the shadows. No one I knew wanted to be a coach. But that was John Lynch's abiding goal, and while he waited patiently for the dream to take shape, there was nothing to do but follow Frank, like a teenager on the trail of a rock star.

At the fundraiser, Mahovlich began his talk by asking Judy to stand and be acknowledged as the daughter of his biggest fan. Frank then proceded to tell stories that had Judy wanting to duck under the table. One time, Mahovlich said, he went to open the door of his hotel room, somewhere in the American South, when the Leafs were on a road trip. He was looking for his morning paper, and there—"like a dog" is how Mahovlich put it—lay John Lynch, asleep and no doubt content in the knowledge that behind the door slept his precious Frank. Mr. Lynch would plot the travel plans of the Leafs, learn their connecting flights, and book a seat on the same plane. Everybody on the team knew about this ardent fan and they must have eyed him with head-shaking wonder, like sailors in mid-ocean gazing up at a gull who has shadowed the ship all the way from port.

One time John Lynch boarded a plane at a connecting point—my father thinks it was Buffalo—and as he walked down the plane's aisle he spotted Frank Mahovlich sitting by himself, reading. Mahovlich, then playing for the Toronto Toros of the World Hockey Association as his career was winding down, told him, "John, you can sit beside me but you can't say a word! Not one word, OK?" John nodded and sat down.

On another occasion, when Bob Baun was coaching the Toros and the team was heading home from a road trip, John tried to get on the team bus at the airport. Baun was having none of it, so John Lynch stood in front of the bus. Finally, Baun relented. He stepped down off the bus, sighed, and said, "Get on, John."

When John Lynch picked out the family plot at the graveyard, he insisted that the grave numbers assigned include the number 27, Mahovlich's old sweater with the Leafs. When Frank Mahovlich was part of the Canadian team that played Russia in the dramatic 1972 series, John Lynch had a splendid suit made to mark the occasion, for, of course, he followed Mavhovlich to Russia. The suit, my father remembers, cost $700—an enormous sum then. The colour was the brilliant red of the maple leaf the players wore on their jerseys; on one sleeve, in white, was the same stylized leaf, on the other the number 27.

John Lynch saw most, though not all, of the series in person. He was appalled by conditions in the hotel rooms, which he was convinced were bugged by the KGB. (There's a story told about Phil Esposito—who shared the same conviction—loosening a suspicious nut and bolt under a rug in his room, whereupon the chandelier in the room below was sent crashing to the floor.) For some reason, John Lynch lost faith in the Canadian team, and he headed home during the series. He never saw Paul Henderson score that winning goal in the last minute of play in game eight.

My brother Tommy remembers a time when he was ten, and Mr. Lynch, who was fill-in coach for the team, was driving him to a tournament. Tommy worried about what he was going to say all that time in the car, for boys that age are uncomfortable with adults they barely know. He needn't have worried. For the whole two hours John Lynch talked of nothing but Mahov and coaching the Leafs.

But maybe coaching was trickier than he thought. John looked the part—dressed to the nines, bold and cocky. But as a fill-in coach, he got the lines on Tommy's team all confused, the game turned chaotic, he yelled at the other coach, they lost. On the way home, in the calm of his gold Caddy, Mr. Lynch returned to his favourite subject.

On the other hand, John Lynch's nephew, Ron Guest, remembers him fondly as a gifted hockey man. "I was on a midget team," he says. "We had lost our coach and Uncle John came in and transformed us from a Bad News Bears team that never won a game to one that never lost. He was a Don Cherry figure who drove a Cadillac Eldorado. This was small-town Acton. Word got out. He came to us after coaching a few games with the Toronto Toros. Everyone was in awe of him. In the dressing room he held nothing back." Translation: He occasionally turned the air blue.

For the next eighteen games, they never lost. He encouraged a "run-and-gun" offence and wanted his players always to be on the puck.

The Toros link is fuzzy, even among Lynch family historians. Ron Guest remembers that his uncle spent time behind the Toro bench, perhaps as an assistant. Ron remembers watching Mahovlich play for the team, along with Paul Henderson and Vaclav Nedomansky.

The irony (one of many) is that in all likelihood John Lynch only rarely laced on skates. He was born in England and was fifteen when his family moved to Canada in 1939. Somewhere along the line, he acquired a passion for hockey and enough knowledge that he could cleverly talk about a game he had never played.

When I asked Judy to talk about her father for this book, I read into her testimony a curious mix of pride (for John was a character and much loved); embarrassment (he was a hockey fanatic and a health nut who drank homemade carrot juice, took mud baths and practised colonic irrigation); and, when all was said and done, regret. "My mother and father," she said, with evident understatement, "were not well suited. We had no choice but to tolerate his passions. He lived in his own world. There was never much money, but he did his own thing as breadwinners at the time were wont to do. But when my mother was dying—she died of lung cancer and my father was very good to her through all that—she said she forgave him for all the lousy things that he did, and he did a lot of lousy things."

After John's wife, Georgie Lynch, died, Judy, Joanne, and their brother, David, chipped in and sent their father to a "dream" camp at Lake Placid where he got to play on the ice with retired NHLers. "He said it was one of the happiest moments in his life," Judy commented, "and he said that Red Kelly treated him especially well."

When John Lynch was sixty-one, Judy and her siblings convinced him to move into a seniors' apartment in Oshawa, a community east of Toronto. She admits it was a mistake. He was still too young for a rocking chair. But he quickly discovered a nearby disco called Illusions, and he would go there three times a week. "He added," said Judy, "a new dimension to the place. He had this zest for life and a lot of energy. The bartender would buy him drinks and they gave him a jacket with the name of the disco on the back, which meant he didn't have to line up to get in. He used to joke that he was dancing with the prettiest girls in Oshawa."

That his heart gave out on the dance floor of Illusions on the Big M's birthday seems too ironic to be believed, but that's how life ended for the man who stalked Mahovlich and who craved Punch Imlach's job.

All through my childhood, my father was an organizer in our church hockey league. The five boys in the family played hockey, and all but David—who was traded by Brazil to Spain in 2001 for future considerations—still play and coach thirty and forty years later. Late in 2001, David sent back an urgent message from Madrid: Send my hockey stuff; a local ex-pats team was looking for players.

Every year we joke about suiting up an all-Scanlan squad: Pop in goal, Tommy and David on defence (only David ever actually played that position), Stephen centring Wayne and me. The fantasy has my mother (who loathes hockey) coaching, Theresa assisting, Rosemarie and Karen working the doors.

There is a lovely story that Roy MacGregor tells in his book *The Home Team* about the Howe family, who *did* play together in the bigs. Typically, the Howe boys would call out "Gordie" when they were on the ice with their father, but in one game an animated Mark struck for open ice and called out "Dad!" who hit him with a perfect pass, and the son went in and scored. In the sometimes tangled country of fathers and sons, this is the stuff of dreams. My own son has played with me in Monday-noon pickup hockey, and I hit him once with just such a pass. Maybe Kurt was pleased; I was made young.

My son, fifteen as I write this, spent the first twelve years of his life living in the country. Home was a village northwest of Kingston called Camden East. Population 250.

Every winter the cycle of freeze and thaw meant that a small rink formed naturally at the bottom of the hill in front of our nineteenth-century clapboard house. Kurt learned to skate there. Then came pond hockey in the nearby village of Newburgh. At the edge of the village, a natural marsh-pond would freeze, and the man who lived adjacent would set nets on this improvised rink and painstakingly flood and scrape the ice. He even rigged night lights overhead so the kids could get in evening games of shinny. I marvelled at his generosity.

Kurt and his pals would spend the better part of whole weekends out there, freezing their feet the way I used to as a kid, but refusing to come in from the cold. Pucks would be lost in snowbanks and found again in spring; other pucks would fall through the sluice gates at the end of the pond, there to confound upside-down ducks slurping through the boggy bottom for food the following spring. Sometimes work preceded play: After snowfalls, Kurt and I would lace up, take wide shovels, and clear the ice. I showed him how to angle the shovel the way a snowplough clearing a road is angled—a trick I had learned on our backyard rink in Scarborough.

At the pond there were the usual complaints about older kids shooting too high and hard, about sides not being fair. But for the most part, the boys found ways of keeping the peace. One Saturday morning, Kurt and his buddy Gil were playing a little one-on-one, each taking a turn in net, wearing Gil's elaborate goalie equipment. Gil's father, George, and I skated on the periphery.

Kurt doesn't remember what provoked the little explosion that occurred that day, but he well recalls grappling with Gil, how they fell upon each other, driving their fists with furious intent. I remember shock, then embarrassment. The two fathers entered the fray, separating the combatants, each convinced that his own son had sparked things.

Was one boy scoring too many goals for the other's liking, so that poking for a loose puck at some point was seen as an insult? Was it a matter of Gil's pride and Kurt's swagger? Was an accidental elbow taken for something else? Or did we—do we—just blame hockey itself?

All I know is, the play turned. Two friends who had been buddies and classmates for years suddenly, and quite uncharacteristically, began to attack each other, like two ants from enemy colonies tossed into a jar.

I remember when hockey scrawled its name on my young body. My right eyelid hangs lower than the left, and I wonder whether the sag will increase. If I hit eighty, will the lid give me the look of a geezer frozen in the art of winking? I took four stitches over my eye when I was a kid of twelve playing road hockey in the schoolyard. Paul Game, who would grow up to become a school principal and a bruising defenceman in Sunday-morning, old-timer hockey, was winding up for a slapshot, and my thought—as I darted in from behind—was to lift his stick and wrest the bald tennis ball from him before he made contact. Maybe that lid closed in a moment of reflex, or maybe my guardian angel interceded. Paul Game's pointed Hespeler didn't lacerate my eye, but came perilously close to it.

That same year, my coach in church-league hockey was a firebrand named Harold Tobin. He was tall and stiff and unyielding, and he expected his boys to act like men. Mr. Tobin had been our baseball coach, too, and when he hit grounders to us in pre-game warm-ups, he lashed the ball. If you failed to snag it with your glove, you were expected to stop it with your body, and I recall the sting of a third-base line drive, the fighting back of tears. But, for some reason, Mr. Tobin believed in me and once surprised me by selecting me for an all-star baseball team. I took Mr. Tobin as seriously as he took the role of coach, whether on the diamond or in the rink.

At the Tam O'Shanter arena, he had beseeched us before one particular playoff game to take out, at every opportunity, a star defenceman
for the other team, a chunky imp named Pat Galand. I knew him from
the schoolyard as an opponent best avoided.

Early in the game I caught him as he sped up right wing and I
levelled him with a clean, hard check. Astonishment all around—at
Galand being decked, and at puny me being the decker. Our bench
erupted in cheers. A minute later Galand held me on the boards at
centre ice, for a few too many seconds—a message to me that he had
my number. Our bench erupted again, this time in complaint.

But the incident I remember most vividly came late in the game
when the coach's son charged Galand as he emerged from behind the
net, kneed him hard in the groin, levelled him. The penalty was called,
and when young Michael Tobin returned to the bench, his father
reamed him out loudly and relentlessly. The boy hung his head. We all
knew he had committed a hockey sin and we felt his humiliation—but
there was something else in the air, too, though I did not yet have a
name for it: hypocrisy. Our coach had stoked us, yet shouldered no
blame when his own son went to that place he was exhorting us to go.
"Not *that* place!" he was saying. "Then *where?*" we might have asked.

For me, hockey has always been bound up in emotion. When I
was still a teenager, I helped Paul Game's father coach a peewee team.
For years, Mr. Game had wheeled that Plymouth stationwagon of
his—the red one with the sharp crazy fins that got about ten miles to
the gallon—into our driveway on Sunday mornings and taken Paul
and me to hockey. Maybe I felt I owed Mr. Game something, so that
later on, helping him coach was a form of payback.

On that team was a boy so big that when he barrelled down right
wing, little checkers would drop like pins in the path of a bowling
ball. Scoring came easy. Mr. Game and I had decided to put the boy
back on defence. Maybe pressure had come from league officials;
maybe we felt that was his natural position—the reasons are lost to me
now, but our move did not sit well with the boy's father. I recall the
shouting in the parking lot of Tam O'Shanter, the boy's father hurling

a vile insult, and Mr. Game's shocking reply. Then Mr. Game made a move on the other man, and I had to restrain my fellow coach. I never saw the boy again.

In 1972, when I was twenty-two and a quick, string-bean forward for the Glendon College hockey team of York University, we were in a final playoff game against another college at York—a Stanley Cup, of sorts.

I was not slick around the net, and never did perfect the slapshot, but I was a buzzsaw forechecker who could drive opposing defencemen to distraction. I had scored two goals in a game we would win 3–1, and towards game's end I pinned a defenceman in the corner, matching his feints and turns. At one point, he grew weary of my pursuit, lost interest in the puck, and brought his stick up with both hands, fists forward, so the stick was horizontal and level with his chest. Then he drove it with all his strength into the bridge of my nose. I collapsed, fell to the ice, and lost consciousness for a few seconds.

I remember the ref's words as I rose slowly to my feet and was helped off the ice: "You guys don't want to play hockey; you want to kill each other."

The code of hockey required that I rest briefly on the bench, come out for my next shift, and finish the game—which I did, though my nose was quite broken. There would follow a trip to a hospital's emergency department, general anesthesia and surgery, a cast-like bandage I wore proudly for weeks in the halls of Glendon College, and, when it was later removed, what seemed like miles of packing in my nasal cavity.

We had won. The beer that our captain's father brought into the dressing room after that game tasted better than any I had ever imbibed. Even as my eyes blackened, even as I took thumb and forefinger and moved my nose sideways—the sandpapery sound of jagged bone on jagged bone imprinting on my brain—I felt the warrior's joy. In 1972, even at that amateur level, hockey was war.

"Scooter" they called me when I played for Glendon, on a team we called the "Gophers." I hoped that pure speed would compensate for my ordinary puck skills. It did not. In one game, cruising at centre, my eyes on the puck and not on the enemy, I was levelled with a hip check. My back was never the same. I remember retreating to the house I then shared with other students, a glass coffee jar full of hot water strapped to my back.

In those years I wore a pair of Tacks. When I was a boy, my skates mostly came from church bazaars or shoemaker's second-hand shelves. I remember a few new pairs, but they were Canadian Tire models, thin on quality. I always wanted Tacks. Where the leather curled around the ankles, Tacks had little eyelets, home to tiny laces you tied over your socks and shin guards. When I was a boy, those little laces were the mark of class, but Tacks were beyond the family budget.

Finally, approaching age twenty in 1969, I got my first Tacks. Andy Raven, that year's captain of the Glendon team, gave me his old pair. I was glad of them, but they were marginally too small, and as the season wore on, the nail on the big toe of my right foot began to blacken at the base. The crescent-moon shape gradually grew to half-moon size and, with spring, evolved to total eclipse, so that during summer swims the nail became a conversation piece. By then the nail had loosened, and I would ease it off, revealing the sordid stuff below. The bruising, which I first thought was mere discolouration in the nail itself, existed, I would learn, quite apart from the nail.

I took an almost clinical interest in this, perhaps because it all unfolded so predictably, like the seasons. The black stuff below the nail was wet and dank, but it would dry and peel off. Below was flesh, naked and pink and new—the colour of newborn mice. A new nail would commence, and by fall it was whole, but hockey would soon blacken it. (The elegant defenceman Paul Coffey used to cram his sockless feet into skates two sizes smaller; perhaps he, too, has toenail tales to tell.)

I wore those Tacks the only time I ever played hockey in Europe. Two Glendon teammates—Andy Raven and Terry Walker—had taken the 1970–71 academic year off to play semi-pro in Holland. On his return to Canada, Andy managed to organize sponsors (Dutch and

Canadian airlines) to fund the Glendon team's trip to Holland during the Christmas break of 1971. Glendon players would be billeted in the homes of Dutch families, and our opponents for six exhibition games would include Andy and Terry's old team in Heerenveen, as well as clubs in Groningen and Germany.

We stood on the blue line in that Dutch rink in Heerenveen before a packed house of 3,500 for the playing of the Canadian anthem. Our hearts stirred at that, and we got an inkling of what it must be like to play for your country—the '72 series between Canada and Russia was only nine months away. Gary Young was on that Glendon team and he remembers "how the Dutch looked at us. Did they see us as typical Canadian goons who would hurt their guys? I remember feeling confused about what part of Canada and Canadian hockey I represented. The goons? The courage? The skill? The passion? And all the time I was mulling that over, the Dutch wouldn't stop thanking us for what our fathers had done in liberating Holland during the war."

Jet-lagged and struggling to cope with the bigger European ice surface, we were badly outshot but managed to pull off a 6–3 victory. And that was our one and only game: The team got caught up in an international feud between European and Canadian hockey officials over the use of former pros at the impending world championship. We were sacrificial lambs, though curious "gophers" is more like it. With a week to kill, we sampled Dutch specialties—speed skating by day, *patat frites met mayonaise* and Heineken by night.

More than three decades later, I still lace up skates every winter, don equipment so old and delicate that I have a private joke: I will quit when the equipment does. So far, my body and my old Cooperalls remain more or less intact, or enough for the laid-back hockey I play.

For a few years in my late twenties, I played no hockey. I had loaned my hockey bag and car to my brother Tommy while I was travelling in Europe, and the gear was stolen from the trunk. But when a former newspaper colleague called to say his team needed one more warm body, I was pulled back and I found a complete set of equipment through the Kingston classifieds. A teenager, more or less my size, was selling everything. He had played Junior C but finally found the game becoming too brutal, the risk of injury too high.

He had used a tube of black paint to write his name in bold capitals on the Montreal Canadiens bag, which barely housed his gear. D. DU CHARME wore number 14 and played in Amherstview, and years later the raised scrawl proclaiming this information lives on, though some paint has peeled away. Now it is DU HARMF who makes the round of rinks.

The Scanlan brothers make rounds of their own, summer pilgrimmages wherein we become Hansons. The Hanson brothers in *Slap Shot,* the Paul Newman film about the fictional Charlestown Chiefs were, of course, real players. Jeff Carlson was a tough guy for the Minnesota Fighting Saints of the WHA, and Steve played both for Minnesota and the New England Whalers after several years in the minors with the Johnstown Jets (read, Charlestown Chiefs). Movie and reality, I am told by former Jets, were not far off each other.

In my own family lore, the Scanlans and the Hansons became intertwined after my brothers' Wednesday-night hockey bunch entered a tournament at Lake Placid, New York, in the early 1980s. As a lark, my brothers Tommy, Wayne, and Stephen formed a line, and the boys on the team dubbed them "the Hansons"—a clever choice. Unlike the Hansons, the Scanlan boys don't fight (though Stever did get tossed a few times for dropping the gloves), but like the Hansons, they "zoom all over the ice," as Tommy puts it, "skating like maniacs and getting no goals. We pass and never shoot."

For fifteen summers, Tommy has organized a Scanlan brothers' baseball trip. This often includes David, who flies in from his home in Latin America to blend business in New York with a weekend dedicated to baseball somewhere in America. The baseball fest involves many innings, stadium hot dogs, late nights, and, back in the hotel, Schlitz on ice and the reading aloud of sports sections.

Since politicians keep tearing down old parks and building new ones, we always have new destinations.

In his *Ottawa Citizen* column, my brother Wayne once dubbed the ritual trek, "a cross between the Traveling Wilburys and *Slap Shot*'s Hanson Brothers." We still refer to ourselves individually and collectively in the third person as "the Hansons," never "we," as in "A Hanson takes pride in buying a cheap ticket at the ballpark and then 'slides down' to a better, vacant seat—preferably behind home plate." This is the height of Scanlan malfeasance, helping ourselves to luxury seats. But it's not really us doing the deed; it's the Hanson in us.

All year long we are Scanlans; on these road trips we are Hansons. This is the enduring influence on my family of a mediocre hockey movie that became a cult classic.

I am trying here to fathom my love for this game, one that has never faded. Football lost me a while back; basketball remains of only passing interest; and even baseball doesn't fire me as it once did. Hockey is the one sport I still play, still follow, still coach, still care deeply about.

Perhaps because, more than any other sport, it's a game of courage. Even those of us who played the game at lowly amateur levels know what it takes to dash into the corner after a puck, with someone twice your size bearing down on you, measuring you for a hit. Each game contains many moments of sacrifice, and cowardice, and sometimes games are won because whole teams offer themselves up. Soldiers in battle know about such allegiance. So do street gangs.

Denis Dupere was a defensive centre with the Toronto Maple Leafs in the 1970s. I remember his wide-skating style, as if there were a horse under him. By the end of that decade, he was spent and he had landed a job as a playing coach with the Nelson Maple Leafs in the British Columbia interior, sidelining as an ad salesman for the *Nelson Daily News* when I was that paper's editor.

Dupere told me that in the NHL, defencemen used their sticks with an eye to human anatomy and protective equipment. They know how to hold the stick like a staff, how to bring that lumber down on any forward parked at the net, aiming always for the small of the back, which is vulnerable because free of padding. Dupere talked about the bruises each game brought, how the damage doubled during playoffs.

The hockey I play every Monday in winter—with a mixed bag of players, fast and slow, old and young, gifted and challenged—is a far gentler version. I like our rink's dimensions—the Harold Harvey Arena is small, so that backchecking is less of a chore. We have come to know each other, or, at least, to know each other as players, and feel free to mock each other off the ice. On the ice a curious politesse governs our actions: Pretty goals are acknowledged by players on both teams; goalies are praised afterwards, no matter how badly they played (best keep their spirits raised for they are tricky to replace); the occasional hook or trip sees the perpetrator offer an instant *mea culpa*, and the victim issue a pardon. Everybody else boos. The cloud of fear I sometimes played under in my youth—during high-speed, contact hockey—has given way to the casual fellowship of gentleman's hockey.

Roy MacGregor, the dean of sports writers in this country and a man just one year older than me, has observed that old-timer hockey—often played at odd hours in empty arenas—recalls "the silly joys of childhood" and continues to offer "a temporary balm against the pressures of the week and the march of time."

The game played for money on hockey nights in Canada is something else.

2

THE
CODE

HOCKEY HAS ITS OWN CODE OF HONOUR. It may be the game's distinguishing trait.

Baseball's dugout presents an image of cool detachment, as light as the hulls of sunflower seeds that players are forever *ptooing*. Football players on the sidelines play the fool for the camera and shout, "Hi Mom!" with two fingers raised in victory signs. Basketball players, on sitting down, slip pelican high-fives to each other, drape towels over long necks, and strive to keep ears from being knocked by their own and others' knees. In all these sports, centre stage and the wings seem casually disconnected.

Hockey players, on the other hand, watch the ice with grim intensity. They miss nothing, especially wrongs done to one of their own. Much of the violence in hockey stems from one form of aggression begetting another. Hockey's code demands tribal retribution. King Clancy, a referee when his playing days ended, knew this and would often issue one penalty for retaliation and another for the original infraction—even when he had not witnessed the latter. Where there is smoke, the Irishman figured, there is usually fire.

Morris Mott played for the beleaguered versions of Team Canada in the late 1960s, before joining the California Golden Seals. He told me that hockey has not just codes, but "codes within codes"—one being that big, tough guys fight each other and not little guys. Mott, for example, a compact five-eight, 165 pounds, would supposedly only be expected to fight men his size. Sounds simple. "Everyone feels the code, but no one knows exactly how it works. That's because," says Mott, "not everyone can agree on what transpired five seconds ago, or five games ago."

Hockey's code may seem elusive, but it is deeply felt. A bond forms between players as they travel, share hotel rooms, practise and play for nine months and more each year. Hockey players are blood brothers, kin who, at least in the ideal, esteem dropping in front of shots, risking injury, sacrificing the body for the squad. John Updike once complained in a *New Yorker* essay—one written in praise of golf—that "ice hockey, fervent though its devotees be, retains a dross of brutal messiness. . . ." Blood flows freely in the game, but players are not supposed to mind.

For the code demands stoicism. Jack Adams, who played for the old Toronto Arenas, a precursor to the Leafs, recalled how "the team trainer kept a pail of cold water and a sponge at the bench, and when a player was cut, he skated to the boards, where the trainer sloshed off the blood, put some sticking plaster over the cut, patted the guy on the shoulder, and sent him out for more lumps."

After one game in 1922, Adams had his cuts attended to at the Montreal General Hospital where his sister Alma happened to be the on-duty nurse. But he was so bloodied and swollen that she only recognized him after seeing his name on the registry.

The "lumps" that Adams referred to came in waves. Goalie Gump Worsley took 1,000 stitches in his career, but always managed his trademark grin. Leaf stalwart Bob Baun, on defence, had his big toe broken more than thirty times. During the Stanley Cup final of 1961, hard-rock Red Wings defenceman Marcel Pronovost—he had the scar-tissue face of an aged boxer—would arrive at the arena on crutches, play every agonizing shift, then have the cast put back on his badly cracked ankle. Hockey's longstanding brothers are *play* and *pain*.

One day Gordie Howe picked up "Black Jack" Stewart's stick and was astonished by the weight of the thing.

"Jack," asked Howe, "how the hell do you shoot with a stick like this?"

"It's not for shooting," replied Stewart. "It's for breaking arms."

One of the first Swedes ever to play in the NHL, Inge Hammarstrom, broke in with the Leafs in 1973. He was listed, perhaps generously, at six-foot, 180 pounds, but not a small man in any case. Leafs owner Harold Ballard would say, famously, that Hammarstrom could skate into the corner with eggs in his pocket and never break one. The "chicken Swede's" counter to those who criticized him for not finishing his checks was to point out, "You have no idea how strong some of the guys are in this league." Hammarstrom had an interesting take on pro hockey. Here he is writing in *Maple Leaf Magazine* in 1976. "Hockey," he said,

> is the most demanding sport in the world. It demands speed, stamina, toughness, and a lot of other physical and mental qualities. It also demands tolerance of pain. . . . Hockey reporters in North America are always concentrating on concepts such as courage, when ninety-nine per cent of the time it is not the moral quality of courage that is at issue but only the physical fact of tolerance to pain. Am I exhibiting any special kind of courage if they knock me unconscious to the ice and carry me off on a stretcher and later I return to the game? No, I am a hockey player. I am like the businessman who goes to work after he has had the heart operation. He goes back because that is his job and that is what he has chosen to do. Courage has nothing to do with it.

Hockey players simply assume that the game involves getting hurt. Lorne Chabot, a goalie in the '20s and '30s—two decades before the mask was introduced—would shave just before a game. "I stitch better," he explained, "when my skin is smooth." Eric Nesterenko, among the most thoughtful men ever to lace on skates, once observed that in hockey, "There is always the spectre of being hurt. If you get hit, you get hit—with impersonal force." He remembers looking on as doctors sewed forty stitches into a teammate's face. *Better him than me* was Nesterenko's response. "We conditioned ourselves to think like that," Nester said. "I think it's a defence mechanism and it's brutalizing."

Babe Ruth watched the Boston Bruins play in 1927 and left the game a grateful man. "Never saw anything like it," he said. "Thank God I'm in baseball, with its peace and quiet."

In 1949, the NHL began painting the ice white. When blood pooled on that surface, the contrast was stark—red on white: our nation's colours.

In 1972, just before that classic series resumed with the Russians in Moscow, incredulous Swedish reporters would ask Canadian players after exhibition games, "Why are you so violent?" It's still a good question, and the answer may lie in the peculiarly Canadian hockey mindset that views hockey as war.

For as long as men have made a living at chasing a rubber disc over frozen water, that ice has been reddened with the blood of players. Pucks cut flesh, as do sticks and skates and fists. The wounds are as much a part of the game as the astonishing speed and jarring body contact. I remember playing league hockey as a boy and looking on as referees slid the blades of their skates back and forth over blood on the ice after some accident or altercation. This is hockey's instinct, hockey's paradox. On the one hand, cover up every trace of blood. The nicety of scraping off the pink slur and taking it away with a shovel is one followed at every rink, from peewee to pro. And yet there is huge pride in the scars and the toll the sport exacts from the body.

When the National Hockey League marked its seventy-fifth anniversary in 1992, it co-operated in the publication of a glossy hardcover book to mark the occasion. Howe, Richard, Hull, Orr, and Gretzky all made the cover. Of the 100 or so black-and-white and colour photographs in the book, not one shows a player fighting or swinging his stick. There is blood in the text all right; Paul Quarrington describes Shore's infamous assault on Ace Bailey. But in *The Official National Hockey League 75th Anniversary Commemorative Book,* there is not one photo depicting blood on the ice. Where hockey violence is concerned, text and images bear no relation to one another. This book was commemorating goals and glory—the airbrushed history of hockey.

Consider another, more exclusively photographic history of hockey—*Portraits of the Game*—and a different picture emerges. Nat and Lou Turofsky, from the 1930s and into the 1960s, took black-and-white photographs at Maple Leaf Gardens where Nat was the Leafs official photographer. "And then there was the hockey," Andrew Podnieks writes in his introduction. "Though the men loved the track, the diamond, and the weddings, their true passion was Maple Leaf Gardens. This was their home, their reason for working, their place of perfect certainty."

Nat's trademark photograph was that of the player braking hard just in front of the camera and throwing up a great curtain of ice. One photo early in the book shows the brothers in their Alexandra Studios on King Street—Lou in a vest with a fat cigar in his mouth and clutching a mittful of glossies, while Nat holds a heavy Speed Graphic press camera in his left hand and points animatedly at his brother with the index finger of the right. Arrayed behind the brothers are half a dozen photos, some of them immediately familiar: a place-kicker in football with one foot high over his head, a bathing beauty, a scramble around the net, a thoroughbred horse galloping for the finish line. Above Lou's head is the photo that interests me.

The photo, shown full-size later in the book, was shot Saturday, November 7, 1942. It shows a dazed and bloodied Detroit player, Jimmy Orlando, leaning heavily on the arm of the referee, King Clancy. The right side of his brow is cut, and the stream of blood has gone down his cheek and onto his sweater. Podnieks calls it "one of the most horrific and most frequently reproduced photographs in hockey."

My overwhelming impression from reading the literature, from hearing the testimony of players from the early to mid-1900s, and from poring over news clippings, is that early hockey was very much like war. The blood flowed freely. The stick, players such as King Clancy and Ted Lindsay liked to say, was the great equalizer. The extraordinary thing about the Orlando incident—and here it has something in common with the McSorley–Brashear incident—is that Nat Turofsky actually went onto the ice to photograph the drama, just as TV cameras, up in the stands, would later on. Sometimes Turofsky got too close to the stick swinging, and his camera was destroyed. At times he was in more jeopardy, as was the case here. The dazed Orlando actually "made a beeline for Nat's camera," according to Hal Walker of the *Toronto Telegram,* who witnessed the incident. Clancy and a player intervened to spare the photographer.

What had set Orlando off was a charge by the Leafs' Gaye Stewart. Clancy caught that infraction but missed Orlando's response—a left hook that downed Stewart. The two made for each other as soon as Stewart's penalty was over, but were separated. The mood between them must have been exceptionally hostile, because Detroit coach Jack Adams came onto the ice to join those restraining Orlando. Despite all the bodies endeavouring to disconnect the two men, they managed to wreak havoc on one another. Podnieks: "Orlando sucker-punched Stewart, who then hit him over the head with his stick. The attack left Orlando dazed and disoriented, a bloodied mess in one of hockey's ugliest hours."

The seventy-three images in *Portraits of the Game* are remarkable for the quality of their composition. And because the players usually wore no helmets, the viewer sees what modern fans are denied: the look on the players' faces—looks of anguish and ecstasy and desperation. You can see teeth clenched, hair flying, almost hear the impact of hips and shoulders and elbows. Some players sport bandages over their cuts; a few wear leather helmets to shield their battered heads; some wear contraptions that were supposed to protect their shattered jaws. The photographs capture mêlées, a fight in progress, a penalty box filled to overflowing, players separated by a large policeman.

The most famous shot in the book has Bill Barilko, who would die the following summer in a plane crash, diving to get his stick on a pass that finds the net, for a goal that won the Leafs the Stanley Cup in 1951. There's one of Johnny Bower clearing a puck, and Podnieks adroitly calls the look on his face a blend of "childlike glee and demented ferocity." On the ice, all eyes are almost always focussed on the puck, but it's the look on the faces that speaks volumes about this game. The zone in front of the net, the photographs show repeatedly, is a dangerous place to be.

The Game, by Ken Dryden, published in 1983, still ranks among the best hockey books ever written. "Mr. Goalie" describes graduating in history from Cornell University with no real sense of history. Early in the 1980s Dryden happened to pick up *The Hockey Book,* written in 1953 by Bill Roche, who had collected the memories of players, coaches, and referees from the mid-1920s to 1940. What struck Dryden with force was that the book's themes—hockey in the grip of big business, the decline of American interest in hockey and yet hockey catering to the American fan, the increase in fighting and brawling—were still central themes thirty years later, as indeed they are now. Each new generation, largely unaware of the history, is convinced that all this is new.

The "dump-and-chase" game, Dryden wrote, had been vilified by those who blamed it on expansion in 1967. But here was Roche citing critics who decried it in the 1950s. Dryden set out to probe the roots of the game and how it was played, convinced that history held valuable clues, that "a link between present and past might tell us why we play as we do."

I am convinced he is right. "The boy becomes a man;" Dryden wrote, "the player a coach, a manager, a scout, a father; a game is passed like tribal history, one voice, one mind." No one was challenging the continuum: "There was simply no other way to play."

But the game did change after its first decades, and especially when the forward pass was introduced. Hockey in the 1800s was a lateral game; what a sea change the forward pass must have meant. But as the game got faster and faster, the game's salient features—finesse and violence, grace and fire—vied for supremacy.

For Dryden, hockey had—it seems a heresy to say this—too *much* speed. Hockey became overmatched and overwhelmed by speed, and defenders saw no alternative but to slow down the opposition. Bobby Orr was one of the few players in the past century who could play hockey as a game of finesse and at top speed. But for the rest, the faster the game gets, the harder it is to play. Speed robs athletes of the time it takes to be creative. Watch an NHL game and count the seconds a puck carrier has to decide on an option. Small wonder most players dump it out, around the boards, shoot it in. No time. No space. No choice.

In the adrenaline game that hockey has become, says Dryden, violence almost makes sense. But adrenaline, he warns, "has its dark side. Fouled or resisted, it turns to anger, frustration, retaliation. And inside a pattern of violence allowed many years before, it sends violence spiralling higher."

The ethic of playing through injury, of playing while hurt, Dryden found, was rooted in early rules that forbade replacements. Hockey originally deployed seven against seven, including a rover, and those fourteen men played the entire sixty minutes, unless one got hurt. Imagine how exhausted they must have been by the end, how slow the pace as a result. Only in 1925, during a Stanley Cup series, did teams begin to substitute entire forward lines. This was seen as revolutionary.

Hockey players went from playing entire games to playing five-minute shifts. Now shifts are forty and fifty seconds. Players are bigger, faster, better conditioned, wiser about nutrition. Yet the size of arenas remains the same as it was a century ago. No wonder there is all that contact and seemingly no room to manoeuvre.

Canadian hockey's "tribal history," to come back to Ken Dryden's phrase, seems rooted in defiance. The Swedish reporters trying to fathom the nastiness of Canadian hockey players might have found the answer in Canadian colonial history.

In the late 1800s, the colonial aristocracy in Canada tried to make cricket our national game. They failed. People in this country rejected the sport that their so-called "betters" sought to impose on them; Canadians wanted a sport that reflected their own pioneer identity. At first, lacrosse was that sport, one inextricably linked to Canada's indigenous peoples and to the harsh conditions of life in this country; lacrosse was a vicious game. And it was a short hop from lacrosse to hockey, the game that was soon seen as the perfect metaphor for life in the hinterland.

The choice of hockey, then, was a charged one, both meaningful and enduring. To embrace the game of hockey in the late 1800s was to show the finger to the powers that be. Hockey violence was thus not gratuitous at all, but revolutionary and subversive in its way—at heart, political. The British would play gentlemanly cricket in their summer whites; the Canadians would play primal hockey in the biting winter wind. In its early days, hockey was condemned by the clergy as "a desecration of the Sabbath," but boys paid no heed and spent Sundays on frozen ponds pursuing a lump of coal, a frozen horse bun or potato, or a wooden puck—the elegant age-rings making each puck distinct, the rough wrap of bark still attached.

One small town would form a team and play the gang down the road, each trying to entice players "from away" by offering under-the-table deals or jobs with bloated salaries. Community pride would launch those first hockey wars. In 1905, for example, the Fredericton Trojans vied with the Marysville Crescents to decide the York County championship in New Brunswick. But when the Crescents didn't get a promised $25 guarantee, they refused to come out for the second period and the game was called. Outraged fans broke windows, ripped out light fixtures, and tossed seats onto the ice. Only at midnight did police convince the mob to go home.

Devotion to the home team became deeply ingrained in the Canadian psyche. In 1941, two Nova Scotia towns fifteen miles apart engaged in a vigorous hockey spat. Glace Bay, the coal town, had the Miners; Sydney, the steel town, had the Millionaires. The Miners bolstered their team by paying their goalie, "Leaky" Boates, $200 to join the army (or to claim he had joined), and thereby legally disappear, allowing for a more talented goalie, "Legs" Fraser, to take his place. The ruse was discovered when Leaky was spotted in nearby Truro, in civvies. As the controversy swirled, Glace Bay retailers set up a roadblock and refused to let folks pass by. There were even rumours of a coal strike, which would have effectively shut down the steel town by denying fuel to the ovens. The feuding even split families. Amateur or pro, small town or big, prairie or coast, Canadian hockey made blood boil.

Garth Vaughan, a retired surgeon in Windsor, Nova Scotia, and a hockey historian who wrote *The Puck Starts Here,* remembers that arenas would use music to quell on-ice fisticuffs. "Whenever a fight broke out that couldn't be controlled," he says, "they had a seventy-eight record of 'God Save the King' that would be played. Everybody would stand at attention until it finished. Then the fight would resume. One night they had to play it three times before the fellas got finished."

Those who think hockey violence was somehow invented by Dave Schultz and the Broad Street Bullies in the 1970s should consider this from the *Renfrew Mercury,* January 28, 1910. (What is noteworthy is the complete absence of moral outrage; as hockey games go, this one in the Ottawa Valley was apparently business as usual.)

The trouble with ["Bad" Joe] Hall started when Hall hit Lester Patrick over the left eye with a stick, making quite a gash. That started bad blood between the Patricks and Hall, and when Frank Patrick cross-checked Hall when the latter was going down the side, a free fight followed. Frank Patrick had the better of the scrap while it lasted, but when the pair were separated the judge of play ruled Hall off for three minutes. Bad Joe became enraged and made for the official with his fists. He was promptly met and knocked to the ice, and for attacking the official was ordered off for the remainder of the game. He made a kick at Kennedy, the official, with his skate, as he lay on the ice, and tore the referee's trousers. Hall knocked a tooth out of Whitcroft's head and in many other ways upheld his reputation of being a bad actor.

Then there is this headline from the *Daily British Whig* in Kingston, Ontario, on January 17, 1918. "Warned Against Fighting. President Calder Tries to Eliminate Pugilism from Hockey."

Richard Gruneau and David Whitson offer a slightly different take on hockey history in their book *Hockey Night in Canada*. They make the point that early hockey was offered by "moral entrepreneurs" who believed that hockey made one a better person, unlike other sports linked with gambling and drinking. But by 1910, hockey was no longer the domain of earnest amateurs. Filthy lucre had entered the sport, and that would change everything. The professional hockey player was born.

Some of the first pro-hockey players toured on a circuit in the 1870s. Businessmen staged "friendly matches" (though these exhibition games were sometimes anything but). Later such games were called "challenge contests." Soon a hockey network was in place, and by the 1890s, these extravaganzas included bands, carnivals, masquerades, skating races. Hockey as circus.

Tribalism is a useful word to describe early hockey: Irish-Catholic and French-Catholic teams vied with English-Protestant teams. The working class challenged the affluent, loggers took on miners, farmers vied with fishermen. Just born, hockey was already charged as race and religion, class, politics, and hometown pride all hotted up the mix.

Here's hockey historian Brian McFarlane writing about what he called the "Battle of Montreal" in the 1920s: "It was explosive. When the English-backed Maroons met the French-supported Canadiens, the on-ice battles were often overshadowed by skirmishes in the stands. Emotions became so feverish that a missed goal or an 'undeserved' penalty would trigger a rash of pushes and punches, with police and ushers rushing in to keep English and French fans apart."

The growth of hockey was fuelled by the creation of the Stanley Cup, a national trophy. McFarlane reports in *One Hundred Years of Hockey* that in the first Stanley Cup championship, played on March 22, 1894, "Both teams freely indulged in tripping and slashing, beginning a century-long tradition." A newspaper report notes that "never before in the history of the game was there such a crowd present at a match or such enthusiasm evinced. There were fully

5,000 persons at the match, and tin horns, strong lungs and a general rabble predominated. The ice was fairly good. The referee forgot to see many things."

This, too, marked early hockey: Referees were both blamed and held in contempt, much as they are now. The aforementioned Morris Mott, a professor of Canadian history at Brandon University in Manitoba, has investigated nineteenth-century hockey in the west. He told me that the referee was less a governor of play than a consultant. During this period, the goal was defined by two posts—the net had yet to be invented—and scoring was often a matter of some dispute. Players would "claim" a goal, the referee and a goal judge would verify the claim. The referee's position, then, commanded little respect, and there are several instances, even in national championship play of this era, of western teams yanking themselves off the ice to protest what they viewed as lousy officiating. In one Stanley Cup game in the late 1800s, a referee—fed up with the abuse—left the rink and had to be enticed back.

In Manitoba, said Mott, who slowed his words for emphasis, games between communities were "*serious business.* Officially, the games didn't matter, but at the emotional, visceral level they did. And the referee was often seen as a scapegoat. Verbal abuse was very, very common and sometimes physical abuse—especially if big wagers were involved."

Rowdy fans in Quebec City in 1895 were so incensed after an Ottawa victory that they dragged the officials back into the rink, trying to make them declare the game a draw. The police had to rescue the terrified crew. By 1897 the total number of fans watching the several Stanley Cup games would hit 18,000—an impressive figure given the then small arenas.

Hockey had moved quickly from an amateur game played on open ponds before few spectators to one played by paid professionals in closed arenas before more and more paying patrons. The stakes were higher, the venues claustrophobic.

For Canada's pre-eminent hockey historian, Bill Fitsell, the move indoors marked a critical juncture in the way the game would henceforth be played.

Bill is a lanky, gentle man in his late seventies, and he seems not to have aged a whit since he and I were colleagues at the *Whig-Standard* in the 1980s. He then wrote an about-town column, light and friendly pieces where Kingstonians could read about themselves, their names in boldface type. To the mild chagrin of those on staff who thought they were writing deeper fare, Bill's "People" column was far and away the best-read byline in the paper.

In January 2001, Bill met me at the International Hockey Museum in Kingston, where he is the resident historian. The yellow-brick building must have seemed, in its youth, a grand complement to the sprawling grounds that include the Memorial Centre, the old but still-beating heart of hockey in Kingston.

Albert Street, where I live, runs south to Lake Ontario, north virtually into the arena. Bill informs me that Don Cherry's family homestead was at 518 Albert, some twenty houses north of mine and within shouting distance of the rink. Four white pillars wrapped in ivy on the porch lend a certain grandeur to the modest house, and the lawn has been replaced by wildflowers, fruit trees, native grasses, and plants. The occupants are as radical as Don Cherry is conservative.

Modern sports museums like the one in Cooperstown, New York, dedicated to baseball, or the one in Toronto, celebrating hockey, are alive with sound and interactive displays. The more modest Kingston museum—sadly debt-ridden and in danger of losing municipal funding—feels like something from the '50s. Even if there is no dust, you sense it. The museum was closed when I visited it, but Bill gave me a private tour.

The glass cases are busy, full of hockey sweaters and souvenir programs from world championships. Upstairs on display boards are early models of skates and sticks (like the "Truro lifter," made in Nova Scotia in 1904), and sweaters once worn by Bobby Hull and Wayne Gretzky. One item I will not forget is a painting that visitors see on the wall as they leave—a fevered, Goya-esque vision in blues and blacks that shows hockey players swirling around a puck. They look demonic, possessed.

Bill wrote a book in 1987 on the history of hockey called *Hockey's Captains, Colonels & Kings,* and he is founding president of the Society for International Hockey Research. His home office in mid-town Kingston has the feel of a miniature museum, with a collection of antique hockey sticks (none more than four feet high), a great many pucks (one made of wood), vast files, and, of course, hundreds and hundreds of hockey books on shelves, the overflow stashed away in a closet. Bill has collected hockey memorabilia all his life. He remembers being at Maple Leaf Gardens in 1936 when Red Horner and Eddie Shore got into a fight, right in front of his family's box seat. Thirteen-year-old Bill scampered to the walkway next to the boards and screening, but he had little interest in the battle; he was gathering the many programs that enraged fans had tossed at the combatants.

Pose a question about any aspect of hockey, but especially its early days, and he'll have an answer—or a clipping will arrive in the mail a few days later. Where, I asked him, did the word *puck* come from?

"It's an Irish term from the sport of hurling," Bill replied. "In this game, which resembles field hockey, you would *puck* the ball in from the sidelines. The Irish moved in great numbers to the Canadian Maritimes, and the term may have originated there." The curious antecedents to hockey, says Bill, may have included ice polo, a sport that originated in Newport, Rhode Island, and *kolf,* a Dutch game played on ice by stationary players who swatted at a small ball or disc with sticks that were curved at the bottom.

I like the long view he brings to hockey. "Fitz," as we used to call him at the newspaper, believes that whatever innocence hockey possessed was lost early in the twentieth century, when hockey turned from a playful game on a pond to an organized sport played for money and a prize—the Stanley Cup. The advent of television in the 1950s dramatically heightened audience numbers, but by then fighting had long been part of the package.

Bill's gift to me on the day of my visit was two fat files on hockey violence, some of the clippings dating back to the early 1900s—many with Bill's own jottings in the margins. With newspaper and magazine clippings from every decade, the files offered a window into an entire century of fierce and fearsome hockey. "For some reason," Bill joked, "one of the file folders is red."

At one time, said Bill, pushing was an offence in hockey. It was only in 1915 that fighting was introduced as an infraction in the rulebook. "Once hockey moved into a confined area," he noted—and this detail, I think, is critical—"that's when the stick work and the fisticuffs began." It's a point that other observers have raised over time—this notion that while the basketball court, the soccer pitch, the football field, and the baseball diamond offer players at least the illusion of operating in an open space, the hockey rink is a much smaller, more confined environment. The boards and the glass enclose the players, hem them in.

Former McGill Redmen coach Charlie Baillie told a Montreal reporter in the 1980s that during a long pro-football career he had precisely one fight. "When somebody gave me a good hit in football," said Baillie, "I'd usually pat him on the butt. When I got hit in hockey I had to retaliate—immediately." And then he makes a telling point: "It's the only game with boards, a confinement that increases the intensity. Nobody can step out of bounds; it's something like being thrown into a pit. . . ."

The playing grounds for other sports feature air on all sides. A quarterback running up the sidelines can always duck out if he sees a lineman bearing down on him. A soccer player under duress can always boot the ball out of bounds. Basketball at least offers the illusion of space beyond the court proper, thick though that space may be with patrons. A baseball diamond could accommodate about seven hockey rinks. Hockey can seem, by comparison, claustrophobic. Baillie's pit image hits like a dart.

In the Kingston hockey museum is a black-and-white photograph of players lined up across the ice at the palatial Duquesne Gardens in

Pittsburgh, Pennsylvania, in 1905. It must have seemed strange for those players, in their striped sweaters and knee-length knickers, to operate in that fishbowl of a place. Those men, who had learned the game on rivers and ponds, suddenly found themselves *inside.*

European rinks, Bill told me, would remain longer and wider, possibly because of the influence of the old game of bandy—an English game played on ice. North American rinks stayed small, and as the players grew bigger and faster with every passing decade, the rink appeared to shrink. For the small, no matter how swift, there was no place to hide from the bully.

And bullies there were. "Commentators," wrote Gruneau and Whitson in *Hockey Night in Canada,* "frowned on repeated incidents of hacking, tripping and excessive brutality evident in open fighting on the ice and in mob scenes involving fans and players. There are stories of four deaths on the ice in eastern Canada in 1904." More hockey deaths would be recorded in 1905 and 1907.

In 1907 hockey was being both denounced and hailed as "the bloodiest of modern games." In a match that year between the Ottawa Silver Seven and the Montreal Wanderers, so much blood was spilled on the ice that a headline in the Montreal *Star* referred to it as "an exhibition of butchery." In one account, "'Baldy' Spittal [of Ottawa] was said to have deliberately tried to split Cecil Blachford's skull by bringing down his hockey stick upon it with all his force using both hands. Blachford was carried off with his blood pouring on the ice."

Apparently, you could hear, throughout the arena, the crack of Spittal's stick on Blachford's head, a blow that left him unconscious. Blachford took several dozen stitches; Spittal got ten minutes. The game then turned even more savage, with some players hauled off to jail and later bailed out.

The McSorley hit on Brashear in 2000 would hardly have merited a mention in 1907.

During that era, Ontario Hockey Association president John Ross Robertson would lament coal tossing by fans in Lindsay, bottle tossing in Peterborough, and "the inadequacy of police protection in smaller towns."

In the early years of the twentieth century, organized hockey was already out of control. In 1916, a player with the 228th Battalion known as the Northern Fusiliers (briefly a team in the National Hockey Association) created headlines when he became embroiled in a fistfight at centre ice—with the referee. That same year, a Toronto-versus-Quebec game was marred by a brawl that saw Quebec fans hurling bottles at the Toronto players as they ran for their train. The first year of the NHL would set the tone for what followed. A reporter in the *British Gazette* observed in 1926 that professional ice hockey appeals "to those who like their sports served up red-hot." In the game that reporter witnessed, the visiting captain reportedly butt-ended another player, then with one punch knocked down the referee, who rose to his feet and hit the player with an effective right. Hockey and boxing had intertwined, like strands in a rope.

Andy O'Brien was a magazine journalist whose stories I used to read as a teenager. In *Headline Hockey,* he was on the road with the Penticton Vees at the World Hockey Tournament in Cologne, Germany, in 1955. The tone is approving, even epic: "As rugged as the Rockies, as raw as the winter that swept down from those thunderous hills, were the Penticton Vees." Later, O'Brien calls them "rough and tough and born to turbulence." *Time* magazine, on the other hand, reported that the Canadians' behaviour in the tournament "both on and off the ice was anything but ambassadorial."

The *Communist Daily Worker* in London was appalled by what was to have been a friendly pre-tournament exhibition game in Czechoslovakia: "The name of Canadian ice hockey stinks in Czechoslovakia after last night's game in which the Penticton Vees battered, slashed and punched their way to a 3–3 draw with the Czechoslovakian national side . . . the thousands of people who were stunned by the thuggery on ice in the end rightly booed them off the ice."

Early in the genesis of Canadian professional hockey, there developed a code that saw opposing players treat each other as enemies in war. Hockey literature is suffused with that metaphor, one often used with a tincture of pride. In the political tempest that was the world tournament of 1955, the Canadian team was trying to wrest back the title from the Russians, who had won it the previous year in their first try.

Andy O'Brien found himself years afterwards forced to defend the behaviour of what he called "the madcap Vees." Hockey is simply like that, he argued. "It's no pantywaist game; rather it's by nature violent, a 30 m.p.h. skating sport with padded men and sticks and bodily contact permissible." Here, again, was that fatalism Dryden referred to: Players and coaches and scribes saw the game in a certain savage light. Hockey as war was the only way to play the game.

But also critical to hockey's code was seeing the game as one of courage, so that heart mattered at least as much as skill. Like Maori warriors who made faces at the enemy, hockey players understood from an early age that some players—and whole teams—could be frightened off the puck. Like no other sport, hockey works by intimidation.

A part of hockey tradition is the notion that the NHL is the highest you can go in the hockey world (though the way Czech national teams win world championships should give pause to such claims of supremacy). New entrants to the NHL are severely tested, and some found wanting. But when you do gain entry to this elite club, some-times you are congratulated by those who did the testing.

Camille "The Eel" Henry, who played in the NHL between 1953 and 1970, most of that time with the Rangers, was a slender five-nine, 152 pounds. He remembers the first game he played against Detroit when Ted Lindsay dealt a two-hander to Henry's forearm. But The Eel gave as good as he got, and afterwards Lindsay skated by him and said, "Kid, you made it. You're all right." Henry would survive because he refused to back down. Still, The Eel was plagued with injuries throughout his long career, and only twice played the entire seventy-game season.

Ironically, Henry as a coach would show no particular feeling for the small, skilled player. The old New York Raiders of the WHA, coached by Henry, were unable to beat the Quebec Nordiques in 1972—a team with small, quick forwards. "They can skate," Henry told his team, "but if they get hit right from the start, they're not going to skate as fast and they're not going to go into the corners and that's half the battle won." He sent out his best pugilist to box the ears of his chosen Nordique victim.

Jim Dorey played for the Leafs in the late '60s and in the WHA. At a banquet one night in Kingston, Dorey, now in his mid-fifties, described a game in his first year, in 1968, when a Pittsburgh Penguin forward named Ken Schinkel laughed at him for taking his fourth minor penalty of the game, and assured Dorey he was headed back to the minors. Their ensuing fight led to a bench-clearing brawl and a total of forty-eight minutes in penalties to Dorey alone—then a Leafs record. "One fight seemed to lead to another," he recalls. "I couldn't get off the ice."

Later, in the dressing room, Dorey looked up and saw coach Punch Imlach and Leafs executive King Clancy headed his way. "I figured I was done," says Dorey, "that they would give me thirty minutes to clean out my locker and get out of town. But Clancy patted me on the shoulder and said, 'Way to go kid; that's the kind of hockey we want to see around here.' He handed me a $100 bill and said, 'Take off for the weekend and have yourself some fun.'"

For more than a century, fighting has been a feature of pro hockey and much amateur hockey. Many people are convinced that will never change. And yet much has already changed. Fisticuffs in the NHL have fallen mainly to specialists; elite players such as Mike Modano, Steve Yzerman, and Mats Sundin are spared the indignity. But intimidation, fighting's cousin, has always been an equally central element in the game.

Witness the first round of the NHL playoffs of 2001. In one game, New Jersey Devils defenceman Scott Stevens caught rookie Shane Willis of Carolina with his head down. Result: a concussion. Next game he would send another Hurricanes player, veteran Ron Francis, out with a concussion. Stevens did the same to Eric Lindros and Daymond Langkow in 2000. Four players concussed by Stevens in two years. *Hockey News* editor Steve Dryden wrote of "a body count piling up" and declared Stevens the most devastating bodychecker in the history of the game.

All four levelling checks were deemed legal hits. And coincidence or not, when the Hurricanes had finally had enough and went after Stevens en masse several times ("Bring it on," Stevens had said, anticipating revenge), they pulled off an overtime victory.

There is a prevailing notion throughout hockey's history—whether it's true or not hardly matters—that a team refusing to respond to another team's violence has conceded defeat. Ted Lindsay recalls a playoff game against Montreal in which he and Bernie Geoffrion had squared off after Maurice Richard blindsided Lindsay with a punch to the jaw. "I thought someone had dropped the organ on me," he said. "I went right down on my knees in slow motion. Well, the Canadiens went on to beat us, and after the series Richard said in the paper that that was the punch that won the Stanley Cup for Montreal. I could believe it. I think our team lost something when nobody came off the bench to get Richard."

It's still true that "nice" does not win playoff games. But only when I pull back from watching the games and think about what is actually transpiring on the ice does the savagery of playoff hockey hit me. The Dallas–Edmonton series in 2001 looked to be not only the most up-tempo series of the lot, but also the most belligerent. The Oilers' Ryan Smyth looked like a prize fighter when it was done: eleven stitches over his swollen eye, nine more over his left ear. Jason Smith, his teammate on defence, took a puck in the face, and the CBC-TV crew showed him being stitched in the hallway. The bravery and stoicism of Smyth and Smith were peddled much like beer and cars are in the commercials. Over on the other side, Mike Modano suffered a broken nose and thirty-five stitches from the puck he took in the face. Unseen were the welts and bruises and lacerations elsewhere on players' bodies. In that hazardous zone in front of the nets,

Derian Hatcher (six-five, 230 pounds) of the Stars cut a swath, while the Oilers' Georges Laraque (six-three, 255 pounds) wreaked havoc of his own.

My brother Wayne, who writes a sports column in the *Ottawa Citizen,* said the Senators, who clearly had no stomach for gladiator-style hockey, will need a heart transplant for them to be effective in next year's playoffs. The Sens need "grit"—a word I heard over and over again that spring. Grit was what the Leafs acquired when they got Shayne Corson and Gary Roberts. And yet my brother, a lifelong fan of the game, is left with a bitter taste in his mouth. In the wake of the Sens' devastating defeat, the *Hockey News* opined that the team "had better get some players with jam. . . . These pretty boys can't win when it counts." Hockey, at least the kind played from April to June, becomes militaristic. Victory—not to the swiftest or cleverest but to those most able to stomach hand-to-hand combat.

Bobby Smith was six-four and weighed 210 pounds when he broke into the league in the late 1970s; he was later general manager of the Phoenix Coyotes and is now a scout with Carolina. I thought his take on the game was remarkably astute: "More than any other sport," he once said, "hockey is a war. In football, you see players helping one another up. In baseball, they chat away at first base. In hockey, you get unfeigned animosity; it's barbaric. In fact, one of the things I've always liked best about it is that it's a test of a person's courage, and to be successful at it, it's not enough to be a good skater and shooter—you have to be able to withstand the violence and the intimidation."

And that's why even knowledgeable scouts and managers sometimes make bad choices. John Ferguson, a horseman as well as a hockey man, once remarked on the uncanny similarities between picking a good horse and picking a good player. "You're looking for strength, speed, balance, desire. . . ." Sometimes all the pieces in the puzzle are there— size, athletic gift, uncommon quickness—but that little spark, that fearlessness that lets a player streak without hesitation into a corner or fall down to block a shot, is missing.

Players know that sooner or later they may be challenged to a fight, and sometimes by players who have studied boxing. Keith Magnuson, who played wild and woolly hockey for the Hawks in the 1970s, took boxing lessons from Johnny Coulon, a former featherweight champion who ran a gym in Chicago. Marty McSorley mentions, in a cagey sort of way, spending time in boxing gyms. Al Secord donned boxing gloves and learned the manly art. "Muzz" Patrick of the '30s Rangers was once Canadian heavyweight champion.

In other sports, pure talent will let you into the club of the select. The history of the NHL is littered with the names of "sure things"— players with immense potential and promise who discovered that they lacked fortitude. One of the cruelties of hockey is that it insists that those who play at the elite level have grit in spades.

Bobby Smith recounted how even in pre-game warm-ups, players would threaten to break the other guy's arm. Other times they would comment on someone's looks or what was said in the press. "The trick," said Smith, "was to say just enough to irritate the guy, break his concentration, maybe intimidate him a bit, but not enough to get him cranked up."

In the 1970s, a dynasty was built on intimidation. The Philadelphia Flyers had, it seemed, an entire team of bullies. In an exhibition game in 1976 against Moscow's Central Red Army, the Flyers so manhandled the Russians, dropping a number of them early on, that the Soviets left the ice; there was a long delay while they pondered returning. Two days later, the Soviet youth newspaper *Komsomolskaya Pravda* ran a cartoon showing hulking Flyers coming onto the ice wielding huge clubs. The Flyers, much like wrestlers, had nicknames: Dave "The Hammer" Schultz, Bob "Mad Dog" Kelly, Andre "Moose" Dupont. Visiting teams coming to Philadelphia would tiptoe around the arena, clearly fearing serious harm. Some players would insist they weren't well enough to play, citing an injury or sickness—"the Philly flu" the press called it.

"Whenever I walked through that big, black door leading into the visiting locker room at the Spectrum," recalled one Vancouver defence-man, "I thought I was walking through the gates of hell." Rick Smith, a Kingstonian who played defence with the Bruins through the 1970s, once described "the twinge of fear" that was always associated with the Spectrum—a "rough place," he called it, "a danger zone." Here's Fred Shero, coach of the Flyers, in 1975: "If we can, we'll intimidate our rivals. We try to soften them up, then pounce on them. . . . There are lots of ways to play this game. Our way works."

Bobby Clarke was a natural captain for these Flyers. In 1968–69, Clarke's Flin Flon Bombers were playing a national championship against the St. Thomas Barons of the Western Ontario Junior League. So traumatized were the Barons that they refused to play any more after trailing in the series three games to one. It wasn't the first time (and will not be the last) that a team would fold its tent—literally, as the Barons did, or virtually, as many teams do—when the opposition declares itself capable of just about anything.

In 1972, John Ferguson was a Team Canada coach looking on as Valery Kharlamov sparkled for the Russians. Ferguson tapped Clarke on the shoulder and said, "Kharlamov's hurting us badly. Go over and break his ankle. Put him out of the series." On his next shift, Clarke did just that with a slash.

"Cowboy Bill" Flett, a teammate of Clarke's on the Philadelphia Flyers, says he once told new Leaf Inge Hammarstrom during a pre-season exhibition game that his arm would be broken if he touched the puck. "He was two steps behind me," says Flett, "the rest of the night."

Larry Zeidel, the legendary hatchetman in the American Hockey League (he also spent several years in the NHL in the '50s and '60s with Detroit, Chicago, and Philadelphia) once proclaimed, "The easiest way to win a game is by intimidation. You have a holiday. You don't even work up a sweat."

Zeidel says they used to have a name for stickmen in the NHL. They called them "surgeons," and with good reason. In 1968 Zeidel was with the Flyers and Eddie Shack was a Bruin when they engaged in a stick-swinging incident at Maple Leaf Gardens. That winter, the roof of the Spectrum in Philadelphia had collapsed under the weight of snow, and the game was moved to Toronto.

Andy Raven, soon to become my teammate at Glendon College and now a prominent Ottawa labour lawyer, was finishing his third year as a stick boy at Maple Leaf Gardens, where he always worked with the visiting team. Shack and Zeidel went at each other right in front of Andy, and his memories of the incident are vivid. "I met Shack years later," Raven says,

> and he told me he was responding to an earlier butt-end in the ribs from Zeidel. At one point, they just started swinging their sticks like axes. The Gardens erupted, because Shack was a former Leaf. They stood at centre ice, making contact with each other's heads. The ref and linesmen couldn't get close. [Shack and Zeidel] chased each other around the ice. It was a spectacle, and the Gardens was going wild, but all of a sudden everybody realized they were going to kill each other. The crowd stopped cheering and you could hear a pin drop. The only sound was the sound of stick on bone. It lasted five full minutes. In those days, the Leafs dressing room was only for the Leafs, so the Bruins had to use the room the Marlboros used—across the ice from the bench. I helped Shack cross the ice and met the trainer at the other side. He needed stitches in four different places.

Leafs' guiding light Conn Smythe was said to admire guts even more than he did a team member's loyalty to him. He once observed that "The difference between a hockey player and a football player or a baseball player is that hockey guys play if they can breathe."

Derek Sanderson's father used to collect his son's stitches in a jar. "When I reached 100," Sanderson once said, "he threw the bottle away and figured I was tough enough for organized hockey."

Terry Sawchuk, the brilliant and tortured goaltender, used to pickle what he lyrically called "old pieces of me" in jars: one for lost teeth, another for bone chips, one for his appendix.

Johnny Bower's wife, Nancy, remembers when her husband was playing in Cleveland in the 1950s and lost nine teeth during a game.

"They took him off," she says, "and used a flashlight so they could see inside his mouth to stitch it and to clear out what they could find of the teeth, then they froze him up and sent him back on the ice." In hockey, teeth seem a small price to pay for a win.

Since 1923, Royal Military College (RMC) in Kingston has played a hockey series against the U.S. Military Academy (at West Point, N.Y.). RMC handily won the early games, though lately it's gone the other way. When the series is played in Kingston, flags draped in the stands read, "Remember the War of 1812." Bill Fitsell, understated as always, says, "It's advertised as war on ice, and they deliver." In 1997, a CBC-TV reporter asked the West Point goalie, "What would you do to beat RMC?" He replied: "I'd be willing to stop pucks with my bare face. I'd just like telling why I lost my teeth."

Hockey has always been a blood sport. I read about Hal Laycoe stick-fighting with Maurice Richard, Red Horner jousting with "Wild Bill" Ezinicki, Wayne Maki versus Ted Green, Ted Lindsay versus the world. The list of such encounters is long, and there is something in the telling, too, that conveys a certain pride. Hockey, the rugged and possessed kind, is very much a Canadian creation. And hockey history seldom makes apologies for the violence; the way the stories are told tends to legitimize, mythologize.

If anything, the modern game is far more ritualistic than ever. For most of the twentieth century, hockey players fought their own battles. They speared and butt-ended, slashed and cut and fought their way, creating space for themselves on the ice, earning respect game by game. Courage was tested regularly, and smaller men were expected to go toe-to-toe with the taller, heavier enemy. Like Ted Lindsay and King Clancy, the light- and middleweights took on the heavyweights and often won their rounds.

"In this game," Lindsay would say, "you have to be mean, or you're going to get pushed around. I kept telling myself to be mean. Be mean."

Lindsay's teammate, Alex Delvecchio, won the Lady Byng trophy for gentlemanly play three times in the late '50s and '60s, but his reward on the ice was sometimes to be taunted as "Miss Byng." When rumours surfaced that he might be traded to Toronto, Punch Imlach turned up his nose. "We don't want any Lady Byng winners in Toronto," said the Leafs coach, "so he's not coming here."

The fist thus became an elemental part of an otherwise fast and elegant game. "The NHL theory of violence," Dryden wrote, "is nothing more than original violence tolerated and accepted, in time turned into custom, into spectacle, into tactic, and finally into theory." Small wonder that so many say of violence in hockey, "It's just part of the game."

3

THE GAME
ON TRIAL

O N THE DAY THAT ALCIDE LAURIN PLAYED his last game of
hockey, not much was at stake. Only bragging rights.

Laurin's team from Alexandria was playing Allan Loney's team in
nearby Maxville in the final game of the season. There had been an
early thaw that year in southeastern Ontario, and on February 24 the
two teams played on the soft ice of an outdoor rink, before several
hundred rowdy fans—including eighty who had come in with the
team by train.

As sometimes happens when small-town rivals clash in hockey, the
game got rough. That year, letters to the editor of local newspapers had
divided over the issue of fisticuffs and brawls in hockey. Some corre-
spondents said the rough stuff was just part of the game; others
expressed astonishment that there seemed to be one law for the street
and another for the rink.

Alexandria was up 5–3 halfway through the game when the twenty-
four-year-old Laurin came in on a breakaway and collided in front of
the net with Allan Loney, a nineteen-year-old defenceman. The two
scuffled, Loney was hit in the face, and his nose was already broken
when his stick came up, then down hard on the head of Alcide Laurin.
Loney would later say that he was dazed and had trouble (as did
witnesses on and off the ice) sorting out the sequence of events. When
Laurin fell and did not rise, fans rushed onto the ice, and Laurin's
brother attacked Loney. When peace was restored, this much was
certain: Alcide Laurin was dead.

Allan Loney, still a boy, was charged with murder and jailed in
Cornwall. Though two other deaths had occurred that year during

hockey games nearby, these other incidents were ruled as accidents. Perhaps this one was an accident, too, but the courts would have to decide. Loney was charged with murder; if found guilty, he would hang.

The year was 1905. All of Canada followed the proceedings through the newspapers. A thousand people had attended Laurin's funeral, adding to the drama. For the first time, a hockey player had been charged with murder because of an incident during play. Though it's hard to say if religion and language played a role in the highly charged game, the papers made much of the fact that Laurin was francophone and Catholic, and Loney the son of a prominent Orangeman.

But was this a case of murder? How could the Crown prove intent? Had Laurin, in fact, been the aggressor? Do players in a violent game implicitly give their consent to be hurt? Before the trial, the charge was reduced to manslaughter, but that did nothing to diminish the spotlight that now shone on the tragedy. "Not only is the prisoner at the bar on trial," said the lawyer for the Crown, "but the game of hockey itself is on trial."

The accused was later acquitted, but only after the jury debated the matter for more than four hours. The judge, who warned Loney that he had had a close call, hoped the case would send a warning to every hockey player in the country. That warning has yet to be heeded.

Dave Seglins, a CBC-Radio reporter who produced a documentary drama on the Loney case and looked into other cases of hockey-related violence and death, is mystified by what he calls "the unique amnesty" that hockey enjoys. "Is hockey," he wonders, "a different realm?"

It seems there is a pattern. Hockey players are invariably charged and hauled into court, but always let off—after the judge issues a stern warning to them and to all who play hockey. In 1969 Wayne Maki of St. Louis and Ted Green of Boston clubbed each other with their sticks, and Green almost died from a fractured skull; both were charged with assault causing bodily harm, both were acquitted on grounds of self-defence. In 1975 Dan Maloney's beating of Brian Glennie left the Leafs defenceman with a concussion and other injuries, but the charge of assault causing bodily harm was dropped in the wake of a hung jury. In 1988 Dino Ciccarelli spent a few hours in jail for twice clubbing another player with his stick, but he remains the only professional player ever to spend any time behind bars.

One amateur player did spend time in jail. In 1973 seventeen-year-old Paul Smithers fought with another player, Barrie Ross Cobby, outside a Toronto arena after a fight-filled midget game. The other boy was kicked in the groin, collapsed, and died after choking on his own vomit. Smithers was convicted of manslaughter and sentenced to six months in jail.

Three years later, a professional player was fined by the courts but not jailed. This stemmed from a WHA game in which the Calgary Cowboys' Rick Jodzio laid a fearful beating on the Quebec Nordiques' Marc Tardif, leaving him unconscious and out for the season. Jodzio was charged in a Quebec court with causing bodily harm with intent to wound, but he pleaded guilty to a lesser charge and was fined $3,000.

The notion of a crime being committed in the course of a game often seems too far-fetched for the courts to handle. The issue of motive, the assigning of blame, even ascertaining what actually happened—all seem perilously elusive and beyond the law. For whatever reasons, the long record of hockey and violence is eerily consistent. If anything, the courts have been harder on amateur players. The pros get off the hook.

Two years after the Loney trial, hockey recorded another death—very close to the scene of Canada's first hockey homicide case, in Maxville. Ed Grenda, long active in the amateur hockey scene around Kingston and an avid hockey historian, calls the region bounded by Kingston, Cornwall, and Ottawa a kind of Bermuda triangle for the several hockey deaths that have occurred there.

On March 6, 1907, the Cornwall Hockey Club was playing the Ottawa Victorias, when Owen "Bud" McCourt was hit over the head by Charles Masson. McCourt later died in hospital. As in the Loney case, murder charges were laid and later reduced to manslaughter; in court the judge heard eyewitnesses insist that Masson was struck by

Ottawa players *before* he dealt his blow. Masson was acquitted, but the jury had this suggestion: "After hearing the evidence, your jury recommends that legislation be enacted whereby players or spectators encouraging or engaging in rough or foul play may be severely punished."

A century later, the courts are still grappling with this question: Does the law of the land apply on the ice? A game between the Boston Bruins and the Vancouver Canucks on February 21, 2000, was a case in point. Marty McSorley's now infamous felling of Donald Brashear, a two-handed chop with a hockey stick to the side of the head, would see the Bruins' defenceman face a charge of assault with a weapon.

Across North America, the intense response to the incident trained a harsh spotlight on McSorley. Thanks to the video replay, which was shown over and over again on television, few missed the assault. And though there were extenuating circumstances (had Brashear's helmet stayed on, there might have been no injury at all), commentators, coaches, players all agreed: McSorley had crossed the line. McSorley himself had trouble comprehending his action. "I'm in shock with what I did," he told a reporter after the game. "That's not the way I want to be remembered as a hockey player."

The *Globe and Mail* devoted an editorial to the matter of violence in hockey. CTV made McSorley's suspension the lead item several nights later. Peter Mansbridge, on CBC-TV, spent an hour interviewing Roy MacGregor on the subject. CBC-Radio's *Cross Country Checkup* waded in. The sports pages of every newspaper in the land were consumed by it.

British Columbia's Attorney General Andrew Petter defended his decision to lay the charge against McSorley, arguing, in effect, that the rink and the street are *not* worlds apart. "The criminal law does not end," he said, "simply because the occurrence took place on an ice surface."

But the results of the trial suggest that hockey's "unique amnesty" still held. In October of that year, Judge William Kitchen found McSorley guilty, but once again a fast and instinctive game had defied easy laying of blame. In his twenty-page ruling, the judge concluded that McSorley was remorseful and that his act was both unpremeditated and impulsive. And so while McSorley was found guilty of assault, his penalty was light—an eighteen-month conditional discharge. No time in jail, no community service.

Hockey may have *looked* as guilty as sin, but the court record of the game stayed clean. And I had to wonder: If the game has forgotten the Loney case, as clearly it has, would the McSorley case also be forgotten in time? Hockey seems doubly protected—by amnesty and amnesia.

I have my own quirky sense of North American sports and, in my mind, I have assigned each game its own colour coding. Baseball is a cool, almost polite game, steeped in ritual and played in shades of green. Football, with its clever deployment of troops arrayed in lines, is brown and mechanized. Basketball, a game that has impossibly tall and regal men doing pyrotechnics in the air, I see as purple.

Hockey is another matter. Hockey is about intensity, a game painted in red. Like no other, the game stirs those who play it.

Consider what happened on February 24, 1996, when the Université de Moncton Aigles Bleus (Blue Eagles) played against another university team, the Prince Edward Island Panthers, in Charlottetown. With the game tied 2–2 in overtime, the Panthers scored a highly controversial goal, and the enraged Moncton players attacked the referee. A news clip of the incident was broadcast all over North America. Charges were laid, long suspensions handed out—some of them five years in duration.

In his thirty-page report on the incident, Ken Dryden said that in all his years in hockey, he had never seen anything like it. "It *felt* dangerous," he wrote. "It frightened me to watch." Dryden also felt a sense of violation, for a cardinal rule of sport had been breached. *You do not touch a referee.* Dryden called the attack on the referee a defining moment in hockey. (Though this was by no means the first case of assault on a referee: Both the amateur and pro games have been marred by such attacks—by both players and fans—since the beginning.)

Several historians have pointed out that hockey was originally a poor man's game, the colonist's revenge on cricket-playing imperialists. Dryden would take that analysis one step further. "Once," he wrote,

> sports existed as an idealized world apart, with its own special, *higher* code of behaviour—sportsmanship and fair play. It was a way for the rich—because only the rich had the time and energy to play games—to teach life's lessons to their children, lessons of hard work, morality and discipline. Lessons to build character, to build empires. But in time, as money, celebrity and national prestige came to enter sports, as sports became more like real life, we came to behave in sports as in real life. By its temptations, we have become tempted. Faced with its choices and conflicts, sometimes we do the right thing, and sometimes we don't.

In his report, Dryden notes that every player has "a stupid point," a level of anger beyond which rational behaviour ceases. And the span between what Dryden calls "out of control *good* and out of control *bad*" is as narrow as the gap in a spark plug. Players, he says, move at great speed in a confined, congested space, all the while carrying wooden sticks. "The heat [of a hockey game] can be controlled," Dryden was certain, "but not eliminated."

One of the Blue Eagles players could barely comprehend how the adrenaline of that game had consumed him. "It was the first time in my life I didn't see a ref as a ref," he told Dryden. "I saw a thief, and he was running out of my house with my TV on his back."

In his evaluation, Dryden cast wide blame for what happened in this particular game—and in hockey in general. The stakes, he believes, have risen too high. Fans invest so much in the home team—their hearts, their souls, their dollars. I happened to be reading the classifieds in the *Globe and Mail* one morning in June 2001 and spotted a tiny ad: "Leafs Hockey Seat Sale," it read. Someone was offering season's tickets, and more importantly, ownership and the right to renew. The cost of two red seats? $45,000. Four gold were going for $169,000, four platinum for $299,000. Some season's-ticket holders, I have read, bequeath their seats to loved ones.

Players, meanwhile, turn games into personal contests and taunt each other. Coaches, Dryden wrote, "have learned to search deeper for slights and hungers, for hot buttons to push that will make us go harder and longer. Face to face with a game we might not win, we find ways to squeeze that extra little bit of performance. Appealing to pride, fear, solidarity, anger, to some higher purpose, and if one prod doesn't work, we try another."

Punch Imlach, the Leafs coach of the 1960s, once set out $12,000 in cash on a dressing-room table during the playoffs—the then sizeable sum that each player stood to gain by winning the Stanley Cup—as part of his pre-game inspirational talk. "See that money!" he shouted. "Those other guys down the corridor are trying to pick your pockets!" Imlach would start three spikes into the wall, describe them as "nails in the other guy's coffin," and, between periods, drive them in a little further if the Leafs had a lead.

Hockey, from the beginning, has been intensely tribal. It is surely no coincidence that that first murder charge in amateur hockey almost 100 years ago featured an Anglo-Protestant team pitted against a French-Catholic one. The Panther–Eagle contest was saturated with just that kind of clannish fervour. The *Bleus* were an *Acadien* team playing in a hostile Anglo environment. Their team captain, Yves LeBlanc, had died before the season in a tragic car accident, but his presence was still felt. His equipment hung at his cubicle in the dressing room, along with his photo-graph. Before every game, the players would file past this shrine and touch his sweater. After an important playoff win, they paused in their celebration to honour their fallen captain with a moment of silence. Someone had made the decision to create that monu-ment to a dead player—maybe to honour him, maybe to spur his teammates. But no one could have foreseen the result. As Dryden would describe it, the rats had been set loose in the box, and no one was controlling the voltage.

This was not "Win one for the Gipper," as in the old gridiron movie about Knute Rockne and Notre Dame. The circumstances must have weighed heavily on every player. Losing would have been catastrophic, and so it was.

It seems that losing, and losing it, go together in hockey. In 1977, an amateur hockey player in Quebec died after taking a punch in a game. The accused got only a conviction for assault. In the early 1990s, a Canadian player in Italy hit an opponent, who promptly died of a heart attack. A charge of homicide was laid, but after a long and tortuous delay, the result was a fine of $1,800.

In the United States, where hockey got a later start than it did in Canada, a similar pattern has unfolded. The courts look sternly at hockey violence, but accused players seem to find the exits. In 1975, for example, a Boston Bruin forward became the first athlete in the U.S. ever to be brought to court for an act that occurred in competition. A grand jury in Minnesota considered a charge of aggravated assault with a deadly weapon.

What had transpired on the ice makes for grim reading. Henry Boucha of the Minnesota North Stars had clashed along the boards with Dave Forbes, who lost the bout. After their respective penalties—two minutes for roughing and five minutes each for fighting—the two men were skating to their benches when Forbes issued an invitation to resume fisticuffs—and then butt-ended Boucha in the eye. Boucha fell to the ice clutching his face, amid "an ever-widening pool of blood," to quote one observer. Forbes then fell on Boucha and rained punches down on him until the Stars' Murray "Muzz" Oliver pulled him off.

Boucha required twenty-five stitches outside the eye, more inside the eyelid. The right eye socket was fractured, requiring eye surgery. Boucha missed nineteen games, and even when he returned he was limited because the injured eye no longer moved in its socket as before. The court would hear all those details, but a hung jury meant that Forbes would go free.

On January 6, 1972, a game between St. Louis and Philadelphia required the intervention of 150 policemen. Blues coach Al Arbour had walked across the ice to dispute a goal as the second period ended, and was actually pursuing referee John Ashley as he walked under the stands towards the referee's room. It was then that a fan, from above, dropped the contents of his beer cup on Arbour's head.

Blues' players came to his rescue, were showered with debris, and started swinging their sticks. Arbour required ten stitches for a head wound, and one of his defencemen took forty stitches in the head. Arbour and four Blues' players were arrested, but charges were later dropped.

Fighting in hockey had reached a new high. The Philadelphia Flyers, known as the Broad Street Bullies, ruled. The team had been manhandled during the playoffs of 1969, and management decided, as a strategy, to bulk up the team with big, mean players. Alarmed at the battles that ensued, Ontario's Attorney General Roy McMurtry attempted to impose on players the same rules of civility that apply on the street. Assault was assault, he reasoned, on or off the ice.

Toronto lawyer William McMurtry (Roy's brother) was asked to investigate hockey in 1975, following a particularly vicious Junior B game. After widely surveying players, coaches, referees—at all levels, from peewee to pro—McMurtry concluded that the game was sick, and that violence had increased markedly in amateur ranks precisely because it was tolerated in professional leagues.

Twenty-five years later, McMurtry still felt the same way. "Hockey," he said days after the McSorley incident, "is the only sport in the history of sport that not only tolerates fighting but rewards it. You breed McSorleys from the age of ten and up, and there may be only thirty or forty in the NHL, but there might be 3,000 or 4,000 who are aspiring to get there. It breeds a culture of violence."

The courts no doubt see hockey as a rough sport where injuries are common. "The conduct of a player in the heat of the game is instinctive and unpremeditated," said a judge in the B.C. Court of Appeal in 1999, "and should not be judged by standards suited to polite discourse." His comment, of course, was completely at odds with the view of that province's attorney general, who had opined after the McSorley incident that the law did not stop where the ice began. Almost everyone in Canada has an opinion on hockey; judges, it seems, are no different.

Hockey, it bears noting, may well be the most dangerous team sport in the world, with the highest injury rate: 37,000 injuries per 1 million participants—football (18,000) and skiing/snowboarding (11,000) lag far behind. A rough comparison of amateur football and hockey in North America suggests that the risk of paraplegia in hockey is three times what it is in football. In 1988 an American medical journal looked at catastrophic sports injuries sustained by high school athletes and found that the incidence of spinal-cord and brain injury was 0.68 per 100,000 players in football—in hockey, the rate was 2.55.

Another study in 1995 by three Minnesota health professionals offered an overview of hockey injuries in youth. They called the article "Gladiators on Ice." Citing their own and other research, they found, for example, that among Canadian peewee teams, the incidence of bone fractures was twelve times higher in checking leagues than in non-contact leagues. A study of 117 hockey players with spinal-cord injuries showed that the most common cause was a shove or push from behind and into the boards. Even so, twenty-six per cent of surveyed peewee and bantam players—who well understood that checking from behind could cause serious injury or death—reported that they would be willing to do so if "angry" or "to get even."

The lesson of hockey history is that the game is inherently dangerous and sometimes violent. But not all players take their lumps and move on. This is new: Players are now pointing fingers and suing—in part, because hockey's latter-day "lumps" are sometimes life-shattering.

We are talking here not about broken bones and stitches, but broken backs and necks. In a recent issue of the *Canadian Medical Association Journal,* researchers found that 243 players suffered severe spinal injuries in the past three decades. Six players died. Dr. Barry Pless, a professor of pediatrics at McGill University and editor of

Injury Prevention, called the numbers "really shocking," especially since the data likely understate the true incidence. Only two such cases were reported before 1982, suggesting either that the rate of injury has soared or that record-keeping before that date was woefully shallow. And, curiously, the rate of severe spinal injury—sometimes leaving victims in wheelchairs—began to rise in 1975 when helmets were made mandatory by the Canadian Amateur Hockey Association. Before then, spinal injuries in hockey were apparently rare.

Consider these five examples:

After Detroit centreman Dennis Polonich clashed with Wilf Paiement of the now-defunct Colorado Rockies during a game in 1978, Polonich was left with a broken nose, a concussion, and several lacerations. The NHL suspended Paiement for fifteen games and fined him $500; not satisfied, Polonich sued Paiement in the first civil case of its kind involving the NHL. The trial heard, in some detail, the impact of the incident on Polonich: breathing problems, loss of taste and smell, and a misshapen face—like that of car-crash victims, said a plastic surgeon who testified. In a decision in 1981, the U.S. federal court jury awarded Polonich $850,000.

In 1992, the B.C. Court of Appeal awarded $3.7 million to Mel Unruh, who was left a quadriplegic after being hit from behind and breaking his neck during a midget game in Vancouver.

In Moose Jaw, Saskatchewan, in 1994, a Junior B player named John Millikin was hit from behind and left a quadriplegic. He sued the Canadian Hockey Association for $13 million. (I've been told the case was settled, but that a non-disclosure provision keeps details private.)

During a junior game in 1992, Bill Muckalt, now with the Ottawa Senators, slammed William Zapf from behind, head-first into the boards, leaving him a quadriplegic. The B.C. Court of Appeal awarded Zapf $4 million in 1995. The same court awarded $3.7 million to another player who was hit from behind in a midget game—neck broken, life in a wheelchair.

Jure Kovacevic, a player with the Ottawa 67's of the Ontario Hockey League, was cross-checked from behind in 1994 and crashed headfirst into the boards, resulting in compressed vertebrae, two broken ribs, and injuries to his shoulders and legs. His dreams of a pro career shattered, he's suing the other player, the other team's coach and owner, and the league itself for $15 million. That case is still before the courts.

The NHL has begun to catalogue serious injury. Dr. Charles Burke, the Penguins' team doctor, heads up the NHL's Post Concussion Syndrome Project. Their data show 104 concussions in the league in 1999–2000 alone. Each player in the league undergoes a battery of neurological tests at the start of the year; anyone suffering a concussion must then undergo the same tests until the post-concussion results match that first test.

Many NHLers have had their careers end prematurely because of concussion: Brett Lindros, Michel Goulet, Pat LaFontaine, Geoff Courtnall, Nick Kypreos, Jeff Beukeboom among them. And what puzzles medical authorities is the phenomenon of post-concussion syndrome—months of depression and inability to focus. This, too, may be new.

Ophthalmologist Dr. Tom Pashby of Toronto has been looking at eye injuries in Canadian hockey after 1972. His data show 1,906 incidents, with 309 losses of sight in the injured eye. In every case, the injured wore no visor or full-face mask. Eight eye-injured players wearing half-visors, Dr. Pashby strongly suspects, wore loose chin straps that allowed too much movement. Since 1972, forty NHLers have been forced into retirement because of eye injuries. In the year 2000 alone, twelve players in the NHL sustained eye injuries, including Bryan Berard of the Leafs, whose career apparently ended with that injury (though he made an extraordinary comeback with the Rangers in fall 2001).

Dr. Pashby's report noted that twenty-four per cent of NHL players wear visors (that number would rise to twenty-eight per cent in 2001). The mystery is why the number is so low. Al MacInnis, a gifted defenceman with St. Louis, once described being struck in the eye by another player's stick. As he headed off the ice, he was unable to resist the temptation to try to see out of the eye. There was nothing, he said, "nothing but black. I couldn't see a thing. You wonder if you'll ever be able to play again. It's the worst thing you could ever go through."

Worrisome, too, is that the damage seems to be spreading, like a contagion. While many stylistic elements of European hockey have come to North America, such as the Russian penchant for circling and involving the defence in offensive play, a flow the other way has also occurred. European hockey, which has always prized skill over rough play and which had known nothing of the tradition of brutality in North American hockey, seems to have shifted tactics. Europeans are now dealing with the tragic consequences of terrible hits—especially hits from behind.

In February 2001 Tomas Zelenka was slammed into the boards by Marian Morava, a much-penalized defenceman. The vicious hit from behind left the Czech Republic pro player almost completely paralyzed, with only the use of his hands.

The Czech Association of Professional Players described the incident as "shocking and inexcusable" and asked players "to realize that life is more important than points. . . . Are we going to further injure and kill each other or are we going to play a sport called hockey?"

In his honour, Zelenka's team forfeited their next game. The players were reportedly in tears and unable to play in any case. Patrik Elias and Petr Sykora of the New Jersey Devils, and Dominik Hasek (then with Buffalo, now with Detroit)—all of them Czech nationals—have contributed to a fund set up for the stricken player.

As old as the game itself is the mixed response to the game, and especially to its rougher side. There's an intriguing picture in an old book about hockey called *The Violent Game*. On the ice a fight is unfolding between the Bruins' Wayne Cashman and the L.A. Kings' Bob Murdoch. It's the reaction of the fans (within ten feet of the fracas) that I'm drawn to. First the women. Several are grimacing; another has opened her arms wide in a "What's this?" gesture; two women on the far right are grimly hanging onto the steel bar in front of them, as if on a roller-coaster ride; a young girl offers open-mouthed shock. Then the men. A bald guy has leaned in for a closer look; another bald guy has pulled back, vaguely appalled; a third man rests his chin in his hand, like a biology professor looking on dispassionately as a tarantula battles a scorpion. No one is looking away.

Is this why those who govern hockey find it so hard to deal with the explosions, large and small, that inevitably occur on the ice? The photograph says it all. There is no consensus about what is unfolding on the ice—whether it's proper or how to proceed.

That may be changing. In the peewee leagues of Kingston, Ontario, where I live, any hit from behind results in automatic banishment from the game; repeated offenders are banished from the league. Some players wear little "STOP" signs on their backs, meant to deter such hits.

What led to this is injury. Several years ago when my son was twelve, his rep team—which played contact only during tournaments—lost a goalie to a separated shoulder, two players to broken wrists, and another to a broken leg. (A "rep" team gathers the best of interested house league players for more competitive hockey.) The team trainer is an emergency-room physician, and there were nights when we parents were glad he was there. In one game, an opposing player went down hard in front of the net, and his horrified father had to look on as the boy lay prostrate on the ice for thirty minutes, and when he was later strapped to a stretcher on wheels, his neck immobilized in a brace. He was later deemed to be fine, but it was wrenching to see him carted off in that way. The silence in the arena was part tribute, part terror.

One can almost accept injury from accident, as this was. But lost tempers in hockey are also responsible for broken bodies. One spring a fourteen-year-old boy in a non-contact league was ejected from the game; in the corridor after the game, he was set upon by two players from the other team. This seemed to me incomprehensible but terribly real: for the incident occurred in the very rink where I play old-timer hockey. I had trouble even imagining such a thing taking place in that friendly old arena. The young player suffered a broken nose, and assault charges were laid.

In recreational leagues all over Canada, the rule is supposed to be "no contact." Most times, these matches are playful and light. Many players sport sizeable pot-bellies and laugh at how many years it's been since seeing their toes. But talk to the men in those leagues, or fathers watching their boys at rinks, and you hear another side: chilling anecdotes about meaningless games punctuated by broken teeth, brawls, and stick work. The police, I am told repeatedly, are regularly called to arenas to settle disputes. The phrase "recreational hockey" begins to sound hollow.

I remember a case in the mid-1970s that made the Toronto newspapers. Two men were playing in a B'nai B'rith businessmen's house-league game when one player hit another and a stick came up. The clipped player then pursued the other man from behind, wrapped his stick around the other player's neck, and began to choke him before they were pried apart. The assailant was charged with assault causing bodily harm and fined $300 or thirty days in jail. The horrified referee later observed that "Some of these guys are not very good players, and the way it seems to work is that the worse a player you are, the more likely you are to take a swing at a guy." His remark hit home to me.

In 1988, at the age of thirty-nine, I was living in Toronto and I played Sunday morning contact hockey at McCormick Arena in the west end with my friend David Carpenter and a group of his buddies, accountants most of them. The hockey was good, and not all that rough, but there was one player who had a reputation. In my head, I called him "Bud"—*B* for big, *u* for ungainly, *d* for dour. Bud did not like to get hit, likely feared being hit, and his defensive and semi-automatic response was a savage elbow or two—and a fist if that became necessary. He played on the other team, and the chemistry between Bud and me was sour. One game, at the blue line, something transpired and suddenly we were eye-to-eye. Had we dropped our gloves? Were we shouting at each other? I can't remember. But I do recall that David, in goal, raced from the net, shouting my name all the way, and gang-tackled me before hostilities could erupt. David thus spared me what would have been my first hockey fight, and, no doubt, my first drubbing. Later in the season, my brother Wayne joined us for a game, and he, too, became entangled with Bud. I had said nothing by way of warning; Bud's elbow somehow found Wayne's head. My brother objected.

But even a clean hit can be provocative, for one man's "clean" is another man's "dirty." Tiger Williams once made a good point about hockey violence. The former Leafs bruiser observed that many players never learned to take a check without starting a fight. "That's a flaw of our game," he said. "Guys have to realize that a good clean check is like a good pass. It's an art in itself." Objecting to every hit offers just one more way for hockey players—the Sunday-morning types as we were, or the pros of Saturday night—to find themselves either in hospital or in court.

Maybe the tally of hockey's wounded has to swell a little more before something is done. "STOP" signs on hockey sweaters and bans on hits from behind only followed a rash of injuries. The sight of a boy being carried off on a stretcher after playing a game he loves: This sends a message.

Will hockey finally fix itself after enough boys and men are hurt or maimed? Maybe the game requires another human sacrifice, another hockey death. Perhaps a case like Allan Loney's would have a different impact now, almost a century later. The irony is that the lawyer for the accused player would likely try to shift the blame, and, as in the Loney case, put the game itself on trial.

The lawyer for Dave Forbes in the aforementioned Henry Boucha case of 1975 did just that. He had argued that hockey—with its insistence on intimidation, on winning at all costs, on accepting grievous injury as just part of the game—was culpable, not his client. The accused apparently struck the jurors as gentle and smart and amiable, so that whatever transpired on the ice seemed out of character. The game, or so his lawyer argued, had transformed him. "You get crazy in the course of a game," Forbes said in court. "It's a continuous battle.

Lots of times players can't account for their actions." His lawyer referred to the "Jekyll/Hyde" effect.

Some reporters at the trial wondered if Forbes was the Lieutenant Calley of hockey—"a foot soldier forced to suffer the consequences of a battle plan ordered by the NHL brass," as *Sports Illustrated* put it.

The magazine quoted from William McMurtry's task force on violence in amateur hockey, which laid the blame squarely at the feet of the NHL. "When the evidence strongly indicates that there is a conscious effort to sell violence in hockey to enrich a small group of show-business entrepreneurs at the expense of a great sport—not to mention the corruption of an entire generation's concept of sport— then one's concern grows to outrage."

"The way things are going," said Minnesota tough-guy Dennis Hextall in 1976, "someone is going to get killed." Many players have since expressed the same fear, using just that phrase. After a particularly brutal playoff game that year between Philadelphia and Toronto, Flyers coach Fred Shero uttered a similar refrain—his fear, though, was not that one player would kill another, but that a fan would kill a player. "Of the 17,000 in this place [Maple Leaf Gardens]," said Shero, "I bet 1,000 of them aren't all there. They let their emotions get to them. They spit on players, curse at them, throw things at them. Some night a guy is going to come in here with a loaded gun."

Rightly or wrongly, that future addled fan's lawyer may also blame his crime, as Forbes did, on the frenzied atmosphere in hockey arenas. If the game can transform otherwise peaceable players, can fans also become victims? Is the league that condones violence somehow culpable? Or is every player ultimately responsible for his own behaviour on the ice? Hockey's next murder, when and if it occurs, may finally answer those questions with a judgment that would end the "unique amnesty" that has, for so long, shielded the game.

THE
ANATOMY
OF HOCKEY

THE CANADIAN AUTHOR DAVID ADAMS RICHARDS must talk hockey wherever he goes. In 1998 he was about to be interviewed by Laurie Brown, an arts reporter with CBC-TV, and he found himself sitting in an equipment truck between the soundman and the cameraman, all of them in animated conversation about the game. The cameraman was Gord Judges, who played on the line with the Montreal Alouettes and the Toronto Argonauts between 1969 and 1983. The soundman, Phil Jones, was a defensive halfback and punt returner with the Als and Argos from '80 to '86. Both men had played high-school football in Scarborough, not far from where I grew up, and had remained good friends.

Jones had a theory about violence in hockey and whatever he said that day must have made a deep impression on Richards: When the writer and I chatted at a charity event in Kingston three years later and I mentioned the hockey book I was working on, that conversation with the two ex-footballers came up early on. Football, Jones had told Richards, features all kinds of breaks in the action, and the contact typically involves one man lined up against another. As he spoke, Richards made two fists and had them clash. This is collision, with a beginning and an end, the whole thing over in seconds. Hockey, though, the footballer opined, features an entirely different kind of action—intense and often unbroken for long stretches, with the contact more often of the glancing and unpredictable kind. Hip on hip, an elbow to the face, a whole-body blow. The hits can come from anywhere—from the side, from behind, out of thin air. A forward who drops his head down for a puckward glance as he brazenly crosses the blue line—especially if he cuts towards centre—may never see the braced and waiting shoulder that will leave him crumpled on the ice. Like a hawk clipped by a truck, or Lindros by Stevens.

I found Phil Jones easily enough, and he remembered the talk and the key distinction he had made: football as collision sport, hockey as contact sport. The distinction seemed profoundly simple and, like many simple concepts, worth pondering. At the age of forty-five, Phil Jones still does some work as a soundman alongside Gord Judges, but in his last year in the Canadian Football League, playing for the Eskimos in Edmonton, he refined a computer game meant to improve an athlete's peripheral vision and reflexes. Called DynaVision 2000, it's now used by several NHL teams, as well as police personnel, driver trainers, and rehabilitation specialists.

My conversation with Jones left me wanting answers to other, broader questions: Just how fast do skaters and pucks travel? How is it that some players can move at top speed while performing intricate manoeuvres? How, really, does the physics of hockey work? Much as a scientist might, I wanted to probe the game I thought I knew and put it under the looking glass.

I learned that a man can skate twice as fast as he can run—forty-eight kilometres an hour—and that a slapshot by Bobby Hull was clocked at 116 miles (187 km) an hour. That's 170 feet per second. A goaltender who moved out ten feet to cut down the angle on Hull also cut down his reaction time—to 0.34 seconds. The time it takes to blink, hardly time to duck.

Dennis Hull, who shot the puck almost as hard as his brother did, once rifled the puck up the boards and it landed in the penalty box, where Ranger defenceman Harry Howell sat. He ducked and fell to the floor, and there were grave fears he had been hit in the head. Howell never wore a helmet. Madison Square Garden fell silent. Then Howell's stick appeared in the air and began to move slowly back and forth, a white towel on the end of it.

Someone once timed Paul Kariya of the Anaheim Mighty Ducks,

moving from behind his net to put the puck in the other net: an astonishing six seconds.

And just as times in track-and-field events have continued to tumble since they were first recorded, hockey has steadily gotten faster. Researchers have scrutinized old film footage and determined, by comparison with modern footage, that even the quickest skaters of hockey history, legends such as Howie Morenz and Maurice Richard, could not have kept pace with mere journeymen today. (Still, Hec "Hurricane" Kilrea, who played for Ottawa, Toronto, and Detroit in the '20s and '30s, was once clocked circumnavigating a 220-yard course at the Montreal Forum in 16.4 seconds, proof that some old-timers were indeed quick. To compare, Mike Gartner—ranked among the fastest contemporary skaters—was timed rounding a rink in 13.4 seconds.)

Players are faster, stronger, better conditioned, and their equipment has gotten lighter and more efficient every year. During a game, a player may lift his skates some 2,000 times and travel the equivalent of four miles. Old equipment was made of leather and cloth and horse-hair, materials that could double in weight when wet. Some goalies would lose 13 pounds in a game, most of it shed in the form of sweat. The advent of nylon and plastic has considerably lightened the load that every hockey player must carry.

Even the sharpening of skates has undergone its own revolution. Most players have their skates sharpened so that the front and back ends are higher than in the middle, the blade touching the ice as a rocking chair does the floor. This works well for forwards and stay-at-home defencemen. But rushing defencemen go for longer, flatter blades (like those of a speed skater), sometimes with a hollow inserted between the edges, to augment their lateral movement.

All the rage, as I write this, is the ultra-light Bauer "Vapour" skate. Old skates were made of leather; today only the heel and eyelets are. The rest of the skate's material sounds like it comes from NASA: Kevlar, graphite, ballistic nylon.

What has not changed is the knack that gifted players have for knowing where they are on the ice—in the way that someone who has lived a long time in one house can navigate his or her digs in the dark. The story is told of Bronco Horvath, a Bruins star of the '50s and '60s, who wanted kids at a summer hockey school to develop just such a knack on the ice. To demonstrate the point, he would stand between the red line and the blue line and, with his back to the net, shoot blindly at it, calling out the post he was aiming for. In five shots, he nailed his target twice and came close with two others.

That story reminds me of a horseman I rode with in Wyoming who always knew where north was—even when there was no sun to guide him, even in dense forest devoid of any long horizon. I could have asked him to close his eyes and spin in circles, but that body compass of his would not be thrown off.

John McPhee, a fine American writer, describes how former basketball player Bill Bradley could do something similar to Horvath's feat. With his back to the basket, Bradley looked McPhee in the eye and threw the ball over his shoulder and into the net, twice. "You develop a sense of where you are," the basketballer said.

Great athletes have such an eye that even subtle changes in their playing environments do not go unnoticed. Dick Irvin, in his book on goalies, *In the Crease*, cites two such examples, one from baseball, the other from hockey. He describes a game in Boston where the cocky slugger Ted Williams took a called third strike—a rarity since umpires tended to trust his eye more than their own. On the bench, Williams grumbled that home plate was out of line, but the smirking among his teammates stopped abruptly when a post-game measurement backed up his contention. Jacques Plante had the same acute sensibility. Beaten for two goals early in a game against Chicago, he insisted, in the dressing room between periods, that the net was set too high. When he leaned against the crossbar, he told his skeptical teammates, it touched him a tad higher than normal. When the referee acquiesced and measured the net, it was indeed found to be out of whack.

An elite player's gift is never solely physical, but some players come equipped with phenomenal biological advantages. Dr. William Tatton, a neurologist at the University of British Columbia, has studied "long-loop reflexes," the ones that let superb athletes perform complex tasks under duress. Imagine, for the sake of argument, that you can do two things at once: juggle several balls and shoot a puck. Now imagine juggling five balls and shooting the puck into a tiny corner of the net while a defenceman whacks at your ankles. This, too, is grace under fire. Wayne Gretzky had the fastest long-loop reflex of anyone Dr. Tatton had ever studied.

It seems that Gretzky was naturally blessed in other ways, too. That slight body of his was tailor-made for the fastest game in the world. Exercise physiologist Dave Smiths at the University of Alberta once decided to test the recuperative abilities of the Edmonton Oilers, when Gretzky was that team's captain. After subjecting Gretzky to a battery of tests, Smith thought the machine had malfunctioned because the results were so astonishing. Though unable to bench-press his own weight of 160 pounds, and though he was the weakest Oiler ("Am I stronger than my mother?" he later asked), Gretzky was far and away the fittest man on the team.

Gretzky himself would acknowledge what nature had bestowed on him, but he was also quick to note that he took his gift to another level—by dint of hard work. "Nine out of ten people think it's instinct, and it isn't," he told Peter Gzowski in *The Game of Our Lives.* "Nobody would ever say a doctor learned his profession by instinct; yet in my own way I've put in almost as much time studying hockey as a medical student puts in studying medicine."

For years, the hardest shot in the NHL has belonged to Al MacInnis of the St. Louis Blues. The defenceman believes that his 100-mile-an-hour slappers owe a great deal to his boyhood custom of shooting 1,000 pucks or more a day against a barn, back home in Inverness, Nova Scotia. Stephen Murphy, a director of product research with Bauer/Nike Hockey in Montreal, is also a biomechanics specialist who did his Ph.D. on the slapshot. He told author Bruce Dowbiggin, in *The Stick,* that "Where you contact the puck on the blade is very important, and MacInnis hits the puck in almost exactly the same spot every time. He's very consistent."

For Gretzky, hockey school began when he was a peewee, with long hours every day at the local arena, on the street, and, of course, on the now almost mythical backyard rink that Walter Gretzky made every winter. Gretzky *père* had, in his head, a deep understanding of hockey, and passed on to his son his uniquely intelligent and analytical approach to the game. He started Wayne off as a defenceman, so the boy could see the pattern of plays developing. Get the long view first. It's called seeing the ice, and no one would see the ice quite like Wayne Gretzky.

In his memoir, Dave Semenko—the tough guy who would respond were anyone foolish enough to actually hit The Great One— talks about Gretzky's remarkable panic threshold, how he seemed to possess unparalleled patience with the puck. Lesser players would fold under the pressure of attacking defenders, cough up the puck, make a dumb pass.

Gretzky was right about most of us seeing hockey as a game of instinct. The speed of the game played at its highest levels is hard for the rest of us to imagine. Numerous scribes, including Peter Gzowski and Eric Duhatschek, have gone out on the ice to practise with the big boys. All have come away shaking their heads at the quickness of the players, even the ones they thought were plodders, never mind the ones with the jets.

My brother Tommy once played a game with Glenn Anderson, in the spring of 1996, when the former Oiler—with six Stanley Cup rings in his drawer—was thirty-six. Anderson had played briefly with the Canadian national team, with a German team the previous fall, and he was working himself back into shape for one last fling with the St. Louis Blues. And since he was pals with one of my brother's buddies, Anderson suited up one night for Wednesday-night hockey.

"I remember a couple things about that game," Tommy says.

He played defence on my team—though, of course, he was a winger in the NHL. He got a pass to me once, somehow thread- ing it through legs and sticks. There was no way he should have got it through, and I blew the pass. At one point we were down two goals and we started giving him a hard time on the bench, and he popped two. But he wasn't turning it on, he was trying to be fair. The only time he turned it on was late in the game when we lost the puck in front of the other team's net. And Stephen [Scanlan]—who is one of the fastest skaters on the other team— got a quick pass at his blue line and took off up the ice. Anderson is way behind the play, almost at the net, and he must have felt badly about the turnover because then he did turn it on. You know that sound that really powerful skaters make? The sound of ice being carved by muscle? Anderson caught Stever by the other blue line. We were all shaking our heads. That's the speed these guys play at.

Afterwards, the normally raucous hockey players were trying to be cool with this sniper who twice notched 54 goals in NHL campaigns. Awe had silenced them. Finally, one of the boys approached Anderson and asked him to sign his stick—"for my son," he said. Pretty soon they were all lined up. "It's for my daughter," some would say, even the ones without kids. But the memory they all took from that game was the astonishing acceleration of an NHLer who was thought to have lost a step.

Maurice Richard had that kind of bold acceleration and never much worried about opposing players told to shadow him. He would practise over and over again the art of bursting into top speed after only three or four strides. He emphasized the need both to give and receive passes in that overdrive. With Richard's acceleration, a pass right on the tape with him breaking for daylight meant he was practically unstoppable.

And, like Gretzky, he had a huge bag of tricks to draw from, some of which he practised, others he conjured on the spot. Despite the increasing tendency in hockey towards systems play, there is still room for creativity—a fraction of a second when it's just you against someone else, striving for the puck in the corner, in close against the goaltender, coming in on a defenceman. When everything accelerates, plans get lost and impulse takes over. "If you don't know what you're going to do," Richard once remarked, "how can the defenceman?"

Hockey genius is enabled not just by natural ability, but by countless other elements—tenacity, heart, imagination, and dull repetition of the same small trick in practice over and over again. All are part of the package. As the following tales would suggest, the grand illusion of hockey is achieved, as all magic is, by both quick hands and a willingness to suspend disbelief.

There is a story told in Andy O'Brien's *Rocket Richard,* a book that dates from the 1950s. The parable nicely conveys how hockey players can be convinced there is gas in the tank, even when there is none. When you're at the end of a shift, when your thigh muscles will not respond and your lungs are crying for air, sometimes it happens that the puck is turned over in the other guys' end; they have a three-on-one break and a line change is impossible. You *must* get back and defend, mind must win over matter. Maybe, you tell yourself—all this in a blink—you're in better shape than they are, your pain is manageable, the mission you share merits the sacrifice. Or maybe you are simply lied to, and you swallow the fib.

In the final game of the 1953 Stanley Cup playoffs, fought between Montreal and Boston, the two teams played to a scoreless draw in regulation time. The series had been a bruising one, and the Canadiens looked exhausted, even though one win would gain them the Cup. In fact, they did win—in overtime—when Maurice Richard assisted on a goal by Elmer Lach and almost killed Lach when the two collided moments after the goal.

On a train years later, O'Brien encountered Dr. Gordon Young, the Canadiens' team doctor. "I've often wondered," O'Brien asked him, "what hypo you used to inject that tremendous surge into the Canadiens."

"That Stanley Cup game," the physician replied, "was really won nine years before, at the Battle of Caen." And he told this story. A month after D-Day, British and Canadian forces encountered stiff German opposition at Caen, France. Casualties were so high that ambulances had trouble keeping up with the wounded, who were placed in ditches on the roadside to await transport to hospital. Dr. Young, then a Canadian army medic, looked on as nuns would approach each man and offer him a cube of sugar laced with brandy. The whole business was done discreetly, the bottle hidden under the nun's skirts and accessed by an elaborate system of ropes and pulleys.

"It seemed to revive the wounded," Dr. Young recalled. Sugar and brandy and a little kindness.

Cut to 1953. The same physician is looking around the Canadiens' dressing room and what he sees is a group of dispirited and physically exhausted men, heads bowed, bodies sagging. Dr. Young wonders if the nuns' trick might work some magic, and he mentions the idea to the coach, Dick Irvin, and the manager, Frank Selke. Both were abstainers but felt desperate enough to try anything—even a "hypo" of sugar and brandy. A minute and twenty-two seconds into overtime, the puck was in the net.

In 1950 the New York Rangers had their own miracle brew. Leone's Magic Elixir was the brainchild of a Manhattan restaurateur named Gene Leone. Despairing at the play of his woeful Blueshirts (and hoping for a little publicity), he blended spices and vintage wine and offered it to the team as "a wonder drink." Frank Boucher remembers different ingredients in the concoction—orange juice, ginger ale, and honey. But whatever was in the drink did work wonders: The Rangers won nine of their next eleven games.

But like the Leafs of the 1970s, who went on a similar run when coach Red Kelly installed a small pyramid under their bench, or the New York Islanders of the same era who were convinced that a fifty-pound bag of elephant dung from the Ringling Brothers Circus was their lucky charm, Leone's magic potion worked only for a brief time.

The notion of time in hockey is a curious one. In the absence of penalties, icings, and offsides, a period of hockey could theoretically last twenty uninterrupted minutes. Hockey and its cousin lacrosse are the only games that allow substitutions on the fly. Football, baseball, basketball, soccer—all these games have pauses, and actual play may last only seconds. Hockey offers sustained action. The game has flow, a sense of timelessness.

Off the ice, time for professional players disappears in another way. Ken Dryden talks in *The Game* about how pro players have no routine at all, but a patchwork schedule built around games and practices and travel. They live in a twilight zone. Dryden: "Awake half the night, asleep half the morning, with three hours until practice, then three hours until dinner, night-time no different from daytime, weekends from weekdays."

The drudgery of modern professional hockey, with teams flying all over the continent for much of the year, exacts a terrific toll. And yet some players manage to get up for practice. Reggie Leach was a sniper with the Flyers in the 1970s. His description of what transpired in practice touches on both the dreariness (the endless hours repeating a manoeuvre) and the leap of faith that can follow.

Leach claimed he could shoot the puck at about the same speed as Bobby Hull's shot. He would rifle slapshots into an imaginary six-inch square in either top corner of the net, hitting on nine out of ten shots. *After* formal practice, he would fire 200 slapshots, occasionally trying to hit the crossbar or the goal post ten times in succession from thirty feet out.

"When I'd shoot," said Leach, "it was as if my eyes were out on the blade of my stick." He had convinced himself that if his eyes could spot a two-inch hole, the stick could surely spot a four-inch one.

Other players talk about the intense focus they bring to even small aspects of the game. In the faceoff circle, for example, some centremen claim they can perceive the skin on the linesman's knuckles go from white to pink as he sets to drop the puck.

Some players, like Brett Hull, actually hold the stick higher up the shaft when they shoot, in order to create what golfers call "whip." One more trick we do not see from our seats.

Oddly, though 90 per cent of Canadians are right-handed, 70 per cent of our hockey players shoot left. In the United States, the figures are flopped: 70 per cent of American players shoot right. "It may be a cultural thing," a hockey stick manufacturer told Bruce Dowbiggin in *The Stick*. "It really is strange."

Stranger still is what some players can do with a stick. When hockey historians discuss Gordie Howe, they invariably come around to his one-punch, nose-fracturing destruction of the Ranger's tough-guy Lou Fontinato. Less well known is this testament to Howe's dexterity, in which his stick seemed an extension of his body. One night in Montreal, Howe deked around all-star defenceman Doug Harvey and then, with the latter draped all over him, used one hand to deal with the load on his back while, with the other hand placed halfway down his stick, he put the puck over Jacques Plante's shoulder. Both benches stared in disbelief.

"The next day," wrote Michael McKinley in *Putting a Roof on Winter*, "Howe's teammates tried the feat in practice, lining up pucks on the goal line, attempting to one-hand them into the top of the net. With no one harassing them and all the time in the world, they couldn't even raise the pucks off the ice."

The other story told of Howe is this one: From one end of the rink, he could wrist a shot to the other end, and the puck would still be rising as it rocketed over the end-glass. Try it.

Or this. When George Plimpton sat in on the Bruins training camp in 1977, he would join them after practice for a beer—the Peter Pan in Fitchburg, Massachusetts, was their favourite watering hole—where they told hockey stories. Plimpton found hockey players to be inveterate storytellers, and the stories the Bruins wanted to tell invariably involved Bobby Orr, who had left the Bruins the year before in the twilight of his injury-plagued career. One story had Orr killing a penalty against Oakland and somehow losing one glove at centre ice, where it lay, as Plimpton described it, "palm up like a huge mail fist discarded on a battlefield." Orr—who has my vote as the greatest player who ever lived for the way he could control a game—continued to rag the puck, picked up that lost glove as he passed it, split the defence, went in on goal, and was thwarted by goalie Gary Smith. The telling point of the story is that when Orr missed, *both* benches groaned.

Since the 1970s, when the six-foot Orr was considered to be a decent-sized defenceman, the anatomy of hockey players has changed considerably. Early players came in a vast range of sizes. In the early 1900s, for example, the biggest pro player was goalie Billy Nicholson, who stood only five-seven but weighed 275 pounds. The smallest player was Dickie Boon, at five-four and 118 pounds.

In 1971 the average NHL player was five-eleven and 184 pounds. Today the average is six-one and more than 200 pounds. Among current players, Derian Hatcher is six-five, Chris Pronger six-six, Chris McAllister six-seven, Zdeno Chara six-nine. In the 1997 draft, no defenceman under six-one was considered by an NHL team. A friend of mine recently went to the Air Canada Centre in Toronto after not seeing a live NHL game in many years. "Have they shrunk the rink?" he asked the person seated next to him. Eventually he realized that the rink is the same size, but the players are far taller and heavier than those he remembered.

A friend, in Boston, owns a collection of NHL hockey sticks from the '60s, and what struck me as I handled them was not just the impossible banana curve of some blades but how small the sticks all seemed. Stan Mikita and Bobby Hull used Northland Custom Pro sticks; Mikita's was a little taller, but both sticks came up to my chest. Even the Victoriaville Pro used by Phil Esposito, who seemed so tall and rangy when he played, only reached my chin. Despite their great gifts, the gods were mere mortals after all.

5

MEASURE
FOR
MEASURE:
HOW TITANS
VIEW
THE GAME

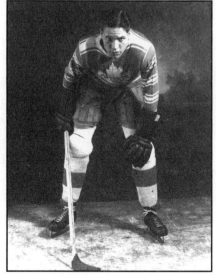

I READ INTO THE TESTIMONY of tough guys (when all are done declaring their fearlessness, that is) something unexpected: a certain squeamishness—genuine embarrassment and regret—about the work they must do.

Enrico Ciccone, a six-five, 220-pound player who was with half a dozen NHL teams in the 1990s (ten goals in eight years) was once asked by a fan if he was going to "kick somebody's butt" in the game that night. "I'd rather they ask me," he later told an interviewer, "'Are you going to play a good game tonight—a good defensive game?' Because fighting is not all of hockey."

Glen Featherstone allowed as how he, too, can't say he enjoyed fighting. Jamie Huscroft didn't mind the fighting, but neither did he enjoy it. His young daughter was mystified by her father's behaviour on TV. "Daddy," she told him, "you're silly. You flip the boys over." She meant the fighting. "We're just having fun out there," Huscroft would say to her. In one interview, he made a telling point: For fifteen minutes after a fight, he could hardly skate and stickhandle. It is said in hockey that goal scorers have "soft" hands and that goons have hands of lead. Fighting makes bad hands worse.

John Kordic complained bitterly about his role in hockey—while freely conceding that without fisticuffs he would have no place in the game. Tiger Williams often said he would love to play eighty games without once fighting.

Like other hockey fighters, Jamie Huscroft worked out in a boxing gym. He trained three times a week in his basement—on a speed bag, double-end bag, and heavy bag. Some hockey players, then, are unique in all of sport, for they must train both for the game and the boxing that goes with it.

Seen in a certain light, fighting in hockey is really a squabble over work—a little like those ugly scenes in the film *On the Waterfront,* where dockyard workers battle among themselves for the few jobs.

In hockey, such fervour can lead to absurd scenarios. A recurring instance has junior players—vying for jobs in the pro leagues by displaying their mettle for scouts—engaging in elaborate subterfuge after nasty contests. This may be the hockey equivalent of urban myth, but several examples appear in hockey literature. Think of those old westerns where the mischievous cowpoke ducks the marshal by sneaking out of Dodge, clinging to the bottom of a stagecoach.

John Kordic—who would die in 1992 at the age of twenty-seven, from cardiac arrest likely induced by a heavy diet of cocaine, steroids, and alcohol—was playing for the Portland Winter Hawks in the early 1980s, when he was ejected from a game and went up into the stands. He had in his hand a single cowboy boot and he beat a fan with it. The police came for Kordic after the game but were told he had already left. In fact, he was stashed in the bus's luggage bin. Brent Hughes, who last played with the New York Islanders in 1997, recalls a similar incident in the mid-1980s, when one of his teammates on the New Westminster Bruins hit an opposing player with his stick and carved him for eighty stitches. Hughes's teammate, too, evaded arrest. The old luggage-bin trick.

What the bad boys of hockey say repeatedly is how important it is for a tough guy to "show up"—to give it his all, every bout. That appears to matter more than whether you win or not, though they do keep score. According to their code, you earn respect simply by answering the bell.

Some players also talk about the moment—what it feels like to be in a fight, with thousands of fans glued to you and your opponent. Brendan Shanahan of the Detroit Red Wings recalls his youth: "The feeling when you're eighteen years old and squaring off is really something. There's a second or two when you are excited and scared and happy all at the same time."

Ken Baumgartner is like many enforcers in the NHL—intelligent and soft-spoken. During his thirteen-year career in the NHL (which ended in 1999), he was well regarded by his fellow players and acted as their spokesman in dealings with the league. He would later study at Harvard Business School. Yet on the ice he was a blend of King Clancy and Eddie Shore, with the latter's feistiness and the former's clown-prince manners. "The Bomber," as he was called, was playing for the Prince Albert Raiders as a junior in the mid-1980s; in one game he grabbed a water bottle from the other team's bench, sat down beside his opponents, and coolly took a drink—which is a bit like entering a bar and taking a swig from a stranger's beer.

Drafted as young as age fourteen, junior players make money for their clubs, though few will ever earn a living from the game. But for as long as they wear jerseys and play before a paying crowd, they live by their own rules, the ones taught them by older players. A certain version of the game is thus passed on, like a tarnished coin.

I heard Harry Neale make a comment during Toronto's 5–1 drub-bing of the Canadiens in February 2001. This followed the second annual Hockey Day in Canada, a day-long televised mix of amateur hockey across the land (shinny on ponds, tykes with toques beneath their helmets) and, that night, three NHL games involving all six Canadian teams. So the remark by Neale, a broadcaster, former NHL coach, and then sixty-four years old, seemed especially telling with so much hockey history and hockey romanticism in the air. "Montreal," he said, "should start something here."

The comment came during one of those milling sessions after play has stopped, a time for issuing threats and invading personal space. Montreal—losers of their past six matches, playing their second game in as many nights, having just traded their best defenceman, a playoff spot out of the question—looked dispirited. Harry Neale was suggest-ing that somebody *do* something. I took him to mean that some Hab should drop his gloves and fight. That no Hab did so spoke volumes for Harry Neale.

Tough guys often surprise in their advice to small fans: Do not emulate me. Baumgartner, for example, urges young players to "Work on your skills." He laments that kids wish they could fight like him. "No," he tells them, "you don't want to, because it's not a life for everyone." Again, that essential regret. A few years ago, Baumgartner was forecasting that fighting in the NHL would diminish with time.

In fact, at last count, fight incidence was not in decline. In fact, fighting was up slightly in 2000–01, with 1,353 major penalties in 1,230 games. Boston's Andrei Nazarov, who stands six-five and weighs 234 pounds, led the league with twenty-seven bouts. By November of the 2001–02 season, the incidence of fighting was up significantly, and the NHL was on a pace to record 1,656 fighting majors—303 more than the previous season.

A headline in the *Hockey News* in November 2001 said it all: "Fighting on rise, goals on decline: Brawlers busier than scorers." Even Don Cherry was complaining that some players were gesticulating dramatically, in the manner of WWF wrestlers. Was this some kinder, gentler Cherry? Or had fighting hit some new low that meant even its champion was squirming?

Despite Baumgartner's prediction, he still believes—and here is a tenet as old as the game—that intimidation works. A third of players, The Bomber once observed, can be intimidated by a fighter's presence, and another third by verbal threats. The rest will not be intimidated at all. Baumgartner is convinced that an enforcer is most effective when he takes a regular shift. Like flying the flag or orchestrating military parades, the display tells the opposition that yours is a team ready and willing to wage war.

It was only while editing two hockey books that I learned how much the pros say on the ice. Chris McDonell—author of *For the Love of Hockey* and *Hockey's Greatest Stars*—would wear out his stationwagon's transmission, visiting current and former players, as he gathered material for 171 profiles, and it wasn't until I read them that I realized how much players yap at each other. They aim verbal darts, they menace and mock and threaten.

Intimidation starts with attempts to throw the opponent off his game by filling his mind with images of horrid outcomes. In the faceoff circle, Ted Lindsay would loudly shout instructions to Gordie Howe to ram his stick through the gut of the winger opposite, naming him, of course.

For Lindsay, the stick was the great equalizer. "I didn't use it much as a weapon," he once said, "it was more to keep the other fellows honest. I've been in a lot of stick-swinging duels—both as instigator and as defender. It's not a good thing, but when the adrenaline gets going you become sort of a Jekyll/Hyde personality. It's like we're in a jungle and it's survival of the fittest. And no one was going to intimidate me."

In his autobiography, cleverly titled *Looking Out for Number One,* Gretzky bodyguard Dave Semenko remembers being top gun in his junior league. If hockey is about players creating space for themselves, Semenko had carved out a rink for himself. "It was," he wrote, "just like public skating."

Gordie Howe knew about creating space. Semenko was wearing a helmet early in his career, when he first encountered, in the WHA, the man they called Mr. Hockey. After the play was whistled dead, Howe skated past him very slowly and ran the blade of his stick over Semenko's helmet, almost a caress and so subtle that few in the arena noticed. And as he did it, Howe said, "Oh, excuse me." Semenko called the gesture "a quiet little message" to a rookie, and it worked. Semenko stayed clear of him.

The sad thing about Semenko and his type is that, in their heart of hearts, they don't *want* to pummel. They want to score goals. Even in practices and games of shinny, a hockey player—no matter what his age or ability—cannot *not* celebrate a goal. "It's hard," said Semenko in his memoir, "for a hockey player to get it through his head that scoring doesn't matter."

Late in his career, during a brief sad stop with the Maple Leafs, under coach John Brophy, Semenko was appalled when Brophy screamed at Basil McRae, on the bench, for going after a loose puck. "Don't even look at that %#@+*&%# thing when you're out there," Brophy yelled. "Don't even think about the puck. You're out there to stir something up. Go fight Joey Kocur."

"Deep down, you want to be a player," said Semenko, "to make the big play or score the big goal." Some may view Semenko and his fight-club ilk as thugs, but they, too, have pride. And my sense is that these big men want the fighting and rough stuff to be *their* idea, that to have it imposed messes everything up. I liken it to someone saying that sex has to be spontaneous or it's no good. "Brophy expected me to be this atomic bomb," Semenko recalled bitterly, "sitting on the bench, ready to explode when he pushed the button."

Semenko argued in his book that "Not very many people would admit they go to a hockey game to see a fight. But not very many turn their heads away when one breaks out. Do you? Violence and gore attract attention. It's human nature. People don't speed up to go past a traffic accident."

Semenko compares having one or two tough guys on the team to nuclear deterrence. But nuclear weapons have only been used twice; hockey fights are as common as acne.

Dave "Tiger" Williams set an NHL record for penalties, with 3,966 minutes. In the 1978 playoff series between the Leafs and the Islanders, Williams took particular aim at Mike Bossy, the supremely prolific scorer who had no appetite for war.

"Tiger was Tiger," Bossy would say later. "He taunted me, threw elbows at me, worked, cross-checked and punched me." When the series was tied at two, Williams reportedly accused the Islanders of crying. He excepted Clark Gillies and Brian Trottier, but called the rest of the Islanders "a bunch of fairies."

In his memoir, *Boss,* Bossy concedes that "Williams was talking about me and as I look back, he was right. I wasn't complaining but I was intimidated. I always was afraid of playing against people who had a total disregard for others. Williams couldn't have cared less if he broke my neck."

In his book *The Hammer: Confessions of a Hockey Enforcer,* Dave Schultz says that "In Philadelphia, every game was like a war and every one of us felt like a soldier going into battle." Still, "The Hammer" conducted his business according to a certain code of honour (though I have yet to forgive him for the beating he laid on Dale Rolfe of the Rangers during a playoff game). Murray Oliver, with the Minnesota North Stars in the 1970s, observed then that there is "a kind of purpose to his aggressiveness. You always know when he's around, but I'm not afraid to turn my back on him in a corner." Oliver recalled catching Schultz with an errant elbow that really hurt, and thinking that his minutes, never mind his days, were numbered. But Schultz told him, "Goddamn it, Muzz, just keep those f----g elbows down from now on, will you?" and he continued after the puck. Oliver worried more about the real goons—players with what he called "that faraway, kind of screwy look in their eyes." I once asked a former NHLer to name someone he played against who matched that description. He mentioned Steve Durbano, who played in the 1970s for St. Louis and Pittsburgh, and for the Birmingham Bulls in the WHA. Players feared him, for they thought him capable of almost anything.

In one of three books by Stan Fischler devoted to profiles of hockey pugilists, there is a picture of Lou Fontinato leaving the ice after Gordie Howe rearranged his face in a fight at Madison Square Garden on February 1, 1959. A line of blood from his right eyebrow has crossed his face, and his lower lip is thick and bloodied, but it's the nose of "Leapin' Lou" Fontinato that draws the eye. A portion of his ample beak has been shoved off to the right side of his face, though the bottom part is more or less where it should be, forming a hideous *S.* And though Lou's eyes are closed, you know they must be registering shock. On the opposite page is a shot taken at the Boston Garden about a year earlier. Fontinato is once again at the centre of things.

Every player has gathered at the penalty box, where Lou is battling a fan. Old-time hockey.

In that brand of the game, justice was invariably meted out, even if it took years. John Ferguson, once ranked by Canadian heavyweight champion George Chuvalo as the best fighter in the NHL, was a stick boy for Vancouver when the Canucks were a Western Hockey League team. Ferguson looked on as Larry Zeidel beat up the team's star, Phil Maloney. "I never again wanted to see any of my boys not back up a teammate in trouble," Ferguson would say later. "You stand up for each other or you fall together." When Ferguson became a player in the AHL, he laid a fearful beating on Zeidel as payback.

Most times, though, justice in hockey is just around the corner. Former St. Louis Blues' team doctor J.G. Probstein recalled his first game in the 1970s. He was taking in the game on the dressing-room radio when Noel Picard came in with a cut over his eye that would warrant eleven stitches. The defenceman was anxious to return, and waved off any local anesthetic.

"Doc," he asked before leaving, "how long you gonna be down here?"

"Till the end of the game," came the reply.

"Good," said Picard, "because the guy that did this to me will be down to see you in ten minutes."

Pity that in some arenas fans cannot hear themselves think. The dumbing down of spectator sports is literally, and loudly, orchestrated. Those who run the big arenas—the music, the lighting, the sideshows—co-operate in the blinkering process. Hockey as pugilism on blades is an easy sell.

In the 1990s, when Bob Probert was with the Detroit Red Wings, he would "box" on home ice to musical accompaniment. "Hit me with your best shot! Fire away!" the raucous music would go. Souvenir stands sold T-shirts depicting Probert's caricature, and underneath, the words "Rock 'Em, Sock 'Em Hockey" and "Real Men Drop Their Gloves." Probert and Troy Crowder of the New Jersey Devils once traded reputations as heavyweight champs. When Crowder first defeated Probert, then lost to another designated hitter, the stage was set for a Probert–Crowder rematch. A sellout crowd turned up in Detroit. The *Detroit News* featured a "tale of the tape"—a listing of fist, chest, and other dimensions, as one might expect to read in the dailies before heavyweight boxers square off.

In Dallas, meanwhile, slugger Shane Churla would be pummelling an opponent and the sound system would play "Macho, macho man! I want to be a macho man!" A massive television screen above the ice showed the fight, then cut to a menacing image of actor Arnold Schwartzenegger warning, "I'll be back." In Anaheim, where Disney runs the Mighty Ducks, a fight would prompt the video-screen operator to run scenes of Goofy and other cartoon characters clouting each other with hockey sticks. Madison Square Garden would show a clip of *Our Gang* heroes Buckwheat and Alfalfa going toe-to-toe with boxing gloves, followed by Jackie Gleason and Art Carney shadowboxing in a scene from *The Honeymooners*.

In Canada, NHL arenas don't offer musical accompaniment to fights. But the nation does contribute in another way. Joe Lapointe, a reporter with the *New York Times,* has observed that most "fighting specialists" are from the junior leagues of Ontario and the Canadian west. Québécois, Americans, and Europeans are much under-represented. Anglo-Canadians as fist fodder.

The first "enforcer" in the NHL, reportedly, was John Ferguson, brought in to protect Jean Beliveau, after the latter was badly mauled during the 1961 Stanley Cup series with the Chicago Blackhawks. I don't buy the theory; Red Horner was a "policeman" thirty years before John Ferguson was an "enforcer."

Norman Morra, a Toronto criminologist with a special interest in hockey violence, dates the evolution of the "goon" hockey player from 1960, when the Hawks' Reggie Fleming was assigned to protect Bobby Hull. "He was getting badly beaten in fights," Morra told me. "The team saw there was no point in having him fighting, and he had to be protected; when Hull was out of the lineup, the Chicago franchise lost money. So what was new was the job description." The fight specialist was born.

In time, the notion evolved that fighting in hockey is a form of entertainment all its own. One hockey fan, a postman in Nutley, New Jersey, aptly named Sandy Vigilante, collects videotape of hockey fights, as others collect matchbooks and dolls.

Don Cherry made a name for himself, and some ready cash, pitching videos that assembled jarring hits and donnybrooks. His imitators are legion. Cruise the Internet and you will find the "Blood on Ice Hockey Game," which "brings all the grit and violence of hockey to your computer screen. Players of the interactive game can take out their frustrations virtually by checking, punching and otherwise mauling their opponents." Other Web sites, such as one called "Knuckles, Blood and Ice," review the week's fights in the NHL and rank combatants.

But if Don Cherry exists to the right of the hockey establishment, Sandy Vigilante operates in a zone well beyond, one that many hockey fans don't know exists. He grew up watching the big bad Bruins and Flyers of the 1970s, and he remembers with shimmering clarity Schultz boxing Durbano. Ever since then, hockey fighting—not the game itself, and especially not the finesse game—has had a fierce hold on his life. Vigilante once had season's tickets to both Rangers and Flyers games and he began to notate fights in 1972, jotting down combatants and winners. Vigilante would also chat with NHL trainers to get their verdicts on bouts. By 1978 he was collecting video. Now he has more than 1,000 hours of hockey fighting—not of games featuring fights, but of one fight after another. Were I to watch the collection from beginning to end, it would take me almost forty-two days and nights of nonstop watching.

One has the sense that Vigilante is not entirely proud of what amounts to an overwhelming addiction. "I'm trying to quit," Vigilante says, "but when I see a hockey fight, my blood boils." Given the choice between a three-week vacation anywhere in the world and three weeks of videotaping what he calls "the old stuff"—hockey fights from his cherished 1970s era—he says he would opt for the latter.

There are many more like Vigilante. Try punching in "hockey fight video" on the Internet; I did, and got almost 9,000 matches. No wonder the NHL walks that delicate walk: making the right noises about curbing fighting—to satisfy those appalled by it—but leaving enough rough stuff to satisfy the other side, like Vigilante & Co., who live for those moments when the gloves are dropped.

In 1986, the *New York Times* did a piece on hockey-fight video collectors, such as Steve Ratinetz, who calls Vigilante "the godfather of hockey fights." Ratinetz operated his four VCRs almost constantly, consulting game summaries so he could fast-forward to the fights and cut the rest. He traded with thirty-six other collectors, such as his friend Tony Blanda, who claimed to have watched 6,000 hockey fights. "It's a hobby," he said, "like stamps." Almost every month, Blanda would put on a hockey-fight party. He would buy ten cases of beer, fifteen pounds of cold cuts, and the gathered would watch two hours of fights, break to eat, then view two more hours. "At that point," he said, "everyone will be pretty much satisfied."

Vigilante is not so easily sated. His addiction has put him on a treadmill. He tapes as many games as he can himself, later stripping away the dross to reveal the treasure—the heavyweight bouts. Friends on both sides of the border also feed him tapes, even of minor-pro and junior games. The Albany River Rats matter as much as the New Jersey Devils.

Vigilante seems likeble on the phone, but when he says that he would "kill" to get his hands on vintage hockey-fight tape, I take him neither literally nor lightly. His passion for hockey pugilism has earned him a certain profile: *U.S.A. Today* once featured him, as did CBC-TV's *The Journal.* When Don Cherry launched a restaurant in Hamilton, Vigilante made the guest list.

Vigilante is, naturally, the repository of some bizarre hockey stories. He tells of an International Hockey League game in the 1970s in which a penalty shot was called and the defending team pulled their goalie and installed their goon. The hapless shooter was sucker-punched before getting close to the net. "They talk about violence today," Vigilante once said mockingly. He has a film of a Montreal–New York game in 1950 in which everybody is swinging away—"with their sticks."

Goonery does sell. Some days the most popular sweater at the Toronto Maple Leafs souvenir shop is not that of Mats Sundin, the creative centreman, but that of Tie Domi, the blocky boxer. His counterpart in Ottawa, Andre Roy, was arguably the most popular Senator until he was traded in March 2002. The autobiography of Tiger Williams, published in 1984, sold more than 100,000 copies. That puts the book in the same league—at least in terms of numbers sold—as Ken Dryden's refined and reflective book on hockey.

For as long as the game has sold tickets, hockey players have fought with their hands, and sometimes their sticks. The Leafs' Red Horner and the Bruins' Joe Lamb, for example, got into a stick fight on December 12, 1932. The resulting mêlée on the ice required the intervention of Boston police. The following year the Bruins and Leafs met in the Stanley Cup semi-finals, one that hockey historian Brian McFarlane called "the most gruelling series in hockey history." Four of the five games ended in sudden-death overtime, and, as the Leafs headed to their dressing room after the first period of the final game, they were attacked by Boston fans. In that game, at 4:46 of the *sixth* overtime period, an errant Eddie Shore pass was picked off by Leafs winger Ken Doraty, who beat Boston goalie "Tiny" Thompson.

Shore brooded over the loss and came to second-guess his "gentlemanly play" in that series. He told reporters he would "return to the rough-and-tumble style of before." This was the preamble to the Ace Bailey incident, and observers later wondered whether the shift in Shore's thinking played any role.

"Absolutely *no* incident in Canadian sporting history," Todd Christie wrote in the *Canadian Journal of History of Sport*, "has ever sparked as much public outcry or received as much front-page newspaper coverage as did the Shore–Bailey fiasco." For two months, readers followed Bailey's condition and debated the issue of violence in hockey.

To understand hockey's past and thus its tangled present, one must grapple with the character of Shore. "Old Blood and Guts," they called him. If Maurice Richard embodied desire, Eddie Shore epitomized rage. When we lose it on the ice—and most who play the game fall prey in some way or another—we follow in Shore's trail. When Shore came undone, as he often did, the results could be savage. The hit for which he became infamous strikes me as a defining moment in hockey, one that merits close scrutiny in order to comprehend the terrible forces the sport can unleash.

Irvine Wallace Bailey was nicknamed "Ace": One of the fastest skaters and slickest stickhandlers in the league, he won the scoring championship in the 1928–29 season. In 1933, he was thirty and at the peak of his game.

The book on Eddie Shore was much longer, even then, and it would grow. In 1939, John Lardner wrote: "For twenty years, man and boy, this evil fellow has been punching people, hitting them over the head with his stick, chewing their ears, butting, gouging, shoving and generally bedevilling his fellow men and always for handsome fees. No one has ever made malevolence pay better money. . . . [He has] developed the role of Villain to such an extent that professional wrestlers gnash their teeth with envy."

Madison Square Garden managers in New York put Shore's face on "Wanted: Dead or Alive" posters. Don Cherry, who saw Shore play and was coached by him in the late 1950s, said that Shore played hockey "like a car out of control in a demolition derby."

"Shore had his own physics," wrote David Cruise and Alison Griffiths in *Net Worth*. In a pre-season practice in 1926—his first year in the NHL—he laid a hit on Billy Coutu, a tough veteran who outweighed Shore. Coutu was knocked out in the collision, and Shore almost lost an ear: Part of his mythology is the story that has the team doctor wanting to amputate. Shore doctor-shops until he finds one who will sew the ear, no anesthetic. Eddie supervises by watching in a mirror, insisting when it's over that the last stitch be taken out and redone.

His list of career injuries included 978 stitches—"He bled almost every night," wrote one columnist—as well as one fractured back and hip, twelve broken collarbones, fourteen broken noses, and five broken jaws. His first broken nose occurred at the age of nine, when he was trying to break a Shetland pony near his family's home at Fort Qu'Appelle, Saskatchewan. When the colt reared, the blood flowed freely from the boy's shattered nose, but that did not stop him. Bloodied but unbowed: That was Shore.

Collier's magazine wrote that Shore filled rinks, his popularity stemming from "the hope, entertained by spectators in all cities but Boston, that he will some night be severely killed."

Reports of what happened that December night in Boston vary only a little. The thing starts with Red Horner tripping Shore, the infraction going unnoticed by the referee, Shore rising to seek revenge. Bailey, meanwhile, has been on the ice for some time, killing a two-man-short penalty. Shore rushes at Bailey from behind and hits him at full speed, as a train would a car stalled on the tracks. And there goes Bailey, looping, his head landing on the ice with a hideous *crack.*

Here's Frank Selke, assistant manager of the Leafs: "We heard a crack you might compare to the sound you remember from boyhood days of cracking a pumpkin with a baseball bat. Bailey was lying on the blue line with his head turned sideways, as though his neck were broken. His knees were raised, legs twitching."

Red Horner's first instinct is to see to his injured mate, but his efforts at straightening Ace's neck fail. Now Horner skates to Shore and hits him with a roundhouse right, though some remember an uppercut to the chin.

"It stiffened him," Selke said, "like an axed steer." Shore falls hard and hits the ice with his head. Now there are two players unconscious at either end of the rink, and I imagine them, arms and legs akimbo, the red halos at their heads still growing, the blood rapidly cooling on the shavings of the ice. At this, the Boston players come off the bench, heading for Horner. Charlie Conacher of the Leafs hops over the boards and lines up alongside Horner, and the two hold out their sticks as they would rifles, with bayonets fixed.

"Which one of you," big Conacher yells, "is going to be the first one to get it?"

The business is not done. Conn Smythe, the Leafs' coach, has led the players carrying Bailey off the ice. When a fan yells that Bailey is feigning injury—"Fake, fake! The bum's actin'!"—Smythe slugs him.

Only minutes after the event, Bailey wakes up. He is like a racehorse coming out of an anesthetic, legs churning, mind still at the track and in the race. "Put me back in the game," Ace pleads. "They need me."

Later, the now conscious but distraught Shore, who has suffered a sixteen-stitch cut to the back of the head, is ushered in to offer his deep and sincere regret. "I'm sorry, Ace," he says. "I didn't mean to hurt you."

"That's all right, Eddie," Ace tells him. "It's all part of the game."

Bailey slips back into a coma and for fifteen days his life hangs in the balance. Neurosurgeons conduct two operations to release the awful pressure from the swelling on his brain, for Bailey's skull is fractured at both temples. During those two weeks, a kind of melodrama unfolds, as if the director of a B-film has been called in to orchestrate events.

There has already been a virtual deathbed scene of forgiveness. There follows a period of mourning, as the end seems inevitable and preparations are made to ship the body; Bailey lapses into, and out of, a coma. There is murder in the air: Armed with a gun and intent on killing Shore, Bailey's father takes a train to Boston, but a police officer catches wind of the plan and intervenes. Through it all, a nurse whispers in Bailey's ear, beseeching him not to give up hope. "Keep fighting, Ace!" says the nurse. "The team needs you."

The NHL would rule that Shore's hit "was of a spontaneous nature with no malice behind it." Frank Patrick, managing director of the NHL, took depositions from all players involved in that game. He noted that Shore's record "does not class him as a vicious player. This is established by the fact he has participated in about

400 games in the NHL and he has never been given a match penalty for injuring an opponent."

I wish Shore were alive to defend himself. I have no desire to bury him a second time, but his record surely says more about the NHL's reluctance to punish players for inflicting injury than it does about Shore's good character. Was the hit on Bailey just another crushing check from a man who dished them out often?

"You play with emotion out there," says Chris Pronger, a superb defenceman with St. Louis. "A lot of times you don't realize the consequences until you calm down and think, 'Did I do that?' It's almost like you're blacking out when you're so enraged. You don't understand what you're doing." Chris Pronger is six-six, 220 pounds. Imagine that frame in a rage.

"Ace" Bailey would recover from the assault, and at the all-star benefit game for him (which would launch the tradition of annual all-star games), he and Eddie Shore shook hands at centre ice in a charged and emotional moment. But Bailey would never play hockey again.

Red Horner was two weeks shy of his ninety-second birthday when I met him in his Toronto condominium. The man who led the league in penalties eight years in succession, from 1932 to 1940, looked like he'd just had a scrap. Two days earlier he had had a cyst removed from his left cheekbone, and he was sporting a swollen eye and a nasty gash where the surgeon had gone in. The look, the boxer's slit eyes, seemed to suit this old hockey warrior.

In his prime, he was a six-foot, 190-pound loose cannon, the perfect complement to his longtime defence partner, King Clancy, whose dainty five-seven carried only 135 pounds—"but 125 of it is heart," Conn Smythe said. In an opening remark, I had suggested to Horner that hockey, more than any other game, demanded courage of its elite-level players.

"You want courage?" he came back, listing Clancy's dimensions. " *That* was courage."

I had read many accounts of the tragedy that occurred the night of December 12, 1933, but most of the major players—Shore, Clancy, Bailey—were dead. Horner alone still breathed. The savage assault on Bailey was perhaps no more sinister than certain others in the history of the game, which had, after all, cost players their lives in the early years of the twentieth century. Nor was Bailey's the first career to be dashed by a vengeful hit. That was, perhaps, just one more cruel moment in a game replete with such moments.

But here is what intrigued me about the Bailey incident and perhaps what gives it legs. Seen one way, the terrible episode feels like a one-act play about justice. One friend comes to the aid of another who has been felled by the enemy; in fact, comes perilously close to dying. If hockey still wrestles with its tribal character, it strikes me that Bailey, Shore, and Horner not only reflected that tribalism but helped etch it in stone.

Loyalty is the virtue that hockey players prize above any other. But the lesson of that night has yet to be learned: The game stirs up unholy emotions and, when not contained, near deadly consequences.

The first thing to know is that Bailey was a smaller man, at 160 pounds, than Shore and Horner, who were two inches taller and thirty pounds heavier; a big man had picked on a small one. Second, the physical insult to one would have been keenly felt by the other.

"The players during our era became close as friends, as brothers," Horner told me (and I thought of Bobby Orr's remark that the Bruins of the 1970s were "a team of brothers"). "We travelled by train and were with each other a lot more of the time than they are today." On the road, players went to movies together in the afternoon, napped in pairs in hotel rooms, ate meals as a group. They were a tight, tight bunch.

Hockey teams may well be the most cohesive units in sport. Other teams—in baseball, football, basketball—may splinter along racial, class, language, or role lines (defence, offence, stars, utility players), with small allegiances forming. Or not. My brothers—Boston Red Sox fans every one—joke darkly that when their squad leaves the ballpark, "it's twenty-four players, twenty-four taxis." Each hockey clan, for better or worse, is all bound up and tangled, like a ball of taut elastic bands.

Horner's recollection of events jibed with the chronicles I had read: Shore dumped and rising in fury, Clancy taking the puck up the ice, Bailey falling back to cover for his defenceman. Shore rushing Bailey from the side and behind, and perhaps thinking that the man he had in his sights was that antagonistic little Irishman with the cocky name of "King."

Horner picked up the tale from there. "Shore was so strong, and he picked Bailey up and he turned him in the air with one knee and one arm." I could see in my mind Shore bending Bailey's body over his waist and tossing him as high and far as he could.

Horner continued. "Bailey came down, his full weight on his head. Bailey's there on the ice, in a convulsion. Shore, meanwhile, skates up the ice and takes his place on defence, staring out." Here Horner mimicked his old enemy: His face took on a cool, grim defiance, eyes narrowed, chin set. There were no rules to govern what happened next. The surprise was not what Horner did, but that Shore never saw it coming. Or did he know and accept it as deserved, in the way that some perpetrators wish to be caught and punished?

"Did Shore smile?" I asked Horner. It seemed a critical detail.

"He may have. I skated up to Shore and I said, 'You can't get away with that, you son of a bitch,' and I hung one on him. He went down flat."

Sometimes, as Horner talked, I would glance over his shoulder at an imposing oil painting—a man plowing a field with a horse, under a vast blue sky. "My father was a farmer," said Horner. "I didn't want to be a farmer."

We sat just off the living room, at a little square card table that served as his office. There were piles of letters and small padded envelopes with pucks inside: fans seeking autographs. Before I left, Horner took me into his bedroom, where a framed photograph five feet wide showed the Gardens under construction. Another display featured dozens of the grander Maple Leafs over the years, their images neatly mounted behind glass, Horner's included. When Red Horner flicks off the switch in his bedroom every night, the last thing he sees is white maple leafs on blue sweaters, the stuff of hockey dreams—at least in these parts. On another wall in the apartment is a gold medal set inside a glass case; the Leafs got them in '32 when they won the Cup.

We all look back through rose-tinted glasses, and this man in the brown tartan cardigan does, too. Early in our four-hour-long talk, Horner said that players in his day rarely raised their sticks above their shoulders; later on, he casually mentioned getting hit over the head by "Red" Dutton's stick one night in New York. A Joe Lamb/Red Horner stick fight has already been alluded to. And when I showed Red Horner the photograph of Jimmy Orlando swooning in his own blood and leaning on referee King Clancy (with the thirty-three-year-old Horner looking on as linesman, his right fist set on his hip and that arm splattered with blood), Horner was keener on talking about the time, years later, that he and Orlando met by chance in Portugal, where Horner had built a summer place.

"Those things happened," he said of the Orlando bloodletting, "even in my time, but very few." As for the Shore incident, it seemed buried: "I don't hold grudges," he said. Of his own play, he observed, "I was aggressive in my own way. I did no fighting to speak of. Fighting did not get far; linesmen and other players would step in." Horner saw himself as a keeper of the peace. "We had two or three smaller players, and I always felt they were being taken advantage of and I would step in and help them." He had his own wry take on Conn Smythe's beat-'em-in-the-alley-beat-'em-on-the-ice maxim. "A lot of players," he noted with a smile, "were no good in the alley." And if George Reginald Horner was the most penalized player of his era, that's because, he insisted, referees called more rigorous games in those days and kept a close eye on any man with a reputation.

"The fans," Horner told me, "loved to see people get hit. They liked to see me get hit—especially in the other rinks." In New York, a fan enamoured of Horner's style of play once sent him a box of Cuban cigars. In Chicago, a band at one end of the rink would play "Who's Afraid of the Big, Bad Wolf?" every time Horner stepped on the ice.

Horner paid dearly for the edge he brought to hockey. He recalled a game against New York in which he suffered a head injury, and though his wife pleaded with him not to play the next game, Conn Smythe and Dick Irvin insisted he would be fine. "I could not keep my head up," Horner told me, his mood more solemn now, "and they took advantage of me. I took a beating that night." He remembers a doctor sewing him up, and the next day his wife, a nurse, examined the wound and found pieces of the stick buried in the flesh. He recalled losing his teeth in Montreal—"down on my hands and knees looking for my teeth on the ice. Can you imagine that?" He remembered young players taking cracks at him—"to get their names in the paper" and build their own reputations by lowering his a notch.

During his career, six vertebrae in his back would have to be fused; both knees would be replaced. He broke his hand—courtesy of a Nels Stewart slash—in only his second game in the league. But he would go on to play twelve seasons, the last two as Leafs captain, and, as Jack Batten once wrote, "[H]is pride in this was immense."

Marty McSorley had already been in Kingston a few days, working out with the Frontenacs, the local junior team whose coach, Larry Mavety ("Mav," as McSorley calls him), is an old friend. In February 2001, I had sent McSorley a note through the team's media man, describing my book as one about hockey as a game of courage and as one fan's attempt to achieve a deeper understanding of the game. In the note, I also assured McSorley that his comments were meant for a book I would spend almost two years researching, and not for quick turn-around in a newspaper. Perhaps, I thought, that would appeal to someone who had been under such intense media scrutiny. Like a politician near the end of his career, he would be mindful of how hockey history would treat him. But after five days, I heard nothing back and presumed he had tossed my fax. Then, at 9:30 one night, McSorley called.

He speaks softly on the phone. My first impression is of a smart, careful man, one who was a tad world-weary. He would make distinctions, challenge presumptions, introduce complexities. Here is a man who once represented his fellow players in union discussions with the NHL brass. At his peak, with Los Angeles in 1992, the defenceman tallied fifteen goals, twenty-six assists, and a numbing 399 minutes in penalties. He was a force. Whatever the image is of the goon in hockey, Marty McSorley brings subtlety to hockey talk. I think of something he told the prosecutor in the Vancouver courtroom in the wake of his hit on Donald Brashear.

"You're being absolute," he said, "and nothing is absolute on the ice." When the Crown attorney suggested that Donald Brashear was "entitled" to stand in front of the Boston goaltender during a power play, McSorley replied, "I question that entitlement." The lawyer pushed the point: But surely a player is allowed to stand further out from the goalie, say in the slot? McSorley replied that only *certain* players are allowed, so that while a goal scorer may, an enforcer may not. I took him to mean that while the scorer was just doing his job by being there, the tough guy was making a point.

Implicit in McSorley's comment is that spectators in the arena (or watching on television) see a very different game from the one players carefully monitor from the bench or on the ice. The elaborate code of etiquette, the breaches and insults little and large, the response to those breaches—all this lies beyond the ken of most fans, save those who have played the game at an elite level.

Clearly, some coaches ignore the code, while some young players don't seem to know it—or is it that so many versions of the code exist? Is it that the code is simply too elaborate, or are the breaches sometimes too obscure, too open to interpretation, so that not everyone is on the same page? What constitutes a violation? Is it a coach sending out *his* tough guy when *their* tough guy is exhausted at the end of a shift? Is it sending a tough guy out, not to fight, but to draw a penalty? Is it suddenly putting your tough guy, normally a defenceman, on right wing?

Marty McSorley and I talked that night for about an hour—about the incident, about the role of fighting in hockey, and much else. All off the record. McSorley was probing me, as a lawyer would a potential juror. I imagine he's learned something from all the time he's spent with lawyers. In his seventeen-year career, McSorley faced eight disciplinary hearings. During his time in the NHL, he clocked more than fifty-six hours in the penalty box; only two players in league history have done more time. Just for fun I looked up the penalty minutes for Dave Keon, a great player notable for his gentlemanly manners on the ice. In a career that spanned more than two decades in the majors, he spent under two hours in the box and in one seventy-six-game season, 1972–73, he took just one two-minute penalty.

McSorley and I agreed to meet at the rink the following Monday after practice, which I would observe. At mid-afternoon that day, I encountered him in a Memorial Centre corridor, wearing a cutoff black T-shirt darkened with sweat from working out in the gym. McSorley was chatting up the Zamboni guy. He greeted me with a smile, then altered plans for the interview after practice, suggesting he could give me more time, if I'd like, in the morning over breakfast. He explained that he and the Frontenacs were getting ready for "a little three-on-three"—a freewheeling scrimmage. And clearly he was looking forward to it.

I sat up in the stands, alone but for three or four regulars—including one I see often at these practices: a guy in a tweed cap, whose cane is the shaft of a hockey stick wrapped with black tape at the top and rubber-tipped at the bottom. An aging rink rat, he will fold his hands over the stick, lean a little forward, and watch with interest.

The Frontenacs came out slowly, one or two at a time. First a goalie and one player. They pursued a ritual, the player lobbing pucks high from the boards and towards the netminder thirty feet away. The goalie attempted to kick each puck, a little like a punter in football. He delighted in distance, but sometimes when he missed entirely, he landed on his bum, which delighted his partner in this exercise.

The Frontenacs were a few points out of first place, and I was curious to know whether they had won their game against second-place Ottawa the day before. My hunch was they had. The last practice I saw had seemed more businesslike. Today they had what hockey players call "jump": They seemed light and loose and playful; some were wrestling in the warm-up, like boys on summer-camp bunkbeds. Later I discovered they had beat Ottawa 3–2 in overtime.

At one point after the warm-up, three players—including big Brett Cloutier, the team's tough guy—surrounded McSorley and menaced him with their raised sticks. He went along with the game, pretending to be under siege, and repelled their feigned blows with his own stick. Then he spun the stick over his head expertly, like a baton twirler. So this, I thought, is what they work on in practice. Earlier, I had watched assistant coach Greg Bignell work on his own little trick, which saw him lay his stick down almost to the ice, the blade over the puck, and then, by some magic, the puck would appear on the upper side of the blade, like a pie cooling on a ladle, and he would bring the puck way back and fling it lacrosse-style into the net. I watched him do it twice, and I still couldn't catch it. Like a good card trick, the sleight of stick was done at blink speed.

But if the Frontenacs were playful that day, maybe it's also because they were all up for the three-on-three. McSorley was out there with the puck, doing a quick pirouette in the offensive zone, giving himself a back pass. It's clever, almost balletic, but in the Ballet Trocadero style, and I swear he smiled as he did it. Later, on another shift, he did it again. A big man at play.

The team had been divided into light and dark sweaters. Both sides wanted to win. Goals, especially nice ones, were celebrated by players at the bench hammering the boards with their sticks. The speed of the game is mesmerizing, yet Dick Cherry, Don's brother, who skates with the boys and who played in the late 1960s for the Philadelphia Flyers, didn't look entirely out of place, despite being weeks away from his sixty-fifth birthday. When he shot on goal and the rebound caromed in off a defenceman, his bench went wild. Dick Cherry went a little wild himself.

Offsides were called by the bench of the team defending, though sometimes those refs found their calls disputed by refs at the other bench. This reminded me of the games I play where offside calls and complaints about infractions are issued loudly from each bench. It's comic and serious at the same time.

McSorley didn't have the speed these guys have ("I never did," he says later) but he hit the lead forward with clean, crisp passes. Right on the tape, as they say. On a breakaway and from ten feet out, he ripped the puck into the top right corner. McSorley smiled broadly and did a little rifle thing with his stick. On another rush, he deked two guys, and the other bench applauded. My abiding sense from this practice was of the players' pure delight. This was high-speed shinny, marked by creative spark and deft passing to ever-circling players.

Throughout the game the boys had obviously been keeping score, and at the end the darks (Cherry's team, not McSorley's) rush out onto the ice and pose, some reclining, others standing behind, all shouting as if they had won a championship and were gathered for photographers. It's a taunt aimed at the losing side.

Like many players who are rough on the ice, Marty McSorley is gentle off it. Some hockey titans are picked for the task because they are as mean-spirited as they are menacingly huge. But a surprising number possess a quiet demeanour off the ice. John Ferguson, to name just one, struck Charles Wilkins—author of *Breakaway*—as "a paragon of discretion, a shy and considerate man, as avuncular as Wiggily, as obliging as Pooh." Yet "Pooh" broke Bobby Hull's jaw and Ken Schinkel's collarbone, and once flattened a linesman.

McSorley met me in the hotel foyer, wearing a black V-necked sweater, jeans, and stylish black boots. I was struck by his impossibly wide shoulders, and the hands, of course. Knuckles like the gnarled upraised roots of an oak. All the equipment you would expect of a hockey pugilist who stands six-two and weighs 235 pounds.

He ordered a breakfast to match his bulk: a pond-sized bowl of porridge, a mess of poached egg whites—"No yolks, they're fattening"—

edged with strawberries, along with two hefty bananas in their skins (a fruit snack for the road), a tall platter of white toast, a large glass of skim milk, orange juice, and coffee—all on the advice, he said, of his nutritionist back in L.A.

McSorley was warm, thoughtful, articulate, yet cautious and careful. Certain things were off the record. "I don't want this," and he meant how he will appear in this book, "to be really negative. I have to be careful." He talked about violence in hockey, for he can claim some expertise in this matter, but he displayed the wariness of a guy on parole. Marty McSorley remembered, acutely, what he had told me off the record. I hoped to sneak into some of this territory, and while he would nibble at my bait, he was not about to be charmed, for he is a charmer himself and knows something of that art. McSorley also possesses a profound sense of hockey politics: He understands how some remarks will be seen as fair criticism and how others will be seen as disloyal to the game. As if "the game" could mean only one thing—the NHL variety.

Sometimes he spoke in hockey aphorisms, but some phrases oppose and repel when lined up alongside each other, like two north ends of a magnet. "I love the game," he said. And then later, "Hockey is a business." He assured me that "I don't ever play with fear," and minutes later told me that "Desire overcomes fear."

Charles Foran, who wrote a magazine piece about the McSorley–Brashear incident in November 2000, sat in the Vancouver courtroom and observed a video replay of their first fight in that game. Foran counted eighteen punches to McSorley's head and upper torso, as he was "pummelled by the younger, quicker player." Imagine how many bare-knuckle fights this man has endured in pro hockey alone, how many blows to the head. Four hundred fights? Four thousand blows? Impossible to guess.

Foran thought Brashear, in court, looked "more like a prizefighter than a left winger." I once watched him fight Andre Roy, but Roy (then with Ottawa) did not just lose the fight; he was never in it. Brashear has jackhammer fists.

Marty McSorley believes there are no more concussions now than before; only that they're being reported. He talked of waking up in the morning after an Oiler game with no memory of the score or of the trainer bringing him home and arranging an appointment with a neurologist. McSorley remembered players, after fights, going to the wrong bench.

My overwhelming impression from that three-hour breakfast with McSorley was of his assured manner and utter belief in intimidation and fighting as natural outcomes of a terribly fast game. And it's all much more complicated, he said, than we think.

At one point, McSorley put down his spoon, quit the porridge, and popped his left wrist joint in and out of position with his right hand. "Quite the party trick," I joked, but my remark fell flat. "No it's not," he said, growing suddenly serious and even testy. There was no danger of him walking off, no prospect of physical harm coming to me. But a door had opened, a shadow had emerged, and I felt, just for a moment, the fear that a player on the ice must have felt as Marty McSorley in his prime doffed his gloves and bore down on him with a purpose.

"Don't mock the role of the enforcer, and don't romanticize either," he said. "It would be cheapened by thinking it's fun and games," and then he offered an example to elaborate. "When a game got chippy, Dave Semenko would skate out and settle a game down just by a threat. He'd say, "Someone's going to get hurt out here." Maybe someone on the other team, a little guy, was doing something to get under Messier's skin or rattle Gretzky. And in McSorley's eyes, that player was putting pressure on his own team's big guy to fight Semenko—which not many cared to do.

But every team has an enforcer, I countered. Do you really believe that having more bullets than the other guy carries any weight?

"I'm really emphatic about this," he said, bristling at my military metaphor. "When a game gets chippy, a fight will settle the game down. It cleans the game up. I've seen it over and over again."

Indeed, sometimes it does—or at least it appears to. I described to McSorley a game I had seen just days before, between the Kingston

Frontenacs and the London Knights. You could plot the chemistry of that game on a chart: fast, elegant beginning; chippy middle; a denouement with a heavyweight bout; return to business. On the other hand, some fights in hockey only lead to more.

McSorley was equally emphatic that Semenko and his ilk would much rather be out there playing and maybe even scoring a goal or two. And thus, the issuing of threats. Classic deterrence theory.

"Fighting is done the vast majority of times because the team needs it," said McSorley as he set out to explain how fights unfold. "There are very few fights between bona fide tough guys, where there hasn't been something in the course of a game that has led up to it. It's not out of bravado. You may have a rookie trying to show he belongs. You do get that. But established guys just don't go out and fight to be macho. Rarely."

What about this notion that no one really gets hurt in a fight? That the players can't get leverage on skates. Isn't that why Don Cherry gives us that little smirk when he talks about players "getting into a scrap"?

"You *do* get hurt," McSorley insisted, before listing the injuries he's suffered in fights. "I pulled a shoulder out in a fight. I've pretty much broken every finger in my hand. Tore ligaments in my wrists, my hands. I've been cut many times. Lost two front teeth. Had my jaw displaced. Anybody who wants to say that we don't get hurt in fights and wants to push the point, I'm sure they'll be welcome additions to the opposing lineup." And, at this, there spills from him a deep, rolling laugh, almost a release, which proves infectious, and my laughter gives his a second wind. Only later do I ask myself: What's so funny about hockey vengeance?

Marty McSorley is a hockey warrior, with a warrior's injuries—the kind you get from clearing strong bodies in front of the net, from dashing into corners with a winger on your tail, from diving in front of pucks, from taking risks. Hip operation. Bone spurs. Calcium deposits. Abdominal tears. Double hernia. Inguinal hernia. Elbow surgery, thumb surgery—eight surgeries in total. That McSorley's regular doctor is an orthopedic surgeon says it all. When he told me he lives in Los Angeles "because my support system is there," he was referring to the medical team of physicians that keeps his battered body running, like a car that's seen many hard miles. "Playing through pain" is a phrase that belittles the medical and psychological trauma that a certain kind of player faces routinely.

Nick Kypreos, a low-skilled enforcer, left the Leafs in 1997 after his New York Rangers counterpart, Ryan Vandenbussche, caught him with a punch, knocked him out, and sent him crashing to the ice in a pool of blood. That punch caused a severe concussion and ended his career. Kypreos is now an on-air analyst for CTV's *Sportsnet.*

The hit man's essential anguish is that of the aging gunfighter worried about some new kid in town looking to make a name for himself. "A lot of guys," says Kypreos, "have problems, anxiety attacks, or they can't sleep. This was a game they loved to play as kids, but now they have to go into Chicago thinking, 'I've got to fight Bobby Probert because if I don't, everybody's going to think I'm ducking him or I'm scared of him.' It's a really tough feeling. You're not thinking about winning or playing a good game. You're thinking about who you have to fight."

They rarely last long, these enforcers. One fighter, Paul Laus of the Florida Panthers, had thirty-nine bouts in the 1996 season, and he would sometimes return home from road trips with hands so sore from hammering the heads of opponents that he couldn't pick up his young children to hold them.

"People see us fight and think nobody gets hurt," says Rob Ray of the Buffalo Sabres. "But the next day your hands are killing you, your shoulders are aching. Your head is pounding. I've been punched so hard I see stars and white dots. You may skate away from a fight and not be bleeding, but it's everything on the inside that takes the real beating."

As we talked, my affection for McSorley grew. At one point I suggested to him, as a friend might, that a thirty-seven-year-old player should not feel obligated to fight twenty-two-year-old rookies looking for a mention in the press. Why not finish your NHL career by sticking to hockey and leaving the gloves on?

"I will fight if I have to," he said. "And if I won't fight, they might as well get a twenty-two-year-old. I am who I am. I react naturally and instinctively. You said I'm not as good a fighter as I was, and I'll be perfectly honest. I'm *not* as good as I was. But I still think I'm better than most guys out there. And if that's what's needed. . . . It's no different than being asked to spend some time on the power play. Am I as good on the power play? No. Was I ever really good on the power play? No. I can't draw that barrier—at this age. That's no good for the team."

McSorley was once quoted thus on the role of the enforcer: "I fought in my first game, just to keep playing, just to stay in the lineup. The fact is I went out to get into a fight that I thought was necessary for our hockey team. Do I have a problem with that? I wouldn't want anybody to do it for me." I wondered what he meant. Was he saying, 'It's a loathsome task I wouldn't want to inflict on anyone'? Or was he saying, 'It's a job that's got to be done and it's for me to do and no one else on my team'?

Roy MacGregor, in *The Home Team*—about hockey fathers and sons—tells the story of Bill McSorley, Marty's dad, "a big, rumbling man with a slow rolling gait . . . wide-open eyes filled with kindness and trust." He ran a 720-acre farm, he and his wife, seven boys and three girls. One day in the field, their border collie chased after a coyote, but he came back later with his tail between his legs, barking at the woods' edge where the coyote smugly eyed them. In one version of the story, McSorley *père* grabs the dog by the scruff of the neck, tosses him in the direction of the coyote and shouts, "You yellow son of a bitch! McSorleys don't back down from anything. Now get back in there and fight." The dog, though, has had enough. He circles quickly and shelters beneath the hay wagon.

The elder McSorley weighed 260 pounds and would sometimes venture out onto the ice when one of his sons was buried under other players in a brawl. In one game, when a McSorley team was both outweighed and outnumbered by another team, the imposing farmer strode out, broke up the fights, and ordered the opposing coach to get his players off the ice. End of story.

Marty McSorley would engage in six fights in his first two days in camp, as a Belleville Bull rookie. Almost twenty years later, McSorley's plan was to play a few games with an International Hockey League team in Grand Rapids, Michigan, (an Ottawa Senators farm team) and to leap from there either back to the NHL, or, failing that, to a pro team in Europe. But wherever he would land, or not—for he had also confronted the fact that his pro career might be over—he would go out as he came in. Like a lion.

I asked McSorley to reconcile the nice guy who was sitting across from me with the hockey player who sometimes loses it. "I *never* lose it!" he shot back. "You don't get mad in a fight. If you get mad in a fight, you'll make a mistake. Talk to boxers or hockey fighters. They don't get mad in a fight. You're so intense, so strongly focussed. You go into it haphazardly. . . ." And his words faded away, leaving me to reach the obvious conclusion.

But then he immediately contradicted himself, or so it seemed to me. He returned to the Brashear incident: "With their bench yelling, us running out of time, so many things going on. . . . When he cut across in front of me and with some of my own [physical] inabilities, everything went wrong. It definitely wasn't intended." The man who never loses it seemingly did so the night of February 21, 2000. McSorley insisted that he didn't lose control, and that a slash aimed at Brashear's torso came up off the shoulder.

Marty McSorley's take on professional hockey is genuine and honest and, above all, heartfelt. It is also self-serving. Naturally enough, he sees a pivotal role for fists and intimidation; otherwise, where is his place in the game? Another vision of hockey would have a great many highly paid pugilists either out of work or making a lot less money. McSorley possessed the talent and the work ethic to play defence on any team in the NHL, but his boxer's manners dramatically increased his value.

"Could the game exist without fighting?" I asked McSorley.

He came back with a question of his own. "Is it too pure a thought?" I found it intriguing that he put his answer as a question, implying somehow that he wasn't entirely sure.

"What if," I asked him, "the refs were simply to call every infraction? Wouldn't the players eventually get the message and abide by the rules?" His answer was the same, but this time delivered as a statement of fact. "It's too pure a thought," he said. "Where is that line? You're constantly reaching for that puck. The refs don't want to be deciding everything. The players can't play in fear of penalties all the time. And fans don't want to see shinny. They want to see guys playing hard." He's right about shinny. The NHL all-star game is as pretty a game of shinny as you'll ever find; it's also supremely boring.

Like many hockey players loyal to their sport, Marty McSorley circles the wagons. He notes that on any given team perhaps only three players do all the fighting, sparing the other eighteen the bother. McSorley also takes potshots at other sports. When I conceded that baseball has the brush-back pitch, McSorley interjected with gusto. "Hey, they have more than the brush-back pitch. They *throw* at each other. Let's get it out there. Catchers get run over at home plate. And if someone in football runs over a quarterback, the other guy's going to get it."

Yes, but in those other sports, fighting means automatic ejection. In those other sports, no team stocks its roster with virtual security guards. The only possible explanation is that hockey is not like other games, and when I suggest this, McSorley nods.

And nod he must, but there was something half-hearted about it. On the one hand, I sensed his pride in what he does: He allows his more-gifted teammates room to manoeuvre, the freedom to "play tall"—without having to worry about the other McSorleys that sit on every bench. It's what's lovable about these imposing men: their profound sense of self-sacrifice and allegiance to their teammates. At one point in our talk, McSorley paused, gathered his thoughts, and said very slowly, "Gretz . . . Gretz really, really *died* to win."

Spoken like a true and loyal bodyguard, the one Gretzky insisted on taking with him when he left Edmonton for Los Angeles in 1988. But I wonder whether, years from now, time will erode that loyalty. Will McSorley resent the almost 3,400 minutes he spent watching from the penalty box? Will there be guilt from all the beatings he laid on other players? Resentment that he had to finish what little guys started?

Cal Botterill, a sports psychologist in Calgary who has worked with several NHL teams and Canada's Olympic team, observes that enforcers have the most difficult job in hockey. "They live by the sword and they die by the sword. It's the law of the jungle. It's only a matter of time before somebody bigger and stronger comes along and takes them out."

Botterill believes that enforcers play a role that is alien to them. They earn a good wage, but pay a high price. "Off the ice," he says, "they're totally different people. What they do on the ice is something that does not come naturally to them. Over the course of a career, it can produce tremendous guilt feelings. They're much more prone to burnout because of the intense emotional situation. It takes a toll."

6

HOCKEY
AS ELIXIR

I N SUMMER 2001, *Canadian Geographic* magazine ran a photo essay about the Blood Indian Reserve in southwestern Alberta. Among the haunting black-and-white photographs is one showing the grave of Bernard White Man Left, who died in 1995 at the age of forty-three. Imagine a small picket fence around a lone monument set off at the edge of the cemetery, the prairie seeming to stretch to infinity, with no sign of a road or a telegraph line, no house or hint that this territory is other than it was in the 1800s, when the Blood rode horses and trailed the buffalo. Bernard White Man Left must have played the game, or at least followed it with a passion, for his monument is two crossed hockey sticks.

Why did he love hockey so?

In late fall 2001, *Globe and Mail* reporter John Stackhouse wrote a fourteen-part series called *Canada's Apartheid,* on Native communities across the country. Part four described how the Cree and the whites of The Pas, Manitoba—"two communities that once were the most racially divided in Canada"—came together when the town formed a mixed-race junior team. At the time Stackhouse was writing, the squad was sporting a 20–1 record and had won the provincial championship the previous three years. "I really believe it was the hockey club that bridged the divide," the mayor said.

In Belfast, meanwhile, hockey is achieving a similar miracle. Irish Catholics and Irish Protestants are sitting beside each other to watch a team of mostly Canadians play the game.

In Manitoba, the town–reserve split was perhaps not as old as in Ireland but nonetheless deeply entrenched, with each side avoiding the other's turf: Natives who crossed the Saskatchewan River and came into The Pas to watch a movie sat in a separate section in the cinema—like blacks in old Mississippi. Now, Crees and whites sit beside each other and cheer the same team—the Opaskwayak Cree Nation (OCN) Blizzard. And thus the headline over the two-page spread in the *Globe:* "The Healing Power of Hockey."

There is a mystery here I am trying to fathom. What I am discovering is that hockey feeds us in some special way. Set aside the violence of hockey, the business of hockey, and what you have is a uniquely Canadian elixir—our game's sustaining rituals, its tall tales and super-stitions and, always, the chance for a laugh.

Here, for example, is a story from one of the funniest men ever to play hockey. After years of toiling with the hapless New York Rangers, goalie Lorne "Gump" Worsley was traded to the Montreal Canadiens. Before that switch, Gump was once asked which team gave him the most trouble. "The Rangers," he famously replied.

During his first game back in New York, wearing a Montreal uniform, he noticed the same little welcome mat that three Madison Square Garden maintenance men had always laid out for him. "Red" De Cesare, "Junior" Gratto, and "Ice Cream Shorty" would paint the ice, the blue and red lines and all the circles, and their last task would be to paint in small neat letters at the back of the net, "Good Luck, Gump." They continued the tradition even after the trade. Fans in the stands couldn't see the note, but Gump would look back there, and smile.

I have no evidence for this, but my hunch is that hockey players come together as teams more than in any other sport. George Plimpton made the same observation while researching *Open Net,* and many stories serve to illustrate the point.

Gump Worsley talks about a New York–Chicago train trip in 1952 when someone on the team started tossing pillows, then everyone joined the fray. One pillow broke and then another. It was snowing in that car. The coach, Bill Cook, heard the ruckus and looked in, said, "Christ, it looks like a chicken farm," and went back to sleep.

Congressmen on the train had to walk through the blizzard to get to the dining car, and complained bitterly. The furious conductor threatened to detach that car from the train and leave it on a siding until the mess was cleaned up. The players got to work.

Here were men, professional athletes, acting like kids on an unsupervised sleepover. When my son, Kurt, was younger, I would take him to tournaments in Toronto, where my sympathies would lie with the poor tourists who lucklessly landed at the same Holiday Inn as all those tykes. While parents would retreat to ad-hoc hospitality suites for beer and pizza and a hockey game on TV, our kids would take over the hallways and play endless games of hockey with miniature plastic sticks and foam pucks. Gump and the boys, Kurt and the boys: It was all of a piece.

Eric Nesterenko knows this to be true. When Studs Terkel wrote his classic book, *Working,* in the early 1970s based on taped interviews with hundreds of people about their jobs and daily lives, he chose Nester to talk about professional hockey. And though Nesterenko touches on the fear and brutality in the game, he also speaks eloquently, in *Working,* about the joy hockey brings to both players and fans. Terkel has enlivened the interviews with his own colour commentary, set off in parentheses.

Nesterenko tells Terkel about a playoff series when the "Cinderella" Hawks beat the favoured Canadiens and went on to win the Stanley Cup. "It was three to nothing, for us, with five minutes left to go. As a spontaneous gesture, twenty thousand people stood up. I was on the ice. I remember seeing that whole stadium, just solid, row on row, from the balcony to the boxes, standing up. These people were turned on by us. (Sighs.) We came off, three feet off the ice. . . ." He adds softly, "Spring of '61."

Nesterenko talks about that sense of brotherhood, the same feeling that likely provoked the pillow fight on The Gumper's train. "Some of the best clubs I've played with have this intimacy," says Nesterenko, "an intimacy modern man hardly ever achieves. We can see each other naked, emotionally, physically. We're plugged into each other, because we need each other. There have been times when I knew what the other guy was thinking without him ever talking to me."

Nesterenko also illuminates that aspect of the game that kids and pros both share—the pure delight that comes with moving at speed over ice. He describes chancing upon a frozen lake, how it lured him out, and he skated, blissfully alone, "free as a bird." Nester said he hopes to do this until he dies.

"I'm in full flight and my head is turned. I'm concentrating on something and I'm grinning. That's the way I like to picture myself. I'm something else there. I'm on another level of existence, just being in pure motion. . . . That's nice you know. [Laughs softly.]"

When *Shinny*, a National Film Board movie, had its world premiere at a five-day international hockey conference held in Halifax in October 2001 (itself a world first), I was sitting across the aisle from two young Finnish academics. Asked to respond to the film, one called it "an eye-opener. I had no idea how deep the feeling for the game is here. It's amazing. In Finland, we don't understand how Canadians feel about the game." Now, he said, he can fathom the emotionalism of Team Canada.

The seventy-minute film moves across the country, from Long Pond, Nova Scotia—claimed to be the site of the earliest recorded game of hockey—to the frozen sloughs of Saskatchewan and north to Nunavut, recording outdoor games of shinny. The opening shot, of a young skater freewheeling on a frozen lake, touched some deep chord in all of us watching. The *sheeek-sheeek-sheeek* of the young man's skates made me want to join him out there on that perfect ice under that cold winter sun, and when the camera—by some miracle of computer engineering—then slipped below the ice, so you heard the skates from below, the elderly hockey historian beside me grew emotional. "I get wet easily," he explained when the lights came up, but he was as teary at the end as at the beginning.

The film—formally called *Shinny: The Hockey in All of Us*—is about hockey rituals: making the backyard rink after that first heavy snowfall, holding a hose at midnight on the community rink, and clearing a foot of snow at dawn with truck and plough, tossing sticks in the middle, and dividing them to make up teams on lake-wide ice. Jean Chrétien is seen playing shinny on the historic rink at Rideau Hall in Ottawa, and he told the film's director, David Battistella, that though he hadn't laced up skates in five years, he was determined to come back more often. This photograph now holds pride of place in the PM's office: In a toque, Chrétien is heading up the hill, away from the rink, with his stick over his shoulders and his skates slung over the blade.

"He *loves* that photo!" Battistella heard through the grapevine. The young filmmaker was wearing a white turtleneck sweater, its red line over the heart very like the one at centre ice. "I set out to make a film about shinny that would help explain the nation," he told us that day in Halifax. "I wanted people, say in Morocco, to understand Canada better." The NFB would later set up a Web site so that people across the country can tell their own tales of open-air hockey; the "shinny community," as Battistella put it, can thus converse.

I asked him how the two-year process of making the film had changed his notion of shinny. What did he know at the end that he did not know at the beginning? "When we went to these places," he said, "we didn't say, 'Toss your sticks in the middle and divide them up.' The rules of shinny are so buried in us. I was shocked that people held it as dear as they did." At the end of his journey, he had forty-nine hours of tape and he faced some wrenching decisions over which stories to cut and which to retain.

Battistella played in a game of shinny on the Bow River in Alberta, with the Rocky Mountains an impossible backdrop. "I gazed in wonder at some of the scenes," Battistella said. "It was an unbelievable personal experience. I had felt betrayed and cheated by NHL hockey. The best of what we are is being taken away. But the fact is, they'll never put their skates on in Arizona and play outside. The climate is on our side. The heart of the game won't be lost because the heart and soul of hockey, which is shinny, is still in us."

One day Battistella was at Rideau Hall doing research and he saw a pair of CCM Super Tacks hanging on a doorknob. They belonged, he learned, to John Ralston Saul, the husband of Governor General Adrienne Clarkson. "I saw those skates," he said, "and I thought, of course." Writer, thinker, provocateur, shaker of hands: Saul is all that, but he's also a Canadian, and he *plays*.

Earlier that week in Halifax, a retired CBC archivist, Ernest Dick, talked about the '72 series, one that ninety per cent of Canadians had watched. He had plucked from the CBC library a public-affairs program, a series called *Weekend*, which had sent out film crews to twelve locations across the country to monitor reponse to that final, eighth game in Moscow.

You see girls in a ballet class doing *piaffes*, with the game on TV in the centre of the room, but when Canada scores, everyone claps, breaks from the wooden barre, and rushes to the TV. All across the land, the televised game is cutting into routine, putting lives on hold. Kids in a classroom shout, "Fight! Fight! Fight!" when a fracas occurs. Diplomats at the Soviet embassy in Ottawa are seen fretting and wincing on a couch. The boxer George Chuvalo, looking young and fit, stands in a bar, alongside the writer Morley Callaghan: Everyone there is looking up at a TV screen. But the best two illustrations of how that series grabbed the nation by the throat were the scenes involving former prime minister John Diefenbaker and a woman I will call "Flora."

Flora sits alone in an Alberta diner, her hair in a beehive, a cigarette or coffee mug invariably at her mouth. You can hear Foster Hewitt's game commentary emanating from the TV set; by its side, the camera only has eyes for Flora. Sometimes her hand comes over her face, as if some horror were unfolding.

Dief sits at home on a couch, but his whole body rocks rhythmically, as if he were on an old and rickety train. His is a face the cartoonists loved, and I have seen it so often that the satirical version and the real article have formed a comic synthesis. The camera loves him, too; it keeps cutting back to him.

"Holy Jeez," he says, in response to some incident on the ice, and the audience that day in Halifax roared with laughter. "Oh-oh-oh," he

says another time, and we split our guts again. His "Oh God!" is
followed by the sight of him clapping, and, finally, the game over, his
deeply satisfying "Well, well, well."

A Newfoundlander, who had been watching with his family at
home, remarked, "Same thing when the war was over, eh?"

"No moment in Canadian history," said Dick, "is remembered as
poignantly as when Paul Henderson scored in 1972." And of all the
people who were asked to comment in that *Weekend* program, he said,
no one was more insightful than Morley Callaghan. The writer
remarked on the high intensity and emotion of the players. Callaghan
was certain: A nation that saw itself as polite and inclined to keep the
peace was revealing its other side.

An American academic in the Halifax audience, Stephen Hardy,
remembered watching that game in New Hampshire, which was offering the same video coverage as Canadians got, but with Boston
announcers. "I always wanted to see history in the making," the
commentator apparently said of that titanic struggle, "but I never
thought it would be Dunkirk."

Dennis Hull describes coming back to Canada after the '72 series
and being taken to meet the then prime minister, Pierre Trudeau. The
players had all been given luggage stickers to match their sweater
numbers, so Hull was #10 and Bobby Clarke #16. Both men
approached the PM, slapped him on the back, and asked him what he
thought of particular goals. Trudeau was well informed and knew a lot
about the series. And there he was, riding around Montreal, high on a
fire truck, enjoying the company of these hockey gods, the numbers
10 and 16 pasted on his back.

Trudeau was like us: When the gods speak, we heed them. Bobby
Orr was once on the ice, observing as the Washington Capitals set up
for a faceoff. Their centreman had directed a rookie defenceman to
move further to his right, but as the player moved he caught Orr's eye.
Orr shook his head, as if to say, "You were right the first time." The kid
went back to where he was, the puck was dropped, and it came right
back to him.

File this story under sustaining rituals. When Mario Lemieux came out of retirement on December 27, 2000, one of the Scanlan boys was there in Pittsburgh to take in that moment. I, on the other hand, was among the millions who saw the game on television, and what we all observed before the game was Mario making his turns in the home end, before the game, and ritually tapping the glass behind the net. His four-year-old son, Austin, a cherubic blond boy wearing a Penguins sweater with his dad's number 66 on the back, would wave in response to each tap of the glass.

Maurice Richard had a similar ritual. His wife, Lucille, would bring one of their three eldest children to Saturday-night games in the Forum, and Richard would wave to them before each period. Like Richard, Lemieux was born in Montreal and likely knows of this custom; perhaps he was paying small tribute in emulating The Rocket. Two hockey legends were thus linked, not separated, by half a century.

My brother Tom, his wife, Sharon, and their children were driving into Pittsburgh the night Mario was to make his comeback, when they spotted a flashing highway sign that offered news, not of a slowdown or construction ahead, but of the *real* news in Pennsylvania. "Welcome Back Mario," the huge sign read.

Tommy has been to many NHL games. He says you might get a few thousand showing up at the arena an hour beforehand to watch the warm-up. This night there were 10,000. The TV audience in Canada was what you might expect for the seventh game of the Stanley Cup finals.

"I went down low in the stands for the warm-up," Tommy told me, "and I picked the right-hand corner, thinking Mario would come out there. He came out the opposite end, as it turned out, but in a way I was glad I had picked wrong. He just charged out onto the ice. It was like being in Spain and seeing a bull charge out of the gate. He had no helmet on. It was just beauty coming at you, with his good looks and size. The crowd was going wacko."

The Leafs, the opponents that night, were also in awe, to judge by the 5–0 score. But so, it seems, were Mario's fellow Penguins. A forward and a goalie were so intent on watching Mario in the warm-up that they smacked into each other, hit the ice, and rose laughing.

Before the game, Mario's number on a pennant was lowered from the rafters. Lemieux's wife and kids were brought out onto the ice (but not Mario), and what Tommy remembers is the look of wonder on the face of the boy in the oversized jersey. In that moment, everyone there, everyone watching, *was* that boy. "It was hokey," says Tommy, "but it was also done with class."

During the game, it was Mario's passing that impressed my brother more than anything. A little backhand pass up the boards, when everyone in the rink was sure he would shoot. A blind pass, right on the money, in front of the Leafs net. A pass to Jaromir Jagr that led to a goal, the timing impeccable. Mario scored, of course, though he had some luck on the play. But what my brother prized was the little things he did. "Things," said Tommy, "I haven't seen since Gretzky."

Sitting high in the stands at Mellon Arena gave my brother the same perspective on the game that Mario has every game. "That's the key," Tommy said. "When I play hockey, I see bodies in the way. Mario has the view from on high. Other players don't." Some interesting scientific work has been done on how elite players see the game: For gifted athletes, the ice surface is a map they see as a whole. And for them, the play unfolds dramatically slower than it does for mere mortals. Wayne Gretzky had called hockey "the study of geometry . . . angles and caroms." Mario Lemieux once likened hockey to a game of chess, but clearly he was a master, always several moves ahead of his opposition. "Before I get the puck," he says, "I look where the players are and try to determine where they will be after. . . . It's easy."

What I noticed at home was the grace with which Mario comported himself in interviews. Long known for his coolness, he was revealing some of the natural passion for the game that he had kept under wraps. So many media people wanted a piece of him, and he was making his answers to the questions, which had to have been mostly the same questions, sound fresh and genuine.

After the game, Tommy watched him skate the length of the ice to shake hands with Leafs coach Pat Quinn and his assistants. Tommy was sure he said something like, "Sorry for all the hoopla."

I was heartened to hear from Mario that one of the reasons he decided to come back was that the league seemed prepared to police the game, to protect elite players and end the mugging. In the press, he had praised Gary Bettman and his officials—"They've done a great job of opening up the game." The first few games back, Mario was seldom touched. But that quickly changed. Boston worked him over pretty good in January 2001, and by the middle of that month Pittsburgh had lost faith in league promises. They brought in three sizable muckers, one a pure fighter. The private police force was once again in uniform. And I began to wonder how long it would be before that pennant with the number 66 on it would once more ascend into the rafters, this time for good.

When Wayne Gretzky played his last game in Canada late in the 1999 season, I was there at the Corel Centre in Ottawa—with my brother Wayne and his son Connor and my son Kurt. I remember Gretz lining up at the blue line for the anthems and thinking how slight he seemed compared to the others—a sapling amid young oaks.

Some have called the space behind the net "Gretzky's office," a quiet zone from which he would send those impossible passes through legs and sticks. And he did that in this game, too. But he would also, whenever the puck was coming out of his end, go directly to the boards at centre ice, stop and wait for the pass that always came his way. Even that year, in the twilight of his career, he was still the on-ice general. Though he would only record nine goals, he still got fifty-three assists. The night was a great gift. We had booked the tickets in advance, and though Gretzy's retirement was rumoured, he had not formally announced it. And so I went to the game unprepared for the emotion that filled the arena. Every time Gretz came over the boards, touched the puck, set up behind the net, a ripple coursed through the place. Every soul there wanted him to score, and he almost did. By the end of the third period, we were all standing, all of us chanting, "One more year, one more year . . ."

It's true what musicians and performers say—that a great mass of people can give off astonishing energy. Artists feed on that. And that modern hockey palace in Ottawa—so like every other hockey palace—soared that night with genuine feeling.

At the end of the game—a 2–2 tie, with overtime, and Gretzky named as first star—all the players on both teams retired to their benches, but not before every Senators player had embraced him. Even up in our lofty corner seats, I could see the emotion in his eyes, see his shoulders sag under the strain. We stood and clapped for about fifteen minutes, long after he had circled the ice and lofted his stick in salute, long after he had gone into the dressing room. Twice we made him come back out, and he obliged, the last time without sweater, elbow and shoulder pads—just the T-shirt. The sapling now looked even thinner.

We didn't want the goodbyes to end, for we were sure we'd never see his like again. And as much as I admired him and his artistry, and wished him well in his retirement, it occurred to me that he wasn't retiring at all. There would be no putting up the feet. Gretzky would go, after only a short delay, straight into ownership with the Phoenix Coyotes. Like one born into royalty, he would still bear the burden of being hockey's ambassador—still be expected to say the right thing, sound the right note, defend the game from those who would dump on it. For a time after retirement, he would write a column in the *National Post*—ghosted, I heard, by Roy MacGregor. It read well, of course, for Roy polished the prose, but the columns were so careful and considered, so *nice,* that it was soon laid to rest.

Only eighteen months after that Canadian farewell in Ottawa, Gretzky was in Vancouver—there to lend moral support at the court appearance of his friend, Marty McSorley. His presence spoke louder than all that he has ever said in lamentation about violence in hockey.

And I wondered, What does Gretzky *really* think? When he's at an Oilers reunion, in a former teammate's backyard after a long day of golf, having an ale with Messier and Kurri and Coffey and Lowe, when Wayne Gretzky tosses off the hockey diplomat's mantle, what does he say?

By showing up at McSorley's trial, I'm guessing he was saying something like, "Marty, you were there for me hundreds of times. The least I can do is stand by you now." One of the greatest finesse players the game has ever seen stood shoulder-to-shoulder with one of the toughest. Grit and grace. They are like two brothers who don't always get along, hockey's strange and tangled bedfellows.

Marty McSorley is not superstitious. During his career, his brand of mischief was to mess with those who were. In the dressing room, a goalie who had laid out his equipment precisely and ritually before going to the washroom would return and find his pads—to his horror—not as he had left them. Some players on the Oilers team would insist on the same order of shooting in the pre-game warm-up; McSorley would tinker here, as well. The more superstitious they were, the more they became targets for McSorley's practical jokes. Hockey players, it seems, are the merriest of sports' pranksters.

Many hockey players have lost teeth from sticks and pucks and fists; in the old days, players would set their bridgework in paper cups atop their lockers. A favourite trick was to swap the cups so the perpetrators could enjoy the sight of their teammates confounded by their suddenly ill-fitting plates. Rookies, especially, would come back to their lockers to find their ties scissored, their shoes missing or nailed to the spot where they had parked them.

George Plimpton describes a classic hockey prank in *Open Net*. On a road trip, a player is awakened by his roommate in the small hours and told that a woman who has seen him play earlier that night has gone to some trouble to secure a room—room 302—in the hotel. Her name is Jeannine and she is desperate to see him. Heart beating, the player shaves, puts on a tie, slaps on some cologne, and proceeds to room 302. The player knocks. After some time, a sleepy and likely not amused man answers the door. The player cannot have been too swift, for even though the man standing opposite him is John Ferguson—his own coach—the hopeful player still asks, "Is Jeannine here?" The story hung around that player like a bad smell for the rest of his hockey life. As his career faded and he played in the minors before retiring, opposing benches would taunt him as he skated by, with the plaintive cry, "Is Jeannine here?"

No wonder hockey players are often a superstitious lot, with all the mischief that surrounds them. Phil Esposito had his own bizarre rituals. He would enter the Bruins dressing room and wink at a red horn hung over his stall—a gift from his Italian grandmother to ward off the evil eye. That black turtleneck he always wore was put on inside out and backwards. And there was more: Espo had a St. Christopher's medal (patron saint of travellers) affixed to his suspenders. The trainer would sprinkle baby powder on the blade of his stick. Any crossed sticks in the dressing room would be uncrossed. Finally, Esposito was ready to play.

John McIntyre, a Los Angeles centreman in the early '90s, used to walk around his car three times and touch each corner before getting in; he never walked through doorways, but jumped through. Jeremy Roenick of the Flyers won't let anyone touch his sticks, and if another player's stick touches his by accident, he'll toss it out or give it away. Donald Audette of Montreal has the same superstition. Petr Klima used to break his stick after every goal, convinced "I only have one goal in each stick." Bobby Orr would make a round of the dressing room before every game, tapping each Bruin with his stick.

But in hockey, it seems that goalies are the oddest of all. Who can blame them? Jacques Plante once neatly captured the goaltender's perspective. "Imagine yourself sitting in an office," he said, "and you make an error of some kind—call it an error of judgment or a mistake over the phone. All of a sudden, behind you, a red light goes on, the walls collapse and there are 18,000 people shouting and jeering at you, calling you an imbecile and an idiot and a bum and throwing things at you, including garbage."

Johnny Bower, the goalie who was already an ancient thirty-four (and thought to be even older) when he joined the Leafs in 1958, used to dream about pucks coming at him from Richard, Howe, and Hull. "They weren't pleasant dreams," he says. "I imagine I did some twitching in my sleep." Even today, in his late seventies, he can be watching a game and his body cannot stop itself from remembering and reacting. "Sometimes," Bower says, "it's as if I can still feel the pads on my legs. When I'm watching the playoffs, I'll move with the goalie, twitch a shoulder or an arm, kick out a leg. Making the save from the easy chair."

Gary "Suitcase" Smith was my fellow student in 1962, when our Toronto high school sponsored his junior team, the Neil McNeil Maroons. He used to doff all his equipment and shower between periods, then don the soggy stuff again. Gary Inness, a former goalie with the Capitals, would line up a precise number of Dixie cups in front of him on a dressing room table, ice in those on the right, water in those on the left. Dave Reece, a backup goalie with Boston in the mid-1970s, would sit on the bench and cease talking precisely one hour before game time—even in mid-sentence—and never say another word until the game was over. If he needed water, he would point down his throat with his fingers. Gilles Gratton, ex of the Rangers and nicknamed "Grattoony the Loony," believed in reincarnation and was convinced that his job as goaltender was punishment for an earlier life in biblical times, when he had stoned people to death. Goalies.

Patrick Roy is careful never to touch the red or blue lines, bounces the same puck on the dressing-room floor all season long, puts on sweater and gloves precisely seven minutes before each period begins, and insists that the same player take the first warm-up shot. That shooter must then stand alongside Roy during the national anthems, until his luck turns sour and another player is given the task.

The goalie on our old Glendon College team, Terry Walker, used to tell the same protracted joke before playoff and other meaningful games, and it actually worked to relieve tension. Terry, now a producer with CBC-TV's *Sports Journal*, would take about ten minutes to tell the tale of pitcher Mel Famey, who—to make a long, long story very short—drank beers before each inning, trying to find the groove on the mound in Milwaukee. The punch line—"It Was the Beer that Made Mel Famey Walk Us"—a twist on an old beer jingle, would elicit as many groans as laughs. On that team, Terry holding court in the dressing room before every game was as much a ritual as us tapping his goalie pads just before the opening faceoff. He had a ventriloquist routine in which he would put his hand in a hockey sock—"Mr. Sock," as he called him—before embarking on inane conversations with the thing.

Guy Lafleur's pre-game ritual involved smokes. Lots of smokes. He used to go through at least a pack a day, and he would light up again between periods. Lafleur had other rituals to ready himself for games. He would sit fully dressed, with skates laced, for five hours before a big game. "It's because he's so hyper," his teammate Steve Shutt would say. "He winds himself up like a coil."

Dave Schultz talks about a night late in his career, when he was playing with the Buffalo Sabres. Both Ric Seiling and Jerry Korab had a ritual of thumping the goalie's pads—in this case, those of Bob Sauvé—before the opening faceoff. The thing is, each wanted to be *the last* one to do it. Korab would start, then Seiling, then Korab again. The referee was beside himself. Finally, the Buffalo coach realized his mistake, and he hauled Korab off the ice and replaced him with a player without superstitions, or at least not that particular one.

"At first glance," Peter Gzowski once wrote, "hockey may seem a curious pursuit for the writerly mind. If for no other reason, it's too damn fast." He argues that the rhythms of other sports—baseball and golf, for example—serve writer and reader both. The scribe can artfully describe moments in the game, the reader can easily grasp them, thus the vast literature on these other sports and hockey's comparatively tiny canon. (Still, *Total Hockey*'s list of hockey annuals, biographies and autobiographies, coaching manuals, history, and fiction numbers more than 1,000 titles.)

These other sports do indeed invite cerebral musings, in part because these other games are so laden with pauses. The mind wanders, metaphysics enters the picture, and the writer looking on may transform the sweet spot on a bat or the aerodynamics of a golfer's swing into metaphors for life. The pursuit of a white ball becomes something else, something meaningful, something lofty. Credit the shape of the ball. Whether dimpled and small or stitched in red, the perfect orb—like the moon—invites contemplation.

The puck is another matter. Black as night, it's a more sinister entity altogether. When the game was young, someone took a black ball and neatly, surgically, removed an inch-thick disc from its centre. Imagine planet Earth cut from space with a laser that vapourizes everything above the Tropic of Cancer and below the Tropic of Capricorn.

Suddenly the ball has become more complicated. Seen from above, the puck is still circular, can still make a claim to perfection. But this new thing has flatness, too, and hard edges. Where the ball has roll, a light and serendipitous quality that makes its flight unpredictable (as any golfer will tell you), the puck has slide, a straight and serious trajectory. As deadly as an arrow. Yet a puck can also flip on its edge and roll crazily, like a pitcher's knuckler.

There is a haircut called "the mullet"—short at the front, long at the back. In many parts of Canada, it's called the "hockey cut." To get this in Michigan, apparently, you tell your barber you want a "Canadian cut." Several films have been made to celebrate this haircut, also favoured by country singers, truck drivers, wrestlers, and lesbians.

Hockey, like all sports, has its own arcane language. We talk about someone deking a defenceman "out of his jock strap" or "undressing" a defenceman. We praise a player's "puck sense," we criticize goalies for "fighting the puck," we decry "puck hogs." The "floater" or "cherry picker" or "goal suck"—funny how we have so many derogatory terms for the slick, lazy player—is someone who skirts the heavy action and glides near centre waiting for breakaway passes. Goal scorers often work from "the slot," that area between the circles in front of the goal. We say of a player who can never put away those chances that "he couldn't put the puck in the ocean." (Bill Fitsell tells me that one of the Patrick boys, or perhaps it was Frank Boucher, once took a player to a pier in Atlantic City, lined up some pucks, and invited him to shoot, and the story—impossibly—has him missing the ocean.)

Some of us extol "fire-wagon hockey" (Andy O'Brien once entitled a book with that phrase, one that describes the all-out attack style of the old Montreal Canadiens). We always worry when the home team sits on a lead and "goes into a defensive shell." Goal scorers sometimes "go upstairs," lifting the puck high into the net or "top shelf"—"where the peanut butter is," as Howie Meeker used to say. Or maybe the shooter goes "five hole": There are the four corners of the net plus that space between the goalie's legs—the fifth hole. In the old days, the phrase "going into the barrel" meant going in to play goal. Bill Fitsell wonders if the expression links to that old symbol of the man who has lost everything, even his clothes, in a poker game and has to walk home—vulnerable and exposed—in a rain barrel. A "healthy scratch" is a member of the team able to play but relegated to the sidelines.

My favourite broadcaster, the sadly departed Danny Gallivan, used to describe "cannonading" shots and "Savardian spinneramas" and players "gaaathering speed" as they came up the ice. We all admire quick players with "good wheels" or "jets." A player visibly rocked by a check is said to have "had his bell rung." Some people still talk about the "Gordie Howe hat trick"—a goal, an assist, and a fight. It's fitting that a game so steeped in history invents its own language and rituals.

Three or four times a year, I play old-timer hockey with some of my Toronto pals, teachers all of them, who play Wednesdays at 4 p.m. in a suburban rink. The calibre is a step up from my Monday gang, the rink is bigger, and I take real joy in playing alongside my friend David Carpenter and his son, Hadley. "Carp," as everyone calls David, has played goal most of his life, but these days he plays out. He calls himself a stay-at-home defenceman, though he looks so at sea out there I tell him that staying up is his real challenge. Still, Carp's father played junior hockey, so the hockey bloodline is good. And it's no surprise that David's son, Hadley, is sleek and quick and creative. He is both a yardstick by which I can measure how much speed I have lost and a reminder of what it was like when I stepped on the gas and the body replied, instantly.

Hadley has scored as many as six goals in one game, but there is one goal that merits a replay. Kind on and off the ice, Hadley would never run up the score, but during one particular game the other goalie had said something to irk him. Hadley took his revenge. On a breakaway, he streaked in, pretended to lose the puck in his skates, and in one motion kicked the puck onto the blade of his stick and roofed it. All of us on the bench dropped our sticks, leaned over the boards, and waved hosannas.

Afterwards, we retired, as always, to a pub called The Half-Time (now called The Wally) where TVs tuned to sports hang in every corner, the chicken wings are cheap and hot (with "suicide" sauce for the brave), and the beer is red and cold and comes several pitchers at a time. Hockey and beer were connected long before Molson and other brewers began their marketing campaigns.

I always thought the beer followed the game, until I discovered otherwise. One reliable account has Howie Morenz—a flash forward for the Montreal Canadiens in the '20s and '30s—drinking beer one afternoon and eating limburger cheese with onions before moving on to garlic and turkey legs. "You stink," reporter Elmer Ferguson teased him, "and you're full of beer. You'll never play tonight." The man they called "The Stratford Streak" scored a hat trick that night for Les Glorieux.

Other stories have the Broad Street Bullies, the Philadelphia Flyers of the 1970s, playing with hangovers. Reggie Leach, at one time a sixty-one-goal scorer, used to make quiet deals with defenceman Ed Van Impe to help cover for him on days when he was feeling delicate. NHLers used to call it "playing guilty." Some things never change. A player tells the author of *Zamboni Rodeo*—a book about a year in the life of a minor-pro team in Austin, Texas—"I've never played with a hangover. Still drunk, maybe."

I mentioned that Carp (who writes crime novels under the name J.D. Carpenter) played goal. On a bookshelf at his home sits a souvenir of the last game he ever played in net: His white goalie's helmet, an elderly model that comprises a basic helmet with a metal screen overlay, looks like something from a car-crash test. Deeply imbedded in the helmet, just above the forehead, is a puck.

Carp never saw the shot, a slapshot from the point. It felled him and knocked him out for about half a minute. "When I regained consciousness on the ice," Carp says, "this oval of faces was staring wide-eyed down at me and saying things like 'Holy shit!' and 'Oh my God!' because the puck was impaled like an arrow in my helmet." The Sunday-morning boys at McCormick Arena then put a few questions to David, to ensure his head was still screwed on correctly, questions like, "What's your name?" When Carp flunked the test, they took him to a nearby hospital where mild concussion was diagnosed.

I wasn't there but I'm guessing that the most distraught guy on the ice that day was Paul Game, my old road-hockey pal—the one who almost took my eye out with his stick. A defenceman, he had hooked up with the Sunday-morning bunch and always played on Carp's team. At the start of each season, the two goalies—Carp and a distillery rep we called Murph—would take turns drafting players until two teams of a dozen or so had been formed. Murph would begin by opting for a sniper; Carp always chose Paul, who went about six-two, 220, and played with a kind of Brad Marsh abandon. Anyone in the goalmouth looking for a loose puck would be set on his can. I remember, in one game, coming in on Paul at the defence, seeing him brace, and deciding I would ignore the puck and hit him with everything I had—all 155 pounds. My gloves and stick went up in the air about ten feet, and days later a bruise the size of a horse's head formed on my hip and thigh.

After the puck downed Carp that day, he and Paul decided they would finish the season and then retire together. And while they did retire from Sunday-morning hockey, and Carp's old helmet was shelved, both men soon found other venues and continue to play the game.

A boy whom Roy MacGregor once coached also has a souvenir on his bedroom shelf. It seems that a teammate, Roy's son, was in the habit of rolling his used hockey tape into a ball and saving it, not tossing it in the dressing-room bin. In time all the other players were adding their tape, as well, and when the boy faced minor heart surgery, the then giant ball was signed by all the players and presented to him in hospital. A month later he was back in the lineup, and the ball became a cherished souvenir of a cherished game.

7
WRITERS AND THE GAME

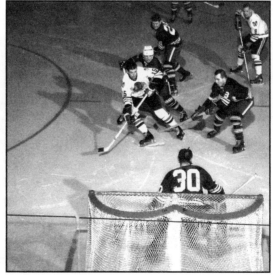

I N A DINER where my Coke comes in the same heavy glass bottle, with a straw, like it did decades ago, David Adams Richards holds forth on hockey. He has his usual: vanilla shake and fries. He lathers the potatoes in ketchup, then forms a steeple with his hands overtop of them, a preamble, I think, to tucking in—a Maritimer's grace before meals.

I'm wishing he would tuck in, because my own meal of two haddock pieces crowning a mound of fries is beckoning deeply to me, the steam rising, the lemon slice yellow and alluring, the fish batter golden and bubbly, the aroma intoxicating. David is speaking and I am listening, even as my own ritual commences. The second I open the vinegar dispenser to anoint the fries, I think of all the rinks in my youth where I have had just this kind of plain food. In my adult life, the accompaniment to TV hockey has often been popcorn and beer. But as a boy, it was arena fries in a funnel-shaped white paper cup and so much vinegar it formed a little dunking pool at the bottom.

Finally, I lose all hope that David will begin to eat. Impolitely, I succumb to my fries. For, by now, he's talking about the '72 series and his own fries have become irrelevant. Aside from some dainty forays into the pile with his fingers, he pretty well ignores them for the next hour and a half. Perhaps he was never hungry to begin with. Or perhaps mere hunger is no match for the passion he feels for hockey.

"Hockey," he wrote in his book *Hockey Dreams*, "is where we finally got it right." He tells me he means only this: that we in this country play hockey as well as anyone in the world and we should make no apology. "You can go to any hamlet in Newfoundland, you can go to

Toronto or Alberta," he tells me, "and any hamlet in between, and walk in on a Saturday night and talk hockey for two hours with people who know the game as well as those who are commenting on the game on TV. There's something in this country that we ultimately love. I was once asked, 'What is the linchpin of Canada?' The interviewer would have laughed me off the air if I had said 'the National Ballet.'"

I had come to David Adams Richards because I knew him as a superb writer, one who happens to possess a deep feeling for hockey. A Christmas party chez Richards once spilled out onto the street and became a road-hockey game when the host took a notion. But there was another reason I sought him out. For almost half of my working life, I have been a literary journalist, for both newspaper and radio, and I had come to believe that writers who create their own imaginary worlds bring a unique sensibility to the real one. Writers are quirky, sometimes insightful, and they typically possess the tools to shape a thought. Creative writers don't necessarily have *the* answers, but more often than not they have *interesting* answers.

Richards has won just about every literary prize this country has to offer. His books give a powerful and complex voice to the dispossessed of rural New Brunswick. But Richards does not romanticize the poor; he is beholden to no one. I read in this writer's rugged and windswept face, in his burly frame and rumpled appearance, a casual defiance.

Richards walks with a pronounced limp, one that forces him as much up as forward with every step. He talks about being born with a bad left leg and left hand, weaknesses that dashed his boyhood hockey dreams. But there's a vigour about him. He has a powerful neck and a barrel body that make him seem younger than his fifty years. I imagine that, during his somewhat wild and troubled youth along the Miramichi River, he was one you didn't mess with. Only his shyness offers any hint of his gentle spirit.

I remember, vaguely, interviewing him in the mid-1980s when I was literary editor at the *Whig-Standard* in Kingston and he was an emerging writer. His high-school fistfights and subsequent refuge in the local library are what I recall from that encounter. In a very real way, literature saved him. But hockey, too, enjoys an important place in his cosmos.

It makes perfect sense that David Adams Richards is besotted with hockey. The concerns that ripple through his fiction—courage, the underdog, the dichotomy in all humans, intensity, loyalty—are ones that characterize much of hockey. Richards has never bothered to hide his disdain for academics and for literature about the middle class—"bores the arse right off me," he once said. His writing, a critic observed, "tries to be accurate, rather than explanatory, because it takes for granted that life is inexplicable; interesting, comic, sad, tragic, ludicrous, beautiful, but inexplicable." One could easily substitute the word "hockey" for "life" in that passage, and Richards would likely approve.

"I love the game. There is something extremely spiritual and non-intellectual about hockey. It's distinctly Canadian," Richards argued. He trashed Canadian intellectuals who worry too much about how our brand of hockey will go down in Europe and elsewhere: "If we want to clean up our game we should do so because we want to and not because some Swedish expert thinks we play dirty."

Richards had no respect for Swedish and Russian "whiners" who complain about "Canadian cowboys on the ice." He bemoaned the stickwork that he claimed was "a child of the Europeans." He said Gary Bettman "wouldn't know a hockey puck if. . . . That he would be the head of the National Hockey League says a lot about what's wrong with Canadian hockey. He has no idea what violence is in hockey." Richards lamented that American fans don't understand the game either, think it's football on ice.

He's on Don Cherry ground here, and while I agree with him that Cherry makes sense a lot of the time, I can't agree that Europeans introduced the spear and the slash to NHL hockey. Canadians were carving each other up with sticks long before the Czechs and Russians, Swedes and Finns arrived. What's perhaps true is that the Europeans laid on the stick as a matter of routine, whereas Canadians slashed with a purpose. Several Canadian friends of mine played in Europe; one talked about the "casual" stickwork he experienced over there; another came back appalled by the nasty stickwork and even skatework—players using the blade to cut the backs of legs. The effect of Europeans entering the NHL in the 1970s was to drive up the level of stickwork yet another notch.

As for Americans, some know the game and some don't, but the same is true of Canada—where street hockey is nowhere near as prevalent as it once was. That, too, is telling.

Richards offered a "maybe so" but then countered. The Europeans, he said, were forced to rely on stickwork to deal with the aggressive forechecking that defined Canadian hockey at that time. "They used the weapons they had. When I first saw that stickwork I was unused to it. I'm far more blasé about it now, which is very unfortunate." Still, Richards lamented the cross-checking and the cutting—more so than the hitting and even the fighting.

"But don't Domi and Brashear set an example for kids?" I asked him.

"Yes, they set an example," Richards said. "But so does Lemieux set an example. Modano sets an example. And Stevie Thomas, who plays a hard game, sets an example. So does Gary Roberts. If I had to pick a hockey hero in the early '90s, it would be Doug Gilmour, who was tough as hell and 170 pounds."

Then I asked Richards the question I had put to several others: Why do hockey players feel so compelled to respond in kind to physical insults? Why is hockey so tribal? "That's what's best about it and that's what's worst about it," the author replied. "Every game is absolutely different. Every game I see things on the ice that are absolutely right and things that are absolutely wrong."

He thinks hockey in this country is complicated and political and religious—"Everyone has their hockey gods and hockey demons"—and it provokes what he calls "affirmation/condemnation."

Our voices were rising a little in the tiny fish-and-chips joint. Two cocksure Canadians talking hockey, each calling on almost fifty years of following the sport.

"Hockey," said Richards, "has been in my blood since I was four years old. In the sixth game of that '72 series against the Russians,

Esposito said there was a change halfway through. He looked at a Russian when he was lining up to take a faceoff and he said to him, 'You are not going to win.'"

"Did the Russian understand him?" I asked.

"I have no idea. But this whole thing that was played out—and I hate to say this because it makes me sound disrespectful—it was one of the most courageous Canadian moments since Dieppe. The players were utterly courageous. The Russians were against them, many people in Canada were laughing at them. They played glorious hockey those last three games in Moscow. And look at the playoffs this year. Shanahan coming back hurt. Modano with his broken nose. If we question that. . . . They asked Mike Tyson, 'Who are the toughest people in the world?' He said hockey players, hands-down tougher than boxers. Look at Howe, Orr. They wouldn't have been as great without that mean streak. Lemieux and Gretzky didn't have it, those don't-fuck-with-me eyes. But Richard had it."

As for the fighting, "Do I get rid of it all? I'm not sure I want to get rid of it all." Richards struggled to describe the delicate chemistry that governs hockey, and he worried, as do others, that if you excise fighting from the game, maybe the hitting goes, too. Something essential, he warned, might be lost were the game to be radically changed.

Richards was throwing in his lot with those who argue, to explain hockey violence, that there is something unique—a hot and intrinsic quality—to the game. He talked about being asked in 1998 to write a piece on the men's Olympic team, and preferring instead to write about the women's team—because he liked their style. Richards remembered talking to some of the Maritime members of that team and feeling intimidated "because they were Olympians." But more than anything he remembers the Canadian players' palpable loathing of the American team. "It was in their friggin' guts. You could feel the tension when I asked about Cammi Granato of the American team. If the fists could fly . . . and they might yet. I once got into an argument with a woman on *Imprint* [an Ontario television program] about women's hockey, and she took the moral high ground." The woman was insisting that women's hockey was a purer game, a finesse game. Richards ripped into her. "I said the Yanks would rather beat the Canadian players than eat. They would eat them alive if they could."

Finally, Richards remembered something that a Swedish player—it may have been Mats Naslund, the diminutive sniper with the Canadiens in the 1980s—had once said. He believed that to win the Olympics or a world championship, you should stock your team with Russians. But if you want to win the Stanley Cup, load up on Canadian players. "It's what they play for," Richards said, "all their lives." Such is the power in this country of a tall nickel-alloy barrel with a bowl made of silver and gold. A Canadian man would do almost anything to get his name on that cup.

The theory of riding Canadian heart all the way to the Stanley Cup sounds dated now, for every team has its stock of Americans, Europeans, and Russians. But there is one staggering statistic to note here: The Conn Smythe trophy—awarded to the most valuable player in the Stanley Cup playoffs—has been won by a Canadian player thirty-five times in the thirty-six years of its existence. The Cup as Holy Grail.

I have never met the gifted Saskatchewan writer Guy Vanderhaeghe, but we have corresponded. While researching a book several years ago about the horse–human connection through time, I wrote him because I had been moved by a section in his novel, *The Englishman's Boy*, about Hollywood film directors using tripwires to get those dramatic horse-and-rider falls in old westerns. Guy wrote me promptly and pointed me towards several useful books. Much later, while reading Roy MacGregor's book on hockey fathers, I saw the touching piece that Guy had written, so I knew he played the game. Again, I wrote him, this time putting to him the question that this book seeks to answer: Why is hockey so violent?

His letter, dated September 10, 2001, follows:

I'm not sure why hockey is such a violent game. Any reasons I could postulate are the obvious ones. It is played mostly by young men who are at the peak of their testosterone levels, and coached by older men who would like to recover the memory of their salad days. Just like lacrosse was supposed to train native boys for war, I suspect hockey is a system to separate the truly "manly" from the weaker, more "effeminate" males. What should be a celebration of speed and finesse is (at least in this country) a celebration of toughness and stick-to-itiveness. How many hockey commentators have praised our players for their ability to win games in the corners? Think about it, that's a pretty small area of the rink. I've always been of a divided mind on these questions. I have a sympathy for toughness and grinding; both are worthy of emulation depending on how they are defined. But a hired enforcer strikes me as something else. He's employed to fight someone else's battles. Of course, this assumes that there will always be battles.

I think the culture of the game has a lot to do with the violence, but so does the nature of it. The blood does get heated in a way it doesn't in baseball or basketball; high-speed collisions do incite a certain eagerness to retaliate. Assholes on ice and chippy play lead you to thoughts of retribution. Just a couple of years ago I fell into a confrontation in which the desire to smash a taunting, leering ape was so strong I was temporarily homicidal.

The fighting and stickwork could be stopped if the penalties were severe enough, but I doubt they ever will be because most hockey people, tacitly, and often publicly, assume they are "part of the game." Outrage is frequently expressed by hockey people when violence which would never be condoned on the street is threatened with prosecution in the courts. Hockey is assumed to somehow be exempt from the rule of law. And hockey culture is unlikely to change because there is so little internal criticism. Parents appalled by its violent nature steer their kids into other games like soccer. Theoretically, hockey could be a game like soccer if it rewarded speed and skill rather than put a premium on force. What would happen if the "instigator" of a fight got a five-game penalty? But that would make it a pansy game.

The last remark, I was sure, held equal amounts of bitterness, resignation, anger, and satire. Recalling that "taunting, leering ape" had perhaps stirred Vanderhaeghe, reminding him of the great divide between what the game can be and what it often is.

Born in 1951, he says his inadequacies as a player have become more pronounced with age, "and now that I don't even have an infrequent burst of speed to encourage me, I've lost heart." He was hanging up the blades. As he put it, "This is my hockey season of apostasy. I'm not going to play this year. I don't know why but with every passing winter I've lost interest in the game."

Few hockey players get past high school, though with more college players entering the NHL that's changing. Few, then, possess the language and poetic sensibility of, say, Ken Dryden, hockey's reigning intellectual. But before he came along, there was a player who both understood the game and who could define its delicate edges. His name was Eric Nesterenko and he played in the NHL for twenty years, with stints in Chicago and Toronto in the '50s, '60s, and '70s. "Nester the Pester" we used to call him when we watched him as kids.

In a striking profile in his book *Breakaway,* writer Charles Wilkins praises Nesterenko as "a man of renegade imagination." A rebel in every way and twenty years ahead of his time, he ate pasta and salad and carbohydrates before a game—conventional wisdom now—when his teammates were devouring red meat. Nesterenko used aerobic training when everyone else "played themselves into shape." And he struck a unique arrangement with a reluctant Blackhawks manager that let him attend university in Toronto and London for the 1956 and 1957 seasons and fly in to Chicago for games only. In New York, he would hang out in The Village, talking to reporters and writers such as Jimmy Breslin and Norman Mailer. Nesterenko would later write a book for young readers based on his life in hockey, and he told me he may yet get to the memoir whose skeleton is tucked in a drawer. I can legitimately, then, call Nesterenko a writer. Few writers, let alone players, can match his eloquence on the subject of hockey.

Now sixty-nine and a ski instructor based in Vail, Colorado, Nesterenko spends time every year hiking, sometimes alone, in the Wind River area of Wyoming, where I've ridden on week-long horse treks several times. He told Wilkins that human beings need a great deal of silence, which he finds up in the mountains. Here was a man of depth and intellect—and, it appears, searing honesty.

Not a small man at six-two and 197 pounds, he said he played pro hockey "in constant fear. So much so that that fear became an old friend. It's a tremendous stimulus; you have to court it at the same time as you try to dispel it. Fear of being humiliated, fear of losing, fear of getting hurt. Those are the big three."

Nesterenko never denied that fear. "One of my tricks was simply to *let the fear in,* imagine the worst thing that could happen to me . . . before long it leaves you in what I call a cold, calculating rage." The rage left him focussed and able to play.

He described early in his career being brought to his knees after Bert Olmstead speared him. The veteran looked down at him and said with a smile, "Welcome to the league, kid." Ted Lindsay used his stick to remove several of Nesterenko's teeth, and Terrible Ted, too, found Nester's anguish amusing. The rookie knew he had to retaliate or he'd get more trouble down the line. That was, and is, the rule of hockey.

But he also talked about the pure exhilaration of the game, how "time would just slow right down for me; I'd feel terrific joy and well-being, totally disappear into the moment. . . . I felt as if I was somebody else, a remarkable feeling. It's one of the things I've always lived for."

Nesterenko was the subject of a novel, *The Drubbing of Nesterenko,* written by Canadian author Hanford Woods, published in the early 1970s. The novel's teenage protagonist is an ardent fan of Nesterenko's, and the story's salient event is fact: a beating that John Ferguson laid on Nesterenko during the Stanley Cup final of 1965. Woods describes how the entire city of Montreal "revelled in their mean, stupid triumph."

The game turned on that moment. Luck had not decided the game, nor had skill or even courage. It had been decided by one man's drilling fists. You have to wonder how other players, then and now, coped with their demons.

The Woods book features some fine writing, and it captures the notion that, whether true or not, we who watch and play the game believe that fights *do* shape outcomes. And in pitting Eric Nesterenko, one of the great intellectuals of hockey, against John Ferguson, the epitome of "no prisoners" hockey, the author had chosen well.

The conceit of the novel is this: The young narrator sees his hockey hero, Eric Nesterenko, savaged in a hockey fight and struggles to recover from it. (One has the sense from *Breakaway,* Charles Wilkins's book, that Nesterenko was unaware of the novel inspired by the beating he suffered.)

Ferguson, writes Woods, "was enraged at Nesterenko, his abstraction, his unconcern at winning or losing. Ferguson had to win, now and always. Winning was life and losing death, and winning sanctified whatever means used." Ferguson continues hammering Nesterenko "after he was little more than butchered meat." The colour of Nester's blood on the ice is "the deepest black."

And when Woods writes, "The outcome of the series was determined by the fight," I thought of other playoffs series, ones in my own memory banks, in which a fistfight shaped results. What kind of game is this, in which finesse yields so blithely to a menacing fist?

After Nesterenko was dispatched to the medical clinic in the old Montreal Forum, he returned, to his credit, to the fray. But the Canadiens eye him one way, his fellow Black Hawks another. The Montrealers, writes Woods, viewed him with "swaggering contempt." Those on the bench, meanwhile, "were malevolently alert to the signal defeat of his broken posture. He skated through the resignation of his teammates who, with eyes lowered, were already fixing him as the scapegoat of the defeat inevitably settling upon them. . . ."

After the game, won, of course, by Les Glorieux, team captain Jean Beliveau paid tribute to Ferguson—"to the work of his hammering fists." But the myth prevailed, that the "superior skills" of the flying Frenchmen had won the day, not "an aberrant rush into force."

"The arena," Nesterenko told Wilkins, "is a survival place." Word of the beating got around the league, and next season "every thug on every team" ran him. "The shark mentality," Nesterenko called it. "One guy'd taken a bite outta me, they all wanted a bite."

He had to re-establish what he called "his space," the respect for personal territory that all hockey players know about. It's why skating through the crease is seen as so offensive, so disrespectful. Nesterenko regained his space by issuing a threat to every young kid on opposing teams who eyed that space. "I know you're coming after me," Nester would tell them on the ice during stoppages in play, "and if you do, I'm going to hit you over the head as hard as I can with my stick." Nesterenko was thirty-five when Ferguson randomly chose him for slaughter; Nester would play another six years in the league.

Nesterenko also gets a mention in *The Good Body*, a novel by Canadian writer Bill Gaston that appeared in 2000. This is a lively and insightful book about a hockey pro not quite tough enough or good enough to make it in the NHL. Bobby Bonaduce, the novel's central character, is also a rarity—a literate player (indeed, he gets into a grad school English program while trying to reclaim the wife and son he had abandoned while playing hockey twenty years earlier).

Gaston captures the wit that hockey players display in various ways—sometimes by having Bonaduce spout clichés while being interviewed, as a perverse form of mockery. Language is not their forte. Gaston's character notes one exception: Eric Nesterenko.

A player hoping for advancement, Bonaduce adopted a gritty style, one Gaston nicely captures in words: "Slash, spear, elbows always up. I'm meaner than you. Drop the gloves first, get in the first punch. In front of the net be a constant menace, a fucking monster. Your goalie's your helpless naked mother and nobody gets near. It wasn't so hard; you'd been living on the edge of malice to begin with." I like that phrase, "the edge of malice." Gaston either played a lot of hockey or researched well.

Here is Bonaduce describing the various kinds of toughness in hockey. Each team has at least one big man who can fight, with his "head high, face calm, sometimes even that cultivated look of boredom. Cocksure as a dog who gets paid to piss." But, eventually, and sooner rather than later, his hand-speed declines and younger players start using that high head as a punching bag—"the father bested by the child."

Then there are the wing-nuts, the players whom Murray Oliver talked about, with "that screwy far-away look in their eyes." The fear these men instill, Bonaduce says, is the fear of the unknown: "The game of hockey is licence for some truly crazy men to inflict pain. These men can't be summed up or described. They're all different, because one aspect of crazy toughness is that it's a kind of genius and it doesn't repeat itself."

Bill Gaston made me think of a certain Belleville Bull player, in 2001, whose ritual at the faceoff was to plant his stick between his opposite's legs and then let it drift up towards the groin. The insult struck me as profound because it was so routine and delivered before play had actually begun. The Kingston Frontenacs' wingers who suffered this ignominy made a mild show of complaint; this, too, fell into routine. The Belleville player had a reputation, he was capable of anything, and the Kingston wingers dared not emulate their tormentor.

In *The Last Season,* a novel published in 1983, Roy MacGregor gets inside the head of Felix Batterinski—a fictitious goon who acts out his role alongside real players, the brawling Philadelphia Flyers of the late 1970s. As the character's name suggests, there's much winking going on here (the enforcer's junior coach is one-eyed Sugar Bowles), but MacGregor does a nice job of conveying the mindset of a bruising Canadian hockey player and of those who encourage that style.

Bowles tells Batterinski all about the legendary Ottawa Valley bad boy Sprague Cleghorn and urges Felix to emulate him. In a pre-game talk, Sugar says, "These guys like to carry the puck and they like to make the pretty play, but they don't seem as keen when the going gets rough." And then he tells Batterinski to "set the pace" and to remember Sprague Cleghorn (who claimed to have sent fifty hockey players off the ice on stretchers). Later, Sugar offers Batterinski that old Canadian hockey dictum: "Talent is what begins hockey games, heart is what wins them."

MacGregor takes potshots at American fans who idolize the brawler. Batterinski sounds an awful lot like Dave Schultz playing in the Philadelphia Spectrum, "where the good play was seldom realized but violence always expected." MacGregor has the Flyers playing the Russians in Philly, as indeed happened in 1976, and in one scene Valery Kharlamov actually winks at Batterinski—to show he understands the goon and is amused by the goon's standing. When Batterinski responds in anger, he is held by linesmen and finds himself at the boards, only inches from his screaming fans, who are pounding on the glass. And the goon—who is portrayed sympathetically here—comes to a sudden realization: "I'd never been this close to my fans before, never seen what they looked like. Never cared. But I saw now, and I knew finally that I was not Batterinski. *They* were."

Bobby Bonaduce and *The Good Body* resurfaced in Halifax in the fall of 2001, when hockey historians, academics, doctors, former NHL players (Jean Beliveau, for one) gathered for a symposium. "I didn't think you could talk hockey for five days," I told the barmaid at a Barrington Street pub one evening during a pause in the palaver, "but apparently you can."

Paul Martin, an Edmontonian finishing his Ph.D. in Canadian literature, gave a talk on hockey and literature. Hockey, he suggested, provokes all kinds of stories and analysis and commentary. Yet the game's richness and complexity, Martin believes, leaves us behind, struggling to "express the inexpressible." The game of hockey, like life itself, "always manages to escape being pinned down or explained once and for all."

Bill Gaston's character understood that. Martin quotes Bonaduce: "On the ice," he thinks to himself, "is where it really happened. All senses sparking, working at the widest periphery, aflame with danger and hope both, seeing the whole picture, the lightning-fast flux of friends and enemies, the blending of opportunity and threat. Words didn't stand a chance here. Words were candy wrappers, dead leaves."

Martin is a longtime pal of another speaker at the conference, a Calgary poet named Richard Harrison, who had written a book of hockey poems called *Hero of the Play*. If the confluence of hockey and literature had a voice that week in Halifax, it was the voices of Paul Martin and Richard Harrison.

Martin had lost his grandfather just weeks before the conference, and I liked what he said of him, a Saskatchewan wheat farmer and once-gifted athlete who "lived this tension between the expressed and the inexpressible." Martin remembered him, on the one hand, as a wonderful storyteller, and, on the other, as a man who lived "a great portion of his life in a monk-like state of silent contemplation." He would watch games on TV with the sound off and even in the company of his grandson, watching the Oilers live, Poppa (as Martin called him) said little. "He watched the ice like he watched the land. Anyone who believes the Saskatchewan prairie is boring to look at, my grandfather and I will tell you, hasn't looked at it closely enough. It is a complex ecosystem in which one can observe many things happening at the same time. For my grandfather, hockey was the same way."

Richard Harrison began his talk not by reading several poems, but by reciting them in the Russian manner of performance. He then described being asked to speak, in 2000, at the Calgary Booster Club's Sportsman-of-the-Year dinner, which that year honoured The Legends of the Game—Maurice Richard, Gordie Howe, Jean Beliveau, and Bobby Hull. Harrison was to write, and read, a poem for and about each man, who would then make a speech and sign a jersey for a charity auction to follow.

In the poems, Harrison described tall Beliveau "coming over the horizon like a mast" and Richard going in on goal "with his eyes ablaze and bituminous black." Each time Hull "touched the ice," Harrison wrote, "he was every boy in love." Finally, he described how he once saw Gordie Howe "flick a stick full of rinkchaff" over the head of a collector seeking autographed pucks at an old-timers' game, how he "sent the snow in a perfect arc," all the while fixing his gaze on the man.

Harrison met each legend before the event so each could see the poem beforehand. Harrison chatted with Beliveau about violence in hockey, he heard Richard's lament that his legs "were gone," and he read Howe his poem because Gordie had forgotten his glasses. Hull was at the centre of a little crowd, and when Harrison was introduced, The Golden Jet said, "A poet, eh? All I know about poetry is Robert Service." And Harrison paints a picture of what happened next as Hull, "in that gravelly-laughing voice of his," began to recite:

Hull: "A bunch of the boys were whooping it up in the Malamute saloon . . ."

Harrison: "And with a gesture of his outstretched arm and his scarred, bent fingers spread as far as he could unbend them, he described the length of the bar from where we stood out into the hotel corridor."

Hull: "The kid that handles the music-box was hitting a jag-time tune . . ."

Harrison: "And he asked me, "You know this?" and I nodded, and he went on, drawing out the syllables because this was, like any good story, worth bringing to life in the telling . . ."

Hull: "Back of the bar, in a solo game, sat Dangerous . . . Dan . . . McGrewww. . . ."

Harrison: "And there he was, Bobby Hull, whose shot could knock a man off his skates and back into his own goal reciting something of the immortal of my art . . ."

The forty-nine poems in *Hero of the Play* venture to capture "the inexpressible": the joy of skating in a rink in Africa; the shock of recognition that comes when the narrator discovers that a hotel employee there *plays*, and how the narrator's mere mention of the name "Bobby Hull" propels the two of them into a palm-on-palm handshake; the poet carrying a hockey stick (borrowed from the Canadian embassy) through the streets of Abidjan, Ivory Coast, and people staring like "inland farmers who had never seen the sea stared at Ulysses with his oar."

Harrison's fellow poets, he told us that day in Halifax, were at first mystified by his quest for higher meaning in the game of hockey. Essentially, they said, What's a sensitive guy like you doing in a hockey rink? "Hockey," Harrison told us, "is seen as a game of violence and not as a game of the mind. The thinking is that hockey is a brutal sport, appealing to base emotions."

Later, I asked Harrison: Just what *did* Beliveau have to say about hockey violence? Beliveau's comment, he replied, was that players were taking too literally the command to finish their check and that certain players—call them goons if you like—weren't really following the sense of the play. They had their own agendas quite apart from the play, agendas that were spawning violence. Harrison likened hockey brutality to "prison justice," in which the cons make the rules. "The danger," he said, "is that prison justice is always in flux. You lose order."

In *Zamboni Rodeo*—a book about a minor-pro team in Texas called the Ice Bats—an enforcer named J.T. "Thumper" Thompson sums it up nicely: "Everybody's gotta play their role. Sometimes I have to go out there and take the law in my own hands. If the ref lets something go I'll say, 'Hey, if you don't take care of it, I'm gonna have to take control.'"

Beliveau's observation was close to that of Morris Mott, who was also at the conference. Mott argued that violence erupting naturally from the play was one thing; "staged" violence was another. He wanted to see more rewards in the game for speed and creativity, but he also suggested that if fighting is to remain a part of the game, perhaps players should practise it on skates, as they do passing and shooting.

Beliveau was in Halifax accepting an honorary degree from St. Mary's University (whose Gorsebrook Research Institute had organized the conference), and I heard him say just before the dinner how much he regretted all the stickwork in the NHL. And then the wise old statesman of hockey joined a long chorus of people when he said, "Somebody gonna get killed."

CBC-Radio's *Air Farce* used to feature a dumb hockey player called Big Bobby Clobber, and the stereotype of the dense plodder has long been a fixture in hockey culture. In Bill Gaston's book, Bobby Bonaduce's hockey buddies make playful theatre of that notion, sputtering clichés into microphones and hiding their innate intelligence. The players' private joke on the world.

In his book *My Career with the Leafs and Other Stories,* Brian Fawcett toys with a similar idea. In the whimsical title story offered as autobiographical, a thirty-year-old poet makes the Leafs and learns, among other things, "the unwritten law of hockey. You're supposed to pretend you're really dumb." Our hero is interviewed by Howie Meeker on *Hockey Night in Canada* (the book was published in 1982) and earns the wrath of everyone in hockey when he replies as a poet might—and not as a player should. In Fawcett's nutty glimpse inside the dressing room, Tiger Williams is a closet reader of Etienne Artaud, Darryl Sittler loves Henry James—"said it helped his passing game"— and George Ferguson is keen on Rainer Maria Rilke. All the Leafs, in fact, hide large hardcover books in their hockey bags, but Fawcett irks them when he lets the cat out of the bag on national TV.

Ferguson warns Fawcett that for his sins he will henceforth be blacked out—"no television interviews, and as little newspaper cover-age as they can give you. What you *will* see will all be bad."

The Canadian poet replies, "I'm pretty used to that."

Mordecai Richler, in *On Snooker,* the last book he wrote before he died in 2001, naturally enough ranges beyond the billiard table. Unbridled and acerbic (he calls Wayne Gretzky "one of the most boring men I ever met"), Richler was also a hockey fan. He jabs at those who contend that obsession with sports is the sign of a weak mind. The review in the London *Spectator,* for example, of Richler's novel *Barney's*

Version was warm and generous. The reviewer's one complaint was that the book "rather strains credulity" when it offers as protagonist Barney Panofsky—a cultured man who knows much about George Bernard Shaw and Samuel Johnson and P.D. James—but who is also "obsessed with ice hockey." And so it goes. Hockey players and hockey fans: dismissed as dumb and dumber.

Richler quotes a friend, the American essayist Wilfred Sheed, who made sense of the obsession with sports shared by male North American writers of Richler's generation: "Sports constitute a code, a language of emotions—and a tourist who skips the stadiums will not recoup his losses at Lincoln Center or Grant's Tomb."

The mischievous Richler, though, is no blinkered cheerleader. *On Snooker* sees him whack the NHL for what he calls its "mindless expansion into the American sunbelt, a move actually informed by a subtext seldom mentioned. The owners hope eventually to acquire fan support by offering rednecks the only team sport left that is just about 100 per cent white."

Richler wrote magazine pieces about the Canadiens, went on road trips with them, smoked and drank with Montreal's hockey scribes. But as much as he loved the game, he was not in awe of its gods. In *On Snooker,* Gretzky got the Richler backhand; so did Howe. Gordie is painted as proudly giving Richler a tour of his trophy room at home. At one point, Howe says, "I understand you write novels."

"Yes," Richler replies.

"There must be a good market for them," Howe observes. "You see them on racks in all the supermarkets now."

Les Canadiens is an award-winning play written by Rick Salutin (with "an assist" by Ken Dryden) in 1977. Salutin makes an interesting point in his introduction, when he talks about the Canadian hysteria over teams in international competition (this was far more true in the '70s than now). It shows, he writes, and here he's on side with David Adams Richards, "that we have so little we feel is clearly ours that we develop a—to say the least—very intense relationship with what is unequivocally Canadian."

But where hockey in English Canada offers assurance that we at least have a culture (for hockey is indeed about "getting it right") in Quebec, hockey is about "getting back." Salutin quotes Red Fisher, the Montreal columnist who said that the French, since the Plains of Abraham, have been number two, but on the ice, number one—or at least they were for a long time. Salutin sees post-conquest history as one of ongoing but never successful resistance against English rule. And so Quebecers "try to win elsewhere, in a form where you *are* successful."

There is a moment in Salutin's play when a hockey stick turns into a rifle, or so it seems. Reminds me of Ted Lindsay doing much the same to fans in Toronto. My father was in the stands one night and saw him do it.

In May 2001, Rick Salutin, in his column in the *Globe and Mail,* fixed on something Don Cherry had said during a Leafs–Devils playoff game just days beforehand. I, too, had made mental note of Cherry's remark, about violence in hockey dating back to 1918. Salutin wondered if Cherry meant 1917, when the NHL was formed. But he did agree with Cherry that early hockey was brutal: "Most news reports about games in those days read like dispatches from No Man's Land."

Salutin wonders whether the simmering violence lies at the heart of the game's appeal. He wants to know why hockey bloodletting never went out of fashion in the way that bare-faced goalies, or the chewing of tobacco in baseball, did. Is it hockey's uncontrollability that grips us, an ephemeral notion captured in the puck itself? "The puck," Salutin wrote, "has a weird shape, it skips and slides on the ice; the players skid on their skates, they swat at it with oddly shaped sticks." He talked of how there is more "contingency" in this game than in any other, since the puck is so out of control—"and, yet, you must somehow try to control it. Just like the violence."

Salutin also described an old TV movie called *The Penalty Killer,* about a hockey goon played by Michael Moriarty (he later starred on the television program *Law & Order*). Apparently the tough guy almost kills someone on the ice, is charged, and faces time in prison. He wails when he hears that word "prison." The player is astonished, just as McSorley was astonished and Domi astonished—by where the game took them, what they did, the terrible consequences.

Christopher Lasch wrote a book in 1978 called *The Culture of Narcissism,* in which he argued that any cultural form—a language, a literature, a sport—needs a critical mass of audience. A certain number of people must have sufficient interest in, say, the local professional hockey team, to attend games or buy books on hockey. Otherwise, the sport remains a mystery to too many. "An athletic performance," Lasch wrote, "like other performances, calls up a rich train of associations and fantasies, shaping unconscious perceptions of life."

In the absence of that knowledge, what follows is what he calls "the contamination of standards." The less the fan knows, the more he or she is drawn to the simpler aspects of the game. *I can't tell how they scored that goal (boy, that puck is hard to follow), but I sure know who won the fight. Ask me.*

"As spectators become less knowledgeable about the games they watch," Lasch observed, "they become sensation-minded and bloodthirsty. The rise of violence in ice hockey, far beyond the point where it plays any functional part in the game, coincided with the expansion of hockey into cities without any traditional attachment to the sport."

Here is a scene from *Glengarry School Days,* written by Ralph Connor in 1902. There's a passage in which a mother implores her hockey-playing son to stick to the game, even when it turns violent.

"Fighting," she tells him, "is not shinny."

But it's hard, he tells her, "when a fellow doesn't play fair, when he trips you up or clubs you on the shins when you're not near the ball. You feel like hitting him back."

She tells him "that's the very time to show self-control. . . . That's what the game is for, to teach the boys to command their tempers. You remember 'he that ruleth his spirit is better than he that taketh a city.'"

Connor—the most successful Canadian novelist of his era—was, in fact, an ordained Presbyterian minister whose actual name was Charles William Gordon (the grandfather of contemporary Canadian authors Charles Gordon and Alison Gordon.)

Later on in *Glengarry School Days*, one of the players, a boy named Hughie, has his ankle broken by another player's slash. But instead of quitting the game, he insists on going into the net (these were the days when the goalie wore no special equipment). In the five minutes left, Hughie keeps net despite unspeakable pain, and they win the game. Hockey stoicism, early twentieth-century style.

And revenge, hockey style. The player who broke Hughie's ankle is set upon by one of Hughie's teammates, who drops him the second the game is over.

". . . Craven struck him fair in the face, and before he could fall, caught him with a straight, swift blow on the chin, and lifting him clear off his skates, landed him back on his head and shoulders on the ice, where he lay with his toes quivering."

A *New Yorker* cartoon from December 4, 2000: Four seedy, hatted, cigar-smoking characters at a table under a hooded lamp casually plot murder over a handgun. There is a pot of coffee on, and beside it a spent bottle of booze. "Use a hockey stick," the one advises—"make it look like a game."

The author of a scientific paper on hockey injuries, meanwhile, calls hockey "one of the fastest and most violent team sports in the world." Someone once told him that the game is played with clubs, knives, and bullets—sticks, skates, and pucks.

This from Hugh MacLennan, the eminent Canadian novelist, in an essay he wrote in 1954 called "Fury on Ice":

To spectator and player alike, hockey gives the release that strong liquor gives to a repressed man. It is the counterpoint of the Canadian self-restraint, it takes us back to the fiery blood of Gallic and Celtic ancestors who found themselves minorities in a cold new environment and had to discipline themselves, as all minorities must. But Canadians take the ferocity of their national game so much for granted that when an American visitor makes polite mention of it, they look at him in astonishment. "Hockey violent? Well, perhaps it is a little. But hockey was always like that."

The late Canadian author Hugh Hood once took a few faceoffs with Jean Beliveau, to get a sense of the latter's quickness. The awestruck Hood compared the dart of Beliveau's stick to "the motion of a small snake's tongue." The centreman schooled Hood on the various options in the faceoff circle, how he could direct the puck to the net, back to a defenceman, to a winger "exactly where he intended, like a billiards champion."

A friend loaned me his copy of *Rocket Richard*, published by Ryerson Press in 1961 and written by Andy O'Brien. It says something about the place of hockey, and of Maurice Richard, in this country that the book had no type on the cover—just a colour photo of Richard seated against a blue background. Even if the face was not familiar, the Canadiens sweater and the small number nine stamped on the stick were thought sufficient ID.

O'Brien quotes from the William Faulkner piece in *Sports Illustrated* of the early 1950s in which the Nobel Prize–winning author attends his first hockey game, between the Rangers and Canadiens, at Madison Square Garden. At first, he wrote in "An Innocent at Rinkside," the game befuddled him as "discordant and inconsequent, bizarre and paradoxical," but then "it would break, coalesce through a kind of kaleidoscopic whirl into a child's toy, a design." And no one impressed him more than Richard. In him the writer saw the "passionate, glittering, fatal alien quality of snakes."

Few hockey players will concede that fear is a constant on the ice; Eric Nesterenko stands almost alone in that regard. I do not say that other hockey players are dishonest. It may be that the fear is there in all of them, but they dare not name it. They call it by another name. Adrenaline. Excitement. Passion. But none of those words can explain the terrible things that occur in the course of hockey. Only fear comes close. And a fearful man's first thought is self-preservation.

In his novel about the war in Sri Lanka, *Anil's Ghost,* Michael Ondaatje conveys a great deal of medical knowledge—including the workings of the brain. Anil Tissera is a forensic anthropologist who had learned in anatomy class about the amygdala—the nerve bundle housed at the base of the brain. This is what Anil's professor calls "the dark aspect of the brain," home at once to fear and anger and pure emotion. Anil wonders if the name is Sri Lankan, for it sounds to her like the name of "some bad god."

Did the amygdala kick in the night that Shore hit Bailey or when McSorley hit Brashear? If hockey has its own bad god, this might be it.

8

FIGHTING
IN
HOCKEY:
THE CASE FOR
THE STATUS QUO

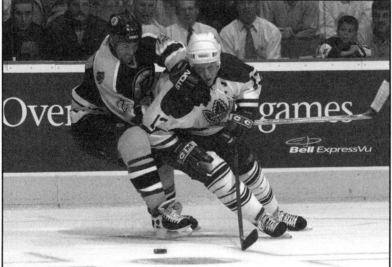

PHIL JONES, THE FORMER ARGONAUT I quoted earlier, with his thoughts on hockey physics, is forty-five. He plays hockey in a Toronto men's league.

"Is there ever any fighting?" I asked him.

"You might get some pushing and shoving," he said, "but anyone who fights is kicked out of the league. And every year there's a draft, so the guy who was your enemy last year might be on your team next year. It's pretty cool."

Jones has also been coaching hockey—girls' and boys'—for a long time, and he is convinced that the key to controlling violence in the game lies with referees and rules. He tells two stories to illustrate his point.

One involves a girl he coaches, an athlete he calls "the Gretzky of girls' hockey." She's Ashley Riggs, a five-two, 110-pound whirling dervish of sixteen years who counted 110 goals and 60 assists in seventy-two games over a two-year period. "She plays with the Olympic girls now and she even scores up there," said Jones. "I have never seen a kid skate like her. And every team wants to slow her down. They hook her, they stick her; her forearms after a game are all bruised and bloody. We've taught her not to retaliate, to get them back by scoring."

These are elite female athletes who are on the ice up to five times a week. Bodychecking or "hitting," as players call it, is not allowed in girls' and women's hockey. But such a prohibition seems only to produce more stickwork. Nothing in the female psyche or gene pool protects these athletes from hockey's intensity.

As her coach, Jones will first try the higher-ground approach. He will appeal to the referee before each game, warning of the abuse

Ashley is certain to take, in hopes the striped shirt will protect her. "I tell the ref, 'We've got the greatest hockey player in girls' hockey playing tonight. Keep an eye out.' And eighty per cent of the time the refs don't get it. It's so hard to get consistency in refereeing. Ashley is so quick. Even when she's knocked down, she rises so fast that the ref will put up the hand and then drop it again. Ashley's talent level means she always gets pounded on."

"What are your options as coach?" I asked Jones.

"We can nail the players going after her," he said. "That sends a message. Or, our players can go after *their* best player. I don't send a player. I may say, 'They're really pounding Ashley tonight' . . . I watch Don Cherry on TV and I think that most of the time he's a jerk. He's inarticulate, almost illiterate. But he makes a lot of sense about hockey. All he's saying is, 'This is how it is and until we come up with a better system, we have to protect our best players.'"

The second story involves Jones's son Joel. He played in the MTHL, an elite boys' league in Toronto. "All he wanted to do was fight," said Jones. "He was thirteen, fourteen years old. He and his teammates would turn their helmet straps inside out, so the helmet wouldn't come off as fast in a fight. The game was to get the other guy's helmet off first. Joel got kicked out of so many games. In minor bantam and bantam he had fifteen or twenty fights in two years. He once broke his hand hitting the glass in the penalty box with his fist. He's a smart kid, but on the ice he was emulating what he saw on TV, the NHL, Don Cherry."

Joel was nineteen when it became clear to him that even if he made a junior team he wouldn't see much ice time. He played high-school hockey in Markham, a Toronto suburb, where the rules are stiff. One fight and you're banished for the year. As a consequence, Joel stopped fighting and has even become a calming presence on the ice. The same young man who blew his lid so often in the past would urge others to stay cool. Maybe Joel matured. More likely, his game changed when the rules did.

Interpreting those rules is the problem. Hockey just might be the trickiest game in the world to police. In a letter to a fan in 1950, then NHL president Clarence Campbell called hockey "the fastest . . . the roughest, and without any doubt whatever the most difficult game of all to officiate."

Firstly, the game unfolds at such a furious pace that clear-eyed detection of fouls is exceedingly difficult. My friend Andy Raven has season's tickets to watch Ottawa Senators games at the Corel Centre. No one I know takes more pleasure in seeing live NHL hockey. "This is heaven for me," he said one night as we settled in to watch a game. Andy sits at centre ice, second level, and he insists—after trying all sorts of others—that they're the best seats in the house. But one time he sat down below, seven rows up from the ice, and he was astonished at how much faster the pace seemed the closer you got to the action.

"We tend to watch hockey," Andy told me, "from above and the side, as we do football or soccer, so that the game seems like it's played left to right and right to left. In fact, hockey—as anyone who has competed knows—is played up and down lanes that quickly clog. The fan sees all this white space; the player sees a lot of fast, incoming traffic. So most fans can't appreciate the game, how hard it is to play, to make good decisions—and to referee." Andy suggested that were a player in an exhibition game to have his helmet equipped with a miniature camera (as television producers sometimes do with race-car drivers), fans at home would finally get a sense of NHL hockey's pace.

So speed confounds consistent refereeing. There is also the matter of how to interpret the rulebook. Imagine this scenario from a player's point of view. The puck is in the other guy's end, but suddenly the play turns and they're rushing towards your zone. Their five defenders have become attackers in the time it takes to blink. This is one more thing I love about hockey (soccer can make the same claim)—how quick the transition is from protection to penetration, unlike football and base-ball where the offensive and defensive roles are so formalized and the shift so elaborate. In football, only following an interception or a fumble does the offence suddenly become the defence; in hockey that happens hundreds of times each game.

Back to our scenario. In that quick transition, defenders may find themselves a step behind, and those who can, will hook their sticks around their opposites, maybe just for a second or two. Longer infringements risk a penalty; a takedown more so. Some players call this often-sly method of slowing down another player "skiing." It's a deft manoeuvre that takes some of the jump out of the other guy's dash down the ice. Suddenly he's dragging, in pro hockey anyway, a 200-pound shadow. Is "skiing" legal? Is it fair? Is that little hook as much a part of the contact game as a bump into the boards or a hip check? What about the little interference that defencemen always run on forecheckers? When do you call that? The NHL brass directed referees to penalize such interference a few years ago, then backed off. The more I ponder the game, the more I respect what referees do. Each player, coach, fan, and owner knows precisely where that bar of tolerance should lie, and for each one of them, the bar sits at a different height.

Do not be swayed by those who claim to be motivated by their "love of the game" or "the good of the sport." The NHL is about neither love nor sport: It is a business, always has been. Pro hockey is about bottom lines and revenue. The players are often millionaires, though not nearly as rich, most of them, as the owners—or the corporations that jostle to put their product names on the air and along the boards and even on arena rooftops. The whole enterprise ticks along like a car that always starts no matter how cold it is on winter dawns. And you may say that there are too many teams and there's too thin a talent pool, that the fighting has to stop, that the NHL is a flawed thing. But those who keep that old car running cannot agree on how to tune it up or make it run smoother. And they most certainly don't want to trade it in on a newer model when the old one seems to work just fine. The NHL plays, on average, to ninety-two per cent capacity (though official

figures are invariably inflated, like all attendance figures in pro sport).
If it ain't broke, the saying goes, don't fix it.

Dan Diamond, editor of the hockey stats bible *Total Hockey,*
wrote an essay called "Fighting and Hockey: It's Part of the Game!?"
in the 1998 version of the book. The punctuation in that title seems
adroit. The exclamation mark is a nod in Don Cherry's direction;
the question mark recognizes those who decry the violence. Those
two small marks capture pro hockey's profoundly mixed feelings
about fisticuffs on the ice.

In the essay, Diamond describes Gary Bettman, the NHL commis-
sioner, speaking to the Canadian Club at the Royal York Hotel in
Toronto on April 15, 1998. The boss is there to talk about the future
of NHL hockey in Canada, and when he is finished speaking, he takes
a few queries from the audience. Finally, it comes, the one question the
league has grappled with since its inception. What is the NHL going
to do about fighting?

The savvy Bettman conducts a straw poll from the podium, asking
all those in favour of fighting and all those opposed, in turn, to raise
their hands. The room, it seems, is about equally divided. Television
moguls, corporate heads, journalists, and just plain fans in the room
are completely split on how to proceed. The NHL's own market
survey, conducted that month, among thousands of hockey fans all
over North America, has obtained the same mixed opinion: thirteen
per cent of respondents thought there was too little fighting, thirty-
nine per cent believed there was too much, and forty-eight per cent
were happy with the status quo. I take the results to mean that there
is a tide forming against fighting, but still, the survey shows what a
divided nation is hockey fandom.

And so Bettman, like almost every one of his predecessors, is loath
to tinker. A dramatic change in policy could have an impact on ticket
sales: A clampdown on fighting could theoretically bring more fans to
the game; a decline in patronage could also ensue. The morality of
fighting, the propriety of condoning on the ice what merits arrest in
the stands: This is simply not addressed in NHL thinking. The league's

case for leaving fighting in the game, then, is not a moral or a legal one, but purely a business one.

A traffic analogy comes to mind. In recent years, Toronto police have installed cameras at certain intersections where drivers often run red lights. We know what the law says about ignoring red lights, just as we know what's in the NHL rulebook. I cannot imagine a police officer ignoring a driver who runs a red light. But for more than eight decades, pro-hockey players have been running red lights on the ice— and getting away with it. When the game is close or near the end, during the playoffs, whenever the referee simply decides to "let them play," players can hook and slash and do much worse without incurring penalties. The on-ice police, the referees, virtually look the other way. History and precedence work powerfully against whistle-blowing.

The NHL's classic defence for this style of refereeing is to suggest that the violence, in fact, used to be much worse. In 1976, when Ontario's attorney general wanted the rule of law to apply on the ice, NHL president Clarence Campbell replied that "The hockey of today is patsy compared to what it was in the days of the six-team NHL." Old Clarence, I am convinced, was right. Bench-clearing brawls and donnybrooks are mostly a thing of the past. Still, a nasty past can explain, but never legitimize, a nasty present.

In 1992 those who sought to eliminate fighting in the NHL got their best shot. Two position papers were put forward from each side of the fighting debate, with owners, coaches, and general managers weighing in.

Abolitionists argued the following: We will never cash in on the vast revenue from American and European television until fighting disappears. We need to market our players as gifted athletes, not bullies. And how many potential fans shun hockey because of the violence?

The other side countered. If fighting stands in the way of American TV revenue, why is it that longtime TV sponsors, such as Molson Breweries, want no change on fighting? As for the European market, how do you explain that the European game has itself become more physical? And how should players respond to illegal tactics—with a "natural release of emotions through fisticuffs"? or through stickwork?

Moreover, how do you respond when another team targets your star—your *injured* star—for abuse?

Punch Imlach, in *Hockey Is a Battle,* which the Leafs coach of the '50s and '60s co-authored with Scott Young, describes how he would keep the doors to the dressing room closed after some games, to hide his players' injuries from the press. But the secrets were invariably revealed and the other team simply went after his hurt players. "You know a guy has a broken wrist, you hammer him there a few times and you don't have much trouble with him for the rest of the night," Imlach declared. "It's nothing personal. I'd do it myself."

It all sounds so cool and calculated. But there is nothing strategic, or even predictable, about hockey rage. Which is why rational thinking and the game of hockey are such odd bedfellows. In his book *Tropic of Hockey,* Dave Bidini, rhythm guitarist for the Rheostatics and a longtime amateur hockey player, addresses what he calls "the asshole gene" in hockey players. This sounds very like the "stupid point," the Jekyll/Hyde dividing line that Ken Dryden is convinced all players possess. The opportunities for physical insults in hockey, and the range of them, are vast, but certain insults spark contagions. When Canadian pros played the Russians for the first time in 1972, our players were appalled at their tactics: Canadian defencemen had to change their laces often because the Russians were in the habit of kicking, and their sharp blades cut the laces. Dennis Hull recalls a time when he was skating alongside Alexander Yakushev, and the rangy centre spat in his face. How do you stay cool when such a gauntlet is thrown down?

Dave Bidini observes, in his book, that the game seems to harbour jerks who shoot pucks at referees, who destroy their sticks after a bad call, or who go after the other team's smallest player. Bidini confesses that while he has never written an angry letter to a newspaper, called back a waiter to complain about the food, or fallen victim to road rage, he has experienced hockey rage firsthand. "I've spent entire games stalking opponents on the ice," he writes, "seeking revenge."

Bidini describes a game in Toronto between his team of musicians and another team of musicians, after which one of the other players says to him, "Good game, asshole." Bidini loses it, hits the other player from behind, and has to be restrained. In a subsequent game, Jim Cuddy, singer for Blue Rodeo, gets into a wild clash with Bidini. The fight features many of the hallmarks of an NHL bout: a previous assault inviting payback, pre-game verbal taunting, Bidini's hard check on Cuddy, Cuddy erupting. So many hockey fights feature those elements—a history, a stoking of the fire, actual flashpoint, and, finally, the tossing down of gloves and the flying fists.

Bidini doesn't blame Cuddy or the guy who called him an asshole. He blames the game itself. This is what Bidini says of his reckless and dangerous hit on a player from behind: "I was both frightened and awed that hockey had transformed me into someone I'd never been before. Whatever poise and good sense I'd learned had been dissolved by rage. The game had poisoned my heart, flooding it black, like ink poured into an aquarium."

Another man's rage is what you're often up against when you play this game. This, I think, is why hockey is such a game of courage, because the chemistry that Bidini describes is at work in almost every game—and especially in the playoffs. And so it is that victory in hockey often goes to the team with the most courageous and disciplined players—individuals who will sacrifice themselves for the team: go into corners first, take the hit to make the pass, drop down in front of shots, show restraint when it matters most, fight if that seems called for.

Not every player is prepared for the latter eventuality, so sometimes they must actually learn hockey's supplementary skill: boxing. In the late 1970s, an Ottawa 67's fan with some knowledge of self-defence grew weary of seeing hometown players, skilled players, bullied by the opposition. So he taught them the sweet science. Players learned how to punch, block blows, practise footwork. Yet the young players were reluctant to speak with the press and seemed genuinely embarrassed by their schooling in martial arts. Still, perhaps the training boosted their confidence, gave them a little swagger. In hockey, what counts—especially among the community of pugilists—is willingness. "Showing up," they call it.

There are few feelings worse than not showing up—having lost and knowing that the other team was simply braver. The slick New York Islanders in 1978 were a forlorn bunch when the Leafs slipped past them into the Stanley Cup finals. Muscle and desire had triumphed over skill and talent.

Chico Resch, the smart Islander goalie and later a TV analyst, said at the time: "I just don't know if we have any personalities on our team who are willing to do what some of their guys were willing to do: use the stick, take the body, rough it up. When Bossy got hurt, we came in the room and talked about how somebody should go out and get [Jerry] Butler for running Mike [Bossy]. We didn't have anybody to do it. Clark Gillies, he's the biggest guy in the league, but he'd rather play hockey. I don't know. Why doesn't he go out and break heads? Should he have to? Do we go out and get someone who will?"

The absence of rebuttal was widely viewed among the Islanders as the reason for their defeat. What other sport demands that combination of physical talent and intestinal fortitude?

I remember playing in an industrial league in Toronto in the mid-'70s. My teammates included several players from my old Glendon College team. And during a playoff game, we came up against a rugged and ugly opponent. Minutes into the game, I was charged in the corner, hit from behind. I remember a smile on the face of the guy who ran me; I had to be helped off the ice. They were bigger, meaner. Their girlfriends in the stands cheered them every time they ran one of us over.

C.K. Doyon, a moustachioed and eminently likeable player, had the courage to stand up to them, but he lacked size. His fight was short and there was no doubt who had won.

Fear coursed through that bench of ours. This was the dark side of hockey, and I remember with shame that most of us wanted little to do with the puck that day. I remember our coach after the game, livid at our lack of gumption. He was a teammate's father, old enough that he wore a fedora. After the game he paced up and down the dressing room, casting blame and salting wounds. "What happened to you?" he asked at one point, looking straight at me.

It wasn't that we lost; we had lost dishonourably. I can call up, even now, that sour taste in my mouth, but I would rather not. I wish I could call up a different memory, one in which I challenge the jerk who dropped C.K.

And while it would be a stretch to say that I had exacted revenge, at least I could say I was there for him. Hockey, contact hockey played by boys and men, still operates under Wild West rules, in which justice is meted out according to an old code. And until someone finds a better way, I suppose it will have to do.

Some players resign themselves to that fact. Paul Kariya, at five-eleven and 180 pounds, is considered a small player in the NHL. An elite winger with Anaheim, he won the Lady Byng trophy in 1996 and 1997, but by 1998 his penalty minutes were rising (forty minutes as opposed to six just two years previously). The fleet Kariya, who once said, "If I'm playing the game properly, I should never get a penalty," had changed his tune. "Obviously," he was saying in 1998, "I've got to protect myself a little better. I don't think winning the Lady Byng is going to help me any more. I'm not trying to be a tough guy, but if someone's going for my head, I'm going to get my elbow or my stick up to protect myself."

Whatever naïveté Kariya possessed about gentlemanly play begetting same must have vanished when Gary Suter cross-checked him in the face as Kariya celebrated a goal against Chicago on February 1, 1998. Kariya suffered a concussion, lost a chance to play at Nagano with the Canadian Olympic team, and was months recovering.

I remember, too, when Doug Gilmour was playing for the Leafs. Team spark in 1993 owed everything to Gilmour, who played with such courage and determination that he will always occupy a special place in that catalogue I keep in my brain of old hockey players. He was the team leader who would play to the point of exhaustion, starting the season at 170 pounds and draining down to about 155 when the playoffs finally ended. In one playoff game that year, Marty McSorley, then of the Kings, levelled him at the blue line and left him prostrate on the ice. Those who remember the hit describe a crushing elbow to Gilmour's head. And Wendell Clark, who combined toughness with skill, rushed at McSorley and they engaged in a vicious bout.

This was classic hockey justice. You ran our best guy; we rushed to his defence. The Rangers in the '70s did nothing when Dale Rolfe was thrashed by Dave Schultz, and hockey is such a game of momentum and heart that the game, and the series, shifted in that moment.

"That one-sided victory," Fred Shero, the Flyers coach, would later say of the Schultz–Rolfe fight, "was the turning point of the game. Rolfe's beating took something out of New York. They didn't seem to do as much hitting after that."

Some hockey observers see no way to stop fighting, no way out of the conundrum. I'm not sure about that, but this I do concede: It *is* complicated.

Let's imagine that on that play, Gilmour was hurt, and that McSorley was given a five-minute penalty after the referee ruled the play as intent to injure. Is that enough? Even were the Leafs to score with the man advantage, they have paid a mighty price and perhaps lost their best player. Under the current system, it pays to maim the other team's stars.

On the other hand, I can see Los Angeles expressing skepticism over the actual harm done. Soccer players take dives and writhe in pain but miraculously revive after the yellow card is raised. Hockey players, likewise, have been diving for decades—and the invention of a two-minute penalty against it has done little to stem the acting.

I don't envy the referees who must weigh all this. Was he tripped or did he embellish? Was that offender trying to injure? Is the victim truly hurt? Did the bloody lip occur during the incident or beforehand? The referees must decide all this in seconds, with 17,000 fans and sometimes a continental TV audience looking over their shoulders.

In an interview, I put the Gilmour–McSorley–Clark scenario to Ken Dryden, now president of the Toronto Maple Leafs Hockey Club. At first, he said he had no interest in talking about violence in hockey. "What I've written is out there to react to," he said. "I'm not sure I want to keep commenting on it."

I had heard through the grapevine that Dryden had softened his views on fighting. Now in management, the word was he had a political constituency to answer to. Wayne Gretzky had undergone a similar transition: opposed to fighting as a player, inclined to see a place for it as an owner. I was not surprised, therefore, at Dryden's reluctance to tackle an issue that would likely land him in hot water—with other owners, with the Leafs' board of directors, with some fans. But the conundrum of how to respond to malevolence aimed at a star player drew him in. He began to talk, pure Drydenese, turning my questions on their sides, now dismissive, now cerebral, now countering with questions of his own.

Despite my personal misgivings about fighting in the game, I told him, I could not see an honourable alternative for Wendell Clark that day. Can you? I asked. "The only answer," Dryden said, "is to get inside your own skin. You create the scenario. Not as an issue [Should hockey condone fighting?]. That's taking it outside the skin. There is a moment when you decide you are not turning the other cheek. You are responding in kind. When is that moment? What does it take?"

Most people, he said, find fighting in hockey acceptable under some circumstances—"it's the same as the view towards war." And only a small minority, Dryden continued, believe that fighting in hockey is wrong under any circumstances, and an equally small minority would say that fighting is great under any circumstances.

What is so compelling about this issue is that every fight in the game is a declaration of someone's morality—players involved, owners who pay their wages, fans who watch, referees who wade in, league brass if that's called for. But I have never *not* watched a fight. I can deplore all I want, I can lament, I can bemoan the lot of the designated hitter. But my disapproval is hollow, no match for what I feel for this game. There is a point of betrayal, my own line in the sand. At some level, the brutality may overwhelm. But where is the point?

After speaking with Dryden, I went on my constitutional evening walk with my wife, Ulrike, and Dusty, our dog. I was pondering what Dryden had said, and my first response was to categorize it. He had become an apologist, a hockey politician; he was speaking out of both sides of his mouth. But the more I examined my notes, the more I became convinced that he was introducing subtlety and nuance to a complex issue. There *is* another side.

"We are all capable of anger and violent feelings," Dryden had said early in our talk. "No one alive doesn't have the capacity for both feelings. What now? How do we behave *after* those feelings arise? What about the outside hand? Certain other messages come into play: Here are the consequences. I'd better temper my natural reaction because the penalty may be too great. Maybe you respond *within* the rules, with the same clenched teeth, but it's acceptable. You're trying harder, digging deeper, beating that guy, burying him in the psychological and competitive way."

Clearly, some players exercise that option: Hit them and they respond by hurting you on the scoreboard. Others don't. Hit them and they hit back. And I wanted to know the source of that violence. Does the claustrophobia of the rink contribute? Is the contact in hockey so different from that in football, for example? Dryden found the claustrophobia argument "simplistic" and he did not buy the collision–contact distinction that Phil Jones had made, though he did warm to the notion that pauses in football serve to cool off emotions.

"Why is fighting unacceptable in football and *not* in hockey?" Dryden asked. "Is the one difference the stick? An awful lot of anger comes out of things that relate to the stick. Things that have to do with body contact are revealed to be less like cheap shots. But the ones that make you want to throw fists, a lot of that comes from the stick."

Dryden wondered why fighting in hockey became such a prominent symbol for violence in sport. He was sure that the medical consequences of football violence—"the life-lasting stuff, the tearing and ripping of knees and shoulders and heads"—were far greater than those arising from fighting in hockey. Dryden drew a scenario of a 280-pound football player using his entire body as a projectile and finding a moment when the other guy wasn't looking to exact his vengeance.

Then Dryden took out a page listing the Leafs' roster. "Let me do this exercise," he said, and he named off every player and then commented on the likelihood of that player getting into a fight. There were zeroes after the names of sixteen players, four others were sure to get into "a few" fights, and three players—Tie Domi, Shayne Corson, and Darcy Tucker—would undoubtedly get into "several" fights. Wade Belak would later show he belonged in that last group.

The point of the exercise was to illustrate that only a small number of players fight. But by now, Dryden was getting testy, and he suggested that if hockey has no appeal for some people, perhaps they should consider other sports. "But at least understand the real nature of it. What is natural and what is just there as part of an environment."

"Environment?" I asked, "or entertainment?"

Dryden countered that old-timer hockey games, with no one watching, can also erupt into violence.

We talked about the several players who have died playing hockey. And when I said that many contemporary players have expressed fears that someone is going to get killed, Dryden said that hockey players have been saying that since 1875. And he seriously doubted whether the death of a hockey player—even an elite player—would change much.

Why, I asked this lawyer and former goalie, have the courts consistently excused the violent behaviour of hockey players?

"There's your question," he said. "Why? Why has there been no serious punishment? Were all those judges in the twentieth century stupid? What is it that makes you so certain of your position?"

Fact is, I am not certain at all.

In later conversations—just after the Olympics of 2002—Dryden would insist that his views on fighting had *not* changed, only that the issue wasn't a priority for him. He spoke of trying to find "a new way to discuss the issue, and a new moment."

"Fighting happens," he said, "because people get mad. But how come it happens with some players and not with others? How much of it is premeditated? And look at those games at Salt Lake City—so full of passion and yet devoid of fights and even stickwork." Why were those games so pure while others are so sullied?

Ken Dryden's parting words of advice were those of one writer to another: "The answer to all this is *your* answer. In the end you listen to yourself and separate yourself from the clutter. When I was writing my book on schools, I realized, about a month in, that if I didn't have an answer to the question, Why is it that some kids learn and others don't? I had no book. Just a bunch of stuff."

Those who resist any move to ban fighting from hockey insist that the stick and the fist are too tightly woven, that rough play is simply too intrinsic to the game. And they point to history to make their case.

The October 2000 issue of *The Beaver* contained a fascinating article on lacrosse, a game the Cherokee used to call "the little brother of war," for it trained men for combat. If lacrosse is one of hockey's ancestors, as many historians believe, then the two sports have bloodletting in common.

One ethnologist believes lacrosse originated among the Algonquin tribes of the St. Lawrence River valley, not far from Kingston—which some claim as hockey's birthplace. Lacrosse spread to tribes all over North America, with the northern tribes playing it in summer on flat open spaces and in winter on frozen lakes and rivers. French settlers who witnessed this often savage game called it *la crosse,* for the sticks reminded them of a bishop's crozier or *crosse.* First nations people called the game *baggataway,* after the Ojibwa word for "ball," *pagaadowewin.*

William George Beers, a nineteenth-century dentist in Montreal and an ardent nationalist who wrote a book on lacrosse, argued that lacrosse would encourage fitness and bravery in the young men of Canada. "Never was there an ancient or modern field sport that effectually tried the endurance and agility, and every physical instinct as the original game of lacrosse," Beers wrote. "What grand training lacrosse would have been for sword and battle-axe encounter—for splitting helmets from crown to chin—for storming redoubts without fear; in fact, for hand to hand conflict."

In its original form, lacrosse was organized as an alternative to war and to settle clan and family disputes, with heroes of each game hailed as great warriors. These contests sometimes lasted three days, from sunup to sundown. And if the hockey player's meal of choice used to be steak, lacrosse players had their own pre-game rituals. They prepared themselves, spiritually and physically, much as for war. The Cherokee would shun rabbit meat—the flesh of a timid animal—and avoided touching babies, whose bones were thought to be brittle. Women who dared touch a lacrosse player's stick could face death. Vast sums were bet on the outcome of games, from horses and blankets to guns and buffalo robes.

In early hockey, the barriers that separated fan from player were low or practically nonexistent; in lacrosse there were no barriers at all, and spectators were prone to injury from the mêlée. The great art historian of the American west, George Catlin, saw many lacrosse games and he observed that a favourite survival tactic of spectators was to wrap themselves around the nearest tree, "holding on like grim death."

Shamans acted as referees of a sort, but their real task was to count the players to ensure that each team had the same number, which could reach 1,000 in total—with up to six times that number watching. There were few rules other than one prohibiting players from touching the ball with their hands. Tripping, gouging, stick-swinging: All were part of the game. And the man with the ball literally ran for his life, ducking behind trees on a playing field that might stretch for two kilometres.

Sometimes, as in hockey, tempers flared, players dropped their sticks and fought. The colonial version of lacrosse was far tamer, featured more rules, and was played on a much smaller field. But in its savagery and war-like atmosphere, in its essential tribalism, lacrosse as it was played by first peoples in the nineteenth century seems very much hockey's kindred sport.

The *Hockey Research Journal,* published by the Society for International Hockey Research, has considered the link between early lacrosse and early hockey. William Upper pointed out, in the magazine's spring 1999 issue, that Mohawks in the Cornwall area (scene of hockey's first homicide) taught the local white kids how to play lacrosse in the late nineteenth century. Cornwall would win the Canadian lacrosse championship in 1885, 1887, and 1888 and the world championship in 1889. Mohawks were not allowed to play on these teams, but Mohawk "ringers" were often recruited if their facial features and facial hair would permit the ruse. Cornwall teams would also play tune-up matches against Mohawk teams, who competed savagely and taught white players to do the same.

Here's one newspaper columnist describing a lacrosse match in 1911. The violence of the game and the stoicism of the players will be familiar to anyone who follows hockey: "Broken ribs are looked upon as badges of honour. Smashed fingers, gashed cheeks, flattened noses, bruised knees, scraped shins and mashed toes are but mere incidents of the game too trivial to be mentioned. . . . So long as there is life enough left in him to wiggle a finger he is supposed to be in the game."

Upper noted that the same men who played lacrosse in summer played hockey in winter. And it wasn't long before the gentlemanly mores of amateur sport came up hard against the harder edges of professionalism. How curious that hockey and lacrosse—the only two team games in the world that condone fighting—both claim to be Canada's national sport. This in a nation known for the politeness of its citizens and their deference to authority.

If lacrosse was "the little brother of war," hockey makes brothers of men. At an unprecedented gathering of hockey watchers in Halifax in October 2001, one session during the academic proceedings gathered former pros on a panel to discuss life after hockey. At one point, I suggested to them that there is a brotherhood among all who have played the game at the elite level. What is it, I wanted to know, that you share? Most of them reverted to military metaphors to explain.

Bob Boucher, member of the legendary Boucher hockey family and a longtime coach at St. Mary's University in Halifax (he's now retired from hockey), had a good line to describe what hockey players shared. "Beer," he said with a smile. "I know a guy who quit drinking twenty years ago and he *still* can't pass a breathalyzer test." The droll Boucher, who was assistant coach alongside Pat Quinn with the Philadelphia Flyers in the late 1970s, described a tradition at St. Mary's of drinking beer on the bus—when the team won. If the boys ran out, said Boucher, "We knew where all the bootleggers were in the Maritimes. Sometimes that bus would go down some pretty dark and lonely roads after a victory. So when old hockey players get together for reunions, we talk war stories. Stories about travelling together, being together, and having a few pops together. That's how teams form. The stories we tell at those reunions won't be hockey stories."

Bob Warner, who played on the St. Mary's squad and several pro teams—he had a brief stint with the Toronto Maple Leafs in the mid-1970s—talked about the deeply felt camaraderie on those teams. "If one guy was in trouble, the boys would be there. If a guy had no place to go at Thanksgiving, one of us would invite him home."

Trevor Stienburg played right wing with the Quebec Nordiques through the late 1980s, and finished his career in the American Hockey League in 1994. For the past five years, he has coached the St. Mary's team. "True leaders," said this still-strapping young man who looked far younger than his thirty-five years, "stand tallest in the trenches. When I was working as a salesman, I got along with my fellow workers but I had no real confidence that they would be there for me. But if I was being mugged on the ice, I *knew* that my team-mates would be there for me. They'll cross that line. There *is* violence in hockey and there is a secret code that we live by. You take that to your grave."

Stienburg grew up in Moscow, a village north of Kingston and only miles from the village of Camden East, the place I called home for seventeen years. His face brightened when he heard that, but he also wanted to elaborate on the theme of brotherhood in hockey. He had looked of average proportion sitting at the front of the room, but his dimensions changed when I stood next to him. Stienburg is listed at six-one, 200 pounds in *Total Hockey,* and while there is great charm and intelligence about the man, there is also a faint air of menace. The delicate Fu Manchu moustache and Popeye arms warn: "Don't mess with me." And I heard him to say, as well, "Don't mess with my friends."

He gave the example of what he might do if someone were berating a friend of his—off the ice, that is: "I would tell that man this. 'You're entitled to your opinion, but the man you're dissing is a friend of mine and there are things about him you don't know. And if you continue along those lines, I'm leaving the room.'" But I also had the sense that were anyone to insult a teammate on the ice, Stienburg would toss off all that quiet diplomacy, and those Popeye arms would quickly come into play.

Donny McClean played for Waterloo on the Canadian university circuit—and pro hockey in Europe in the early 1980s. These days he's a fire chief for the town of Markham, in southern Ontario; when he married my sister Rosemarie, our family acquired a hockey player up several notches from our accustomed level. Donny is physically imposing, but in a roomful of people, he can be still and quiet—like a duck hunter in the reeds—missing nothing and sometimes biding his time before entering any fray, whereupon he can become a contrarian. Here is what he had to say about the hockey brotherhood and lessons learned on the ice:

> As much as I would rather not have been exposed to threats of violence and acts of violence throughout my hockey career, by standing up to intimidation and facing my fears and seeking out those who would try to intimidate me, I have built up a fortitude that is comforting when dealing with adversity (people or situations) in the ultimate team game—firefighting. No wonder fire departments used to recruit former hockey players. Something about the leaders being made on the playing fields of Eton.

Some hockey players, especially some Canadian hockey players, become someone else on the ice. Like the game itself—which can feature in one forty-second shift as many elements of thuggery as of grace—some players have split personalities. And nowhere in hockey literature is there a more striking example than the *New Yorker* profile of Phil Watson, published February 15, 1947.

Talk about a divided man. Henry Philip Watson was born in Montreal in 1914, the son of a Glaswegian printer who spoke no French and a Québécois nurse who never mastered English. For the first six years of his life, Phil spoke only English, but after spending ten years in a French private school, he forgot all his English. Later, he spoke English with a heavy French accent, and eventually lost that accent and could handle both languages well. But on the ice he would become extremely animated—"Phiery Phil" the headlines read—and utter a tortured mélange: "You damn been-has!" he would shout. "*Pollution!* I run you up two-trees, you no-brains, *mal de tête,* mother of pig, been-has *fils de chien!*"

Off the ice, he always wore a pleasant smile, and with his wavy brown hair parted in the middle, his green eyes and Hollywood looks, he was a man much admired. As a school athlete, he won medals for hockey, baseball, tennis, bicycle riding, handball, swimming, boxing, wrestling, shooting pool, chess, and dominoes—fifty-eight medals in all. As an athlete, he was slim, and it struck me that his dimensions (five-eleven, 165 pounds) were almost precisely mine. Sports writers of the day, astonished by Watson's speed on the ice, agreed that he could go faster once around the rink than the champion speed skater of the day. Picture, then, Watson's gifts, his looks, his charming demeanour.

Now picture this. During a home game in 1940, when coach Frank Boucher was off on a scouting mission, Watson was deputized as player-coach. Watson got into five fights and earned himself twenty minutes in penalties. "The job sort of went to his head," Boucher said later. "Phil apparently figured to win by sending the entire opposition out on stretchers." During the Stanley Cup final game, in the spring of 1940, Watson scored a goal when the game was tied at 2. When the referee disallowed it, charging that a Ranger had a foot in the crease, Watson spat in the referee's face. "Phil goes a little crazy during a hockey game," Boucher explained. Fans in Boston used to throw grapefruit and stink bombs at him; men from print shops would rain lead slugs down on him. Fans in Chicago threw their collapsible chairs at him.

Phil Watson would take out his manufactured front teeth before every game (the originals lost to sticks and fists), but it seems that putting those perfect teeth in a cup was a highly symbolic act. Watson was also parking his civility, his manners, and even, it appears, his normal command of English. "Before skating onto the rink," wrote Robert Lewis Taylor in his *New Yorker* profile, "he stands in the runway a moment, out of sight of the crowd, and takes several deep breaths, his knees quaking, his stomach churning, and his palms and forehead moist. Then, when he pushes on into the lighted arena and feels his skates bite into the ice, he rapidly returns to his normal state of belligerence."

Taylor means, I think, *on-ice* belligerence. Watson's "hot-headed urge to win" took him to a place that many hockey players, though not all, well know. Watson would often acknowledge "with a look of bitter self-reproach, that he gets worked up too often and too violently. He blames his Latin blood, implying that it is an aspect of his nature for which he is not responsible and which he cannot be expected to control."

For all its history as a game played by professionals, hockey has sought out men like Phil Watson—divided men, some of them men with uncommon skill but on the ice, devoid of all civility.

9

FIGHTING IN HOCKEY:
THE CASE AGAINST

EUROPEAN HOCKEY HAS GOTTEN ROUGHER. Is it because their society, like ours, has become more violent? Or did we in North America export our version of the sport across the ocean? Do top European players now emulate our style while dreaming of a big-league paycheque?

This much is certain: Violence in hockey is no longer unique to Canada or North America. Russian games now feature fights and brawls, unheard of even ten years ago; Russian kids watch NHL hockey on TV and no doubt emulate what they see. Even the crowds have learned about hockey savagery. In December 1999, a young Moscow Spartaks fan was beaten to death, and dozens more suffered serious injuries during a clash between fans at a hockey game. And consider the 2001 world hockey championship in which teams from Italy and Switzerland got into a post-game donnybrook; one Swiss player was knocked unconscious. Several players were banned from the world championship in Sweden in 2002, with suspensions ranging from one game to the entire tournament.

Whatever code once governed European hockey has been supplanted by something else. A former NHL defenceman, an all-star in 1994, was commenting on Russian hockey in summer 2001. He was suggesting that NHL-style fighting would clean up the elite Russian league, which he called "the dirtiest league in the world." He added, "There is always a code of honour among NHL tough guys when it comes to fighting. In the NHL, you would never see two guys beating up on one," as he said is common practice in Russian hockey. The defenceman's name? Alexei Kasatonov, a veteran of four

NHL teams and a Leningrad-born graduate of vigilante justice.

There are more like him. A cross-check to the face of Paul Kariya—one of the young and elegant stars of the game—almost ended his career in 1998. Gary Suter got his wrist slapped: a four-game suspension. Before the incident, Kariya had aligned himself with pacifists such as the equally gifted, and now retired, Mike Bossy. Ban fighting in hockey.

But Kariya would later bemoan his team's trade of their designated hitter, Stu Grimson. Likewise, his then teammate Teemu Selanne, an elite player from Finland, was shocked at the fighting when he first came into the league but he, too, has had a change of heart: He finds that having boxers in the lineup makes his life on the ice a lot more pleasant. Several years ago, the *Hockey News* interviewed players at an NHL all-star game and none favoured changes in rules that would diminish the role of fighting.

So many NHL players are convinced that fighting "cleans up" a game that you begin to wonder if they're right. Or is it something like the placebo effect in medicine—you think it works and therefore it does?

Jean Côté, an associate professor in the School of Physical and Health Education at Queen's University, has a special interest in sports aggression. He understands full well the emotions, most of them negative, that can arise in any sport, and especially in contact sport. But Côté does not buy the argument that hockey is a special case, requiring its own unique brand of justice.

For Côté, hockey violence is beyond explaining. "I feel terrible when I'm watching hockey with my seven-year-old son," he told me. "He asks, 'Why are they fighting?' You try to explain it as a matter of frustration, but there *is* no explanation. My wife is from California, and we took her relatives to a game in San Jose. I could not explain to them why they were fighting on the ice. It is *not* part of the game."

Côté has examined hockey violence in a scientific way, by wiring bantam coaches during a game and looking for correlations between what is said behind the bench and what transpires on the ice. Côté's conclusion? Coaches, the history of the game, and how referees call the game all conspire to create a context for violence. "If you punish stick-work," Côté is convinced, "it will stop. The sad thing with hockey is that they seem to punish the outcome, not the behaviour itself. If Marty McSorley hits Donald Brashear in the head with his stick but Brashear bounces right back up, it's a minor penalty. But because he was hurt. . . ."

The key to civilizing the game, says Côté, is first having the will to do it and then taking steps to accomplish it. "If the game is too fast to be properly called, make the rinks bigger, try four a side, put another referee in the stands." The case against fighting in hockey is elaborate and as old as the game itself.

Fighting sets a terrible example. It is summer 2001, and I'm watching Kurt's lacrosse game on a vast field in suburban Kingston. I fall to chatting with a nearby man in a white cowboy hat. He has that slow drawl that country people around here have, and I love his humour. I watch him lobbing a tennis ball to several four-year-olds, ensuring that each one, even the smallest, gets a chance at a catch. And I laugh as he professes aloud not to understand this game of lacrosse. "Why are they all carrying fishing nets and no poles?" he asks the kids. "What about those orange pylon things—don't they belong to construction crews?" And the kids swarm his legs, all clamouring and talking at once, each one vying to set him straight, while he plays thick and uncomprehending. I like his humour because that's *my* humour. It may be Irish.

And I like the way he cheers his own favourite player—Curtis, who may well be a nephew—while applauding the other team's good plays. When was the last time you heard a fan, anywhere, cheer both teams?

We talked about the Stanley Cup final, which had ended just two days beforehand, about who we had been cheering, how he had lost some money betting on Jersey. This fellow had played elite hockey in his youth, with future NHLers Jim Dorey and Kirk Muller. What about the fighting, I asked him. Is there too much?

I admired his modest and considered approach. He didn't weigh in, going right to his stand. "Fighting is a part of the game—they say," he began. And he gave full credit to NHL players for the abuse they endure, for all the games they play, the risks they take. But in the end he came down against fighting for one reason: It sets a terrible example to children. This man clearly had a way with children, understood them, cared deeply about them. And though he loved the game of hockey, the brand shown on TV, he was certain, was badly in need of censoring.

And I thought of Don Cherry's phrase, the one he often uses during his *Hockey Night in Canada* performances, as a preamble to some point of advice. One lesson he hammers repeatedly, and it's a valid one, is about defenders keeping their sticks out of the way of shots, for the puck will invariably hit the stick, take a strange bounce, and embarrass the goalie. "You kids out there," he will say, then make his point. The supreme irony is that the kind of hockey Cherry champions shouldn't be watched by kids. The man in the white hat had it right.

Randy Gregg once made a similar point about children and Don Cherry. A general practitioner and now director of medicine at the Edmonton Sports Institute, Gregg was a defenceman in the 1980s with the Edmonton Oilers. In an interview, Gregg described a particular play during a nationally televised game in 1985 between the Oilers and Blackhawks. Edmonton was two men short and Gretzky was coming in over centre, Gregg advancing with him, even when he knew he shouldn't, then taking the pass and going in alone, deking the goaltender and missing the open net. The soft-spoken Gregg, a rare individual who had combined his studies in medicine with a pro-hockey career, said later he was overcome by the notion that he was in the wrong place at the wrong time, that he had tightened up and shot wide.

Don Cherry later observed in his commentary, "With hands like those, I'd never let the guy perform surgery on me!"

Oiler management demanded an apology, and Cherry did offer the semblance of one in Pittsburgh several weeks later. Gregg described Cherry barging into a room where the players were having their pre-game meal and broadcasting that his comment was all in fun and meant no harm. And he did aim a handshake at Gregg, who refused to look up, let alone shake the hand of the man he calls a clown.

"I'd been thinking," Dr. Gregg said, "about how the things people like Cherry say, in the name of entertainment, can significantly affect the attitudes of children and coaches and parents. In many ways, I think a clown is important; that's why I take my kids to the circus." But when a clown is given such prominence on national television, a stage he uses to ridicule Europeans or players who wear masks or who won't fight, then, said Dr. Gregg, "a lot of damage is being done."

Fighting alienates some good hockey people. Tom Reich, Mario Lemieux's agent, conceded that his client's decision to retire from the game was influenced, at least in part, by all the obstruction and hooking that players inflict on each other and especially on gifted athletes. "They were gang-tackling him in the slot," said Reich. "With Mario it took two guys to stop him. There's a longstanding difference of opinion at the heart of these problems in the NHL. I think Gary Bettman should extend the protection he gave goalies to the puck carriers."

Lemieux came out of retirement, to everyone's joy except that of the goaltenders'. But there is no guarantee that gang-tackling won't send him back to the golf course.

The ever-brash and outspoken Brett Hull, who had been similarly hounded, later took back these remarks but they bear the stamp of his anger: "The games suck. I wouldn't pay to watch them. It's boring. The whole style of the game is terrible. There's no flow to the game at all. There's so much hooking and holding. . . . When a guy like Mario leaves the game and tells you why he's leaving and you don't address it, that's stupid."

The league called in Hull for a chat, and he recanted. It seems the NHL cannot decide what it's selling: poetry or war. Talk to the stars, in private and off the record, and they will tell you how weary they are of the mugging and slashing. Brett Hull's father once withdrew his services from the WHA for one game to protest the violence; he reacted when a teammate was temporarily blinded following a high-sticking incident.

Half a century ago, Maurice Richard was the target. Tommy Gorman, general manager of the Montreal Canadiens in the early 1940s, sent this letter to Red Dutton, then NHL president: "It is quite evident that players are being sent out onto the ice to trip, hold, wrestle and block Richard by any means. Richard can take care of himself in a standup fight, but they have formed a 'Wreck Richard Club' and we are not going to let them get away with it. Maurice is one of the cleanest players in the N.H.L. He is entitled to protection and we ask that referees be instructed to give it to him."

Those who played against Richard may have gagged at Gorman's remark about his clean play. Howie Meeker, who wrote a column in the *Globe and Mail* after The Rocket died, remembered how Richard reacted badly to *any* sort of contact. A decade of mauling will do that.

Richard once knocked out a notorious New York Rangers "policeman" named Bob "Killer" Dill twice—once on the ice and later in the penalty box, when Dill revived himself long enough for round two. A columnist called it the "Dill pickling." All very amusing, but the question is this: Should Maurice Richard score goals, or have to pummel his enemies?

The game, it seems, devours the great. In his book *Hockey's Captains, Colonels & Kings,* Bill Fitsell tells the story of Hod Stuart, heralded by observers in 1907 as "the greatest hockey player in the world." The handsome six-footer was a gentlemanly player and a superb rushing defenceman, the Bobby Orr of his day. Such skill made him a target. In one playoff game, Stuart was set upon by the infamous Alf Smith, whose stick blow to the temple robbed Stuart of his hearing for twenty-four hours. In the final game, six of fourteen Ottawa penalties were for stick fouls inflicted on Stuart. He took three cuts above and below the eye, broke a finger, and worse, had his love for hockey beaten out of him—this after playing "the game of his life" and helping his Montreal Wanderers win the Stanley Cup. Stuart was twenty-eight years old, battered, and disillusioned. "I don't know whether I'll play hockey anymore," he told a reporter that summer in his hometown of Belleville, Ontario. A few days later, there was a tragic accident: Stuart dove into the waters of the Bay of Quinte, struck rocks, and died instantly of a fractured skull. "The king of hockey," as the obituary put it, was dead.

Mike Modano almost lost his life early in the 2000–01 season, when Anaheim defenceman Ruslan Salei twisted Modano, as the latter was cutting at full speed towards the net. Modano went headfirst into the boards. Strained neck muscles and a concussion resulted; he could easily have broken his neck. "If things continue," Modano said later, "I'm not going to play anymore. I still have the rest of my life to live."

The less visible effect of hockey violence is that the game's stars are not allowed to shine. Maybe the front of the net, or the slot, become too dangerous to warrant venturing there. Creative offence loses out to stifling and cutthroat defence. Worse, uncontrolled nastiness inevitably means that elite players get hurt. The effect is the same. Fans are denied the privilege of seeing the best players in the world play the game as only they can. Hockey becomes, instead, a mug's game.

Even wizened members of hockey's tribe eventually tire of it. George Armstrong, the ex-Leafs captain, resigned as coach of the Toronto Marlboros, a junior team, because of all the fighting. Much of it, he was certain, was not spontaneous at all but orchestrated.

"I don't have any proof," he said in 1979,

> but I'm certain that some coaches just send their players out to fight. I'm not saying hockey is any more violent than it has been in the past few years, but it just got to me. The coaches in junior hockey now say fight first, play hockey second.
>
> Fights are fine to me, but only if they come in the course of hockey—not because some coach says to his player, "Go out and pound the crap out of that guy." That bothers me so much it really made me sick to my stomach. You might think these players are men but they're boys, and if their coach tells them to fight, they'll do just that.

A friend in Kingston told me of a player he had coached as a peewee and who went on to play junior hockey: "Years later I met him and he told me that he knew perfectly well why he was in the lineup. He was good with his fists. At the bench, his coach would just tap him, and issue the number of the guy he wanted mugged. Number 16, number 4. . . ."

Jacques Laperrière, a fine defenceman with the Canadiens in the '60s and '70s and coach of a Montreal junior team in 1977, quit for the same reasons as George Armstrong. He left in disgust, appalled at "guys who were no more than bouncers playing the game."

Meanwhile, the rewards for fighting at the so-called elite level are there for all junior players to see. Although some notable fighters in the NHL manage to combine brawn with a reasonable touch around the goal (Tie Domi, Donald Brashear, Chris Simon), even hockey's one-dimensional security guards and bouncers earn handsome wages. The *average* NHL salary in 2001 was $1.4 million (U.S.).

Hockey violence only begets violence. Michael Smith, a sports sociologist at York University in Toronto, wrote a defining book called *Violence in Sport* in 1988. In a clinical and scientific way, he examined aggression in sport and he concluded that, in the wake of aggressive play, both players and fans display *higher* levels of aggression. This will surprise those who argue that fighting releases pent-up frustration and works to keep the peace in hockey.

"It's simply a folk theory that aggressions must be released," Smith once told Trent Frayne. "There's not a reputable social scientist anywhere who'd agree that aggressions have to be let out on the ice. It's total nonsense. Human aggression is learned, not innate."

Smith died in 1994, and his book—though well received and much admired—made no dent on hockey. But during the 2000 and 2001 academic years, a series of seminars were held at York in his honour, to reconsider violence and sport.

York kinesiology professor Greg Malszecki organized the series—triggered by the McSorley hit on Brashear and its aftermath. "When I saw the rationalizations, alibis, and interpretations of McSorley's actions," Malszecki said, "I realized that was an area Mike Smith had attended to twelve years earlier, but his work has not had the attention of late that it deserves. So I wanted to go back and use Mike's work as a benchmark to see what we've learned since then."

Like Smith, Professor Malszecki calls the safety-valve theory "one of our useful myths." He also wonders whether violence in sport does not merely reflect violence in society but contributes in some way. Sport, said Malszecki, has long been viewed as its own domain, separate from society. No one knows the impact of violent sport on society, but the professor does point to one disturbing and highly controversial study that shines a harsh light on athleticism. The study looked at ten NCAA (National Collegiate Athletic Association) schools and found that while 3.3 per cent of male undergraduates were athletes, they accounted for 19 per cent of sexual assaults on campus. The study, of course, begs other questions: Is a certain kind of person drawn to sports, or do sports influence behaviour in some sinister way?

For Malszecki, these are critical questions. He worries that the many positive aspects of sports are no match for the suffocating influence of virility, the overwhelming focus on winning, the rampant use of force.

Mike Bossy, the pure goal scorer with the Islanders in the '70s and '80s and three-time winner of the Lady Byng trophy for gentlemanly play, is convinced "there is a definite correlation between violence on the ice and violence in society. I think what it all boils down to is respect for another human being. I think when you respect someone, you don't want to hurt them, no matter how much you want to win. Nothing is worth paralyzing someone or killing them."

Violence in hockey occurs not just on the ice, but in the dressing room: Hazing rituals are inflicted on rookies, from the junior ranks all the way to the pros. Professor Malszecki says that students in his class have shocked each other with tales of hazing rituals they have endured. The CBC-TV program *The Fifth Estate,* he recalls, focussed a few years ago on one such rite practised by the University of Guelph's hockey team. Initiates were supposed to pluck marshmallows from the bare bums of fellow players—without using their hands. "The rationale," says Malszecki, "was team cohesion—if you would do that, you would do anything for your teammates. But it is a very degrading, unhealthy practice. It's bizarre and renegade and shouldn't take place in an institution of higher learning."

Or anywhere, for that matter. Hazing has been driven off campus and underground by bad press. But it continues. The University of Vermont cancelled its entire hockey season in fall 1999 when details of hazing rituals were leaked. These included so-called "elephant-walking," in which players were made to parade nude around the room holding the genitals of the player behind, much drinking, and players urinating on each other—all of which players tried to hide by lying about it.

Bob Kelly, a raw twenty-year-old rookie with Philadelphia in 1970, describes an elaborate and cruel hoax that was his induction into the Flyers' tribe. Kelly was taken on what he thought was a snipe-hunting expedition (snipes are marsh birds) and he became convinced by some clever and elaborate theatre, in rural Pennsylvania, that a teammate had been wounded by the police, and that he himself was facing deportation and a prison term (Kelly spent an hour stewing in an actual jail cell). There was even a "hearing" before a gruff judge. Kelly's teammates—looking on through a two-way mirror—found Kelly's anguish hilarious, and it later made for a funny story, but his fright was genuine.

Hockey rage has a life all its own. Hockey history is rife with examples of players losing control. I was struck by one case, for it involved very young players in pitched battle and led directly to William McMurtry's impassioned report on hockey violence. The flashpoint was a Junior B game in 1974, between the Bramalea Blues and the Hamilton Red Wings. Here's Doug Evans, father of one of the Blues: "I'd never seen anything like that first game in my life. In addition to what happened on the ice [189 minutes in penalties, five players injured in fights, the team trainer hospitalized with a head injury after a fight in the corridor], women and children in the seats were crying and hysterical, the police were running helter-skelter and one fan was held down on the floor." Two policemen on duty had to call in reinforcements, and eventually fourteen officers were in the rink.

Sometimes the lid comes off early. In a Memorial Cup game in 1979, involving several names that would later figure in the NHL (players Laurie Boschman and Jacques Cloutier and coach Michel Bergeron), the Brandon Wheat Kings and the Trois Rivières Draveurs began slugging it out before the puck was dropped.

Sometimes violence on the ice ripples out into the streets. Here's Andy O'Brien writing in *Rocket Richard* about the incident that led to his expulsion from the 1955 playoffs and the Montreal riot. French fans, wrote O'Brien, "felt no penalty should embrace such a territory, especially since it involved a 'fracas' such as hockey has always known and always will know." Yet "fracas" does not begin to describe the scalping of Hal Laycoe on March 13, 1955.

Here's how Laycoe described the incident. "I even hate to rehash it," he told a reporter before his death in 1998. Richard and Laycoe were friends off the ice, tennis partners. But The Rocket had lost all sense and was consumed by rage.

Richard started the affair by pitch-forking Laycoe in the face. "I reached up—ding—and I got him right in the back of the head," Laycoe continued his story. "If somebody cut me, why, I'd ding them right back. I remember Rocket reached up and touched his head. He saw his blood and, boy, did he come."

Laycoe dropped his gloves, preparing to box, but The Rock, as his teammates called him, was past such niceties. He brought his stick down on Laycoe, nicked his ear, and broke the wood over his assailant's shoulder. "He broke one stick over me," said Laycoe, "then picked up another, broke it, picked up another. I'm standing there like John L. Sullivan, fending off sticks with my hands and arms. Rocket was relentless."

The Canadian filmmaker Brian McKenna once made a film about the incident and what followed, called *Fire and Ice: The Rocket Richard*

Riot. Richard told McKenna: "If you know nothing else about the time I played, know about how violent the game was."

Howie Meeker played for the Leafs from 1946 to 1953, before becoming a broadcaster. In a piece he wrote after The Rocket died on May 27, 2000, Meeker recalled how several of his teeth had been knocked out by Richard, and how The Rocket had carved up fellow Leaf Bob Bailey, because the latter "had simply dared to check him into the boards."

"It's hard to explain," Meeker wrote, "the kind of rivalry that existed in hockey in those days, especially between Montreal and Toronto. It's the nearest thing to war on ice I can think of, and Rocket Richard was the enemy." Years later, as a broadcaster with *Hockey Night in Canada*, Meeker actually got to meet the man and discovered how shy and reserved and decent he was—off the ice.

Another famous incident took place at Madison Square Garden in New York on March 16, 1947. With Montreal leading late in the game and New York facing elimination from the playoffs, the Rangers seemed bent on ruining the Canadiens' chances by roughing up their star players. After a fight, the Canadiens' Ken Reardon was skating off "for repairs," as broadcaster Foster Hewitt liked to say, and was heckled by the Rangers bench. When a fan joined in, Reardon swung his stick at the patron and was swarmed by Rangers security people. At this point, dominoes began to fall. It looked to the Canadiens' bench that their man was being attacked by the Rangers, so they rushed to his aid, and when Montreal players went after fans in the corridor the Rangers entered the fray to defend their fans.

At one point, fifteen fights were simultaneously under way. Players broke their sticks over each others' heads, cheekbones were broken. The fan who had needled Reardon took three stitches to his scalp. Curiously, the referee handed out only three penalties—ten-minute misconducts.

The battle had aftermaths. Reardon later discovered it was Cal Gardner who had cut him in the mouth that night with his stick. A year later the two collided and Reardon broke Gardner's jaw in two places. In 1949 they went at it again, engaging in wild stick-swinging that was followed by a fight. Reardon then co-authored an article with a Montreal sportswriter in which he issued a threat: "I am going to see that Gardner gets fourteen stitches in his mouth," he wrote. "I may have to wait a long time, but I'm patient. Even if I have to wait until the last game I ever play, Gardner is going to get it good and plenty."

Clarence Campbell, league president, forced Reardon to post a $1,000 "good conduct" bond with the league, which Reardon would forfeit if he ever made good on his threat. Reardon never did, but he loathed Gardner even decades later.

Fighting in hockey may be good for business. But is what's good for business good for us? The authors of *Hockey Night in Canada* make a good point:

> The early years of modern hockey featured plenty of violence outside the official rules of the game. The passions that became centred around teams that suddenly began to represent their communities led to frequent violent outbreaks. Playing to primarily male crowds in mining towns and small industrial cities, the early pro game willingly accommodated these violent tendencies and, indeed, began to institutionalize them. As the years went by, the promoters of pro hockey sought to control violence outside the rules only to the extent necessary to avoid widespread public disapproval and to ensure the existence of reasonably orderly audiences. Other than that, the tolerant attitude to violence outside the rules has been rooted in the belief that the occasional fistfight has been good for business.

In 1954 a particularly savage battle erupted between Maurice Richard and Bob Bailey that saw The Rocket twice go berserk. He claimed that Bailey had tried to gouge out his eyes, and he threw a hockey glove at a linesman. Leafs owner Conn Smythe later said famously, "We've got to stamp out this sort of thing or people are going to keep on buying tickets."

Then there was George Gross, a Toronto sports columnist who was being interviewed as part of a panel in Los Angeles during the intermission of a Toronto–L.A. game in the 1970s that had been pitched as a bloodbath. And so it was. An American columnist was appalled. "Hockey without fights," Gross countered, "is like a honeymoon without sex."

What he didn't know was that the interview was being piped live into the arena and shown on a huge video screen over centre ice. A roar erupted as 15,000 fans cheered Gross's turn of phrase.

Gross was merely echoing pro hockey's official position on hockey and violence. At a Queen's University symposium in 1975, Clarence Campbell—two years from retiring as NHL president, a position he held for thirty-one years—reminded his audience of a grim truth. "Hockey," he said, "is a game of violence. This will never change. What we do in the NHL is control the level of violence at an acceptable level. I'm not saying that we condone violence, but it's there. We set a level and control it at that point."

There it was again, that constantly moving bar. Marty McSorley was right. There is nothing absolute in hockey—save the bottom line, which governs everything. "My number one duty," Clarence Campbell said that day in Kingston, "is to keep the NHL a viable enterprise." No poetic rhapsody about "the game," no nod to history, no homage to hockey's gifted athletes. Just fill those arenas, and a certain amount of violence—now more, now less—does the job nicely. That's entertainment.

When Red Horner—the Leafs defenceman who led the NHL in penalties all through the 1930s—was about to be inducted into the Hockey Hall of Fame, Leafs lion Conn Smythe wrote a letter in praise of him. "Red Horner," wrote Smythe, "was one of the best drawing cards in the league. Truly, he helped to establish the National Hockey League as a popular attraction." Frank Selke, Sr.—he managed the Leafs in the '40s and the Canadiens in the '50s and '60s—echoed the sentiment, observing that "many of the fans in outside cities attended the games in the fervent hope that somebody would present Horner with a brick house, letting him have the bricks one by one." Later, Selke called Horner "a good man for selling tickets." Ted Reeve of the Toronto *Telegram* similarly alluded, in a poem, to Horner as a team-owner's dream, for he filled buildings wherever he played.

Our Reginald Horner
Leaped from his corner
Full of ambition and fight;
He broke up the clash with a furious dash
While the stockholders shrieked with delight!

Hockey hate has always made good box office. The history of violence in hockey, plotted in chart form, would look like a roller-coaster ride at a theme park. Fighting and stickwork have been a part of the National Hockey League since its inception in 1917, but the incidence soared when the NHL expanded in the late 1960s. Suddenly, there was work for less-skilled players.

In 1953, when such statistics were first compiled, the league saw an average of .2 fights per game—one fight every five games. In the mid-1970s, during the Philadelphia Flyers' so-called "reign of terror," the figure had doubled. By the late 1980s, when the Oilers ruled, fighting incidence had risen to five times what it was in the '50s—to an average of one fight a game. In the 1990s, rule changes punishing instigators caused the level to drop somewhat, but then it rose again. At the halfway point of the 2001–02 season, the incidence stood at .7 fights per game, up from .6 the season before. Certain players now engage in thirty to forty fights a season. What has changed is the nature of the fighting: Today's battles typically involve players chosen for the role; at least the generalized mayhem has been curbed.

Some remember a brawl that took place in Atlanta in 1972, sparked by St. Louis Blues tough-guy Steve Durbano crashing the crease and sending Phil Myre flying. Myre cracked him from behind with his stick, cutting him, and Durbano was heading off to the clinic when he had a change of heart, returned to the ice, and returned the favour, jumping

Myre from behind. The ensuing brawl involved every player on both benches, goaltenders included, and continued for half an hour.

Hockey News correspondent Jim Huber described the fans' response. "Did they cover their eyes in horror and stalk out in disgust? Did they summon the police, order the game outlawed? Hardly. Within moments, there were 15,078 screaming people on their feet, pushing so close to the fight that they had to be warned not to lean on the glass, screaming their lungs out, throwing beer, pretzels, programs, and anything that wasn't screwed down."

It was Atlanta's first season in the NHL. According to Huber, team management "saw the brawl not as a half-hour interruption of an excellent hockey game but as money in the bank. They began predicting sellouts for the remainder of the season, and the way the fans attacked the ticket agencies the next morning their predictions appeared to have been coming true."

South of the border, there are many informed and avid fans. But hockey is a business, and the task is to sell the sport to the uninformed. What are they told to expect? Ken Dryden, in *The Game*, recalls how billboards went up in southern Virginia when the Tidewater Red Wings entered the American Hockey League. "Brutal, fast, brutal, exciting, and brutal" read one poster; "If they didn't have rules, they'd call it war," read another.

Jason Cohen, author of *Zamboni Rodeo* (about a minor-pro team in contemporary Texas) describes one game that features seven fights. He asks two "slightly tipsy" but clearly animated fans what they like about hockey. "We like the fights," one says in his southern drawl, "because we don't know the damn rules."

Finally, there is the health risk associated with all those blows to the head. In January 2002, researchers at the University of Pennsylvania were warning that some sports—boxing, soccer, hockey—elevate the risk of Alzheimer's disease. Research with mice suggests that repeated blows to the head accelerate the onset of dementia.

Dr. Charles Tator, the eminent Toronto neurosurgeon, told me the Pennsylvania study had its genesis in Holland, where Dutch soccer players who were especially adept at heading the ball were later found to experience an inordinate amount of dementia.

Dr. Tator is professor of neurosurgery at the University of Toronto and president of Think First Canada, an injury-prevention program. I thought he might have an answer to a question that had long troubled me: What is the neurological impact of fighting in hockey?

"There is no doubt that repeated blows to the head take a toll," he said, "and subsequent impact takes an even greater toll. Fighting is one way the brain is injured and for that reason alone we should do away with it. We should take steps to stop *any* contact with the head, and not just by the bare-fisted hand, but by the gloved hand, by elbows, by a shoulder check."

In a two-year retrospective study of twenty-five of his own patients—all hockey players—Dr. Tator found that fighting was one of the leading causes of brain injury. One young man lost his helmet during a fight, hit the ice with the back of his head, and was left with significant memory loss, emotional disorders, and his dream of a higher education dashed. Another player endured ten concussions, five due to fighting.

Dr. Tator lamented the "terrible influence on hockey of Don Cherry" and the refusal of NHL owners to adopt the European rink size, a move that he is convinced would reduce collisions. "The owners *want* collisions," he said. "They think it sells tickets."

Some of what happens in hockey is beneath human dignity. The NHL is a tight ship, with harsh outcomes for those who defy hockey's code. Paul Mulvey of the Los Angeles Kings never played another game in the NHL after refusing his coach's explicit order to join a fight in progress on the ice in 1982. He was a six-four, 220-pound bruiser, and he was not shy about fighting.

What Mulvey balked at was the premeditation on the coach's part. "Get out there and don't dance," Don Perry had told him. Mulvey refused and was banished to the minors. Now forty-four, he is a youth hockey instructor in the Washington area.

"Everything that I was taught—and try to teach—were the skills of the game and the demands of the game and the intimidation in the game," Mulvey says. "I don't mind seeing intensity and I don't mind seeing raw passion sometimes erupt in a fight." But no coach, he believes, has the right to send a player out to fight.

Glen Sather, the veteran NHL coach and general manager, has observed that an honest, spontaneous fight between two players is one thing. But the same two heavyweights fighting each other night after night is "a waste of time."

In hockey, time is on the side of tradition. Hockey players and managers—despite the great influx of Europeans into the game—largely emerge from Canadian junior hockey. Wayne Gretzky's idea, at one point, was to start the change in junior hockey. Give fighters an automatic ejection and a two-game suspension. "We've got to stop breeding animals," he once said.

Actually, animals typically behave better than this: On October 25, 1998, Jeff Kugel, a giant forward (six-seven, 260 pounds) with the Windsor Spitfires in the Ontario Hockey League, lost all composure on the ice in a game against the Owen Sound Platers. During the brawl, Kugel chased another player around the ice and was later banned for life from the OHL.

"I was disgusted," said Owen Sound forward Adam Mair, now an NHLer. "It was like a scene out of *Slap Shot*."

Gretzky predicted in 1989 that fighting would be banned in five to ten years. "No question," he said. His move to California a year earlier and actually living in a place where hockey is not widely understood had painfully driven home the point: Violence gives the game a black eye. "We always talk about the people who come to the games to see the fighting," said Gretzky. "And I was one of the ones who believed that. . . . I wonder if they've ever done an analysis on how many people *don't* come because of fighting." Hockey, Gretzky lamented, "is the only team sport in the world that actually encourages fighting. I have no idea why we let it go on. The game itself is so fast, so exciting, so much fun to watch, why do we have to turn the ice red so often?"

Fighting in hockey is silly. Joe Lapointe, in the *New York Times,* suggested in 1997 that fistfighting be incorporated into the skills competition at the all-star game. His dark image prompts another. If fighting between players is allowed in arenas, why not permit fans to duke it out, as well?

Here is how seriously hockey players—at the amateur, and perhaps rank amateur, level—take the game. Late in 2000, a charity hockey game took place in Edmonton between a team of local police and a team of firefighters from Calgary. Marcel Dionne skated with the Calgary team; Eddie Shack refereed in a cowboy hat. Old-timer rules applied: No hitting, no holding, and goals aplenty. In the last few minutes of the game, a brawl erupted. Dionne left the ice shaking his head. So did Shack, who called the game. "Look, I'm finished," he told them. "I don't need this kind of aggravation."

In 1963 two NHL Hall of Famers—Aurel Joliat and "Punch" Broadbent—were at a hockey banquet in Boston. While recalling a fight the two had had in the 1920s, a spark flew and a fire that had lain cold for four decades smouldered anew, and the old boys were right back into it. Joliat was sixty-two, Broadbent seventy-one. Hockey hate endures like no other. When George Plimpton was a fly on the wall at the Bruins' training camp in the 1970s, he was astonished at the level of animosity that existed between Boston and Philadelphia. "I hate these people," Terry O'Reilly told him in the dressing room before a game against Philly. Plimpton wrote of the "torrent of heat" in that room, and he wondered "how these people ever calm down."

Yet some would argue that a fight on the ice—*most* times—is far safer than a fight on the street. The notion of the hockey player always on the edge and ready to fight at the drop of a hat is part of the gunslinger mentality that players like to think they possess. Many Canadians have never been in a street fight, but almost every male I know who has played hockey can claim at least one hockey fight. Young players I've talked to tell their fight stories with pride; the older ones may admit to shame.

Some enforcers, though by no means all, will admit to a secret: that despite the blood, fighting on ice is typically less dangerous than it looks. Gino Odjick, an enforcer with the Montreal Canadiens, insists that he has only been "hurt" three times in a long, fight-filled NHL career. Ken Baumgartner had made the same point: the blood deceives the onlooker. Consider, too, that players wear protective head-gear, that linesmen step in if a bout gets out of hand, and that most fights are over in about thirty seconds.

Anyone who has ever worked out in a fight gym or with a body bag will tell you that those who have not trained hard for punching are quickly spent. Finally, there is the physics of skates to take away the power of the punch. The initial flurry is short-lived, quickly giving way to wrestling and tugging. There is no denying that hockey players are capable of the devastating knockout punch. Ask Lou Fontinato or Nick Kypreos. But most players skate to the penalty box after a fight, virtually unscathed, rendering the hockey fight more ritualistic than truly reckless. Want reckless? Try acting out your road rage: Pull the other guy over and put up your dukes, and pray he's not a kickboxer, or has a handgun in his glove compartment.

The game actually rewards violence. The Don Cherry school of fighting, McSorley's impassioned defence of the status quo—is this, in part, about job security? If fighting were banned and hockey were recast, Cherry would be out of a job. He is paid to view hockey as he sees it, and he sees the game in tribal terms. With no place for fighting in the sport, every tough guy in the league would not only see a pay cut, many would find themselves in the minors—replaced by faster, more skilled players. And if the minors were also reformed, pure pugilists would be gone from the game.

In the fall of 2001, CBC-TV ran a six-part series on hockey called *The New Ice Age,* one that took viewers behind the scenes at NHL arenas and offered a look, for example, at actual contract talks. Don Meehan, agent for the Leafs' tough guy Tie Domi, is heard to say to Leafs' executive Bill Watters, "He's the best at what he does in the league today," and Meehan asks the rhetorical question, Who else is going to give the Leafs 275 minutes in penalties? And Watters has to agree: "I appreciate what he does for the team." Gordon Pinsent, the series narrator, calls Domi "a fan favourite in Toronto, and scoring goals has little to do with it." Implicit and widely understood by all parties is that Domi's fists put him a cut above players who post similar numbers (I mean goals and assists) but who lack his presence on the ice.

The directors of the series had originally chosen to run three scenes of Domi fighting, using the banter between Watters and Meehan as voice-over. The NHL, apparently worried that viewers might conclude the obvious—that Domi was being paid to fight—objected and bullied the directors into replacing two of the fight sequences. The final cut shows four quick clips: Domi fighting the Sabres' Rob Ray, delivering a rugged hit behind the net, staring down the enemy with linesmen in between, and a return to the Ray fight.

Joseph Blasioli, who co-directed *The New Ice Age,* was not surprised by the league's intervention: "The game in the U.S.," he told me, "is sold as a violent game. You should see some of the TV ads for hockey down there—illegal hits, fights. Yet the NHL is so conscious of its image. They've been wrestling with this a long time." But to "wrestle" with an issue suggests a heartfelt, even noble, stab at resolution. NHL spin doctors, who cast censorious glances at a feature Canadian film but who let the gladiatorial ads roll in the American south, seem not that way inclined.

Meanwhile, the notion of fighting as purely natural or spontaneous and even inevitable in a game of such hot adrenaline—while surely still true at times—begins to unravel. The reward system for fighting is too lavish, too firmly entrenched, too much a factor on the ice. Tie Domi's contract may not spell it out in black and white, but it's there all the same—an expectation of aggression and intimidation, measured in minutes, egging him on.

10
A YEAR
IN THE
HOCKEY LIFE

NOVEMBER 30, 2000. The goalie on my son Kurt's house-league team, a likable kid called Sandy, has rushed to the bench so we can put on the extra attacker in the dying minutes of a game at Harold Harvey Arena. I am an assistant coach, some say bench coach; read, doorman.

The baby-blue–sweatered team—Chalmers United—is a curious mix of talented and ungainly players, with Sandy somewhere in the middle (though as the season has worn on, he's gotten much better). Between periods he comes to the bench and asks someone to squirt water in his mouth, and though we typically miss the target, he happily abides our ineptitude and is ever grateful.

"Ah, we lost," he tells me on the bench as the buzzer goes, "but who cares?"

"Sandy, *I* care," I tell him, though later I regret saying it. I do care, too much. Sandy always has a smile on his face, and I fear I inflicted on him my own high seriousness about hockey.

I hate to lose. Even in our old-timer games played in this same rink, the sides are never the same, but I want to be on the upside of any lopsided score. House-league hockey is supposed to be fun, and while hockey experts in this country now freely admit that we should stress skills development, have more practices than games, focus less on winning—all of which I embrace in theory—I cannot shake off old thinking so easily. It's like the sour smell that invades the inner leather of elbow pads. Invasive. Invisible. Resistant to any attempt at removal.

The team coach is Roger. He is a calm and pleasant man in his forties, committed to hockey and still a player. Sometimes the lid comes off, and a referee or player sees another side of him.

What coaches must struggle to contain are old competitive juices and instincts that were instilled in them as boys—when their coaches were "old yellers." I once looked on from the stands and watched as a coach took a player behind the bench while the game continued, paced back and forth, and loudly dressed him down because the boy had failed to dump the puck out past the blue line. I know that coach. He is, by my reckoning, intelligent and kind and educated, a smart hockey man. What gives?

And yet it's not so mysterious. Watching my own son's games for years, I am reminded often of the adrenaline it generates in me. That spot behind the bench raises the juice level yet another notch. Before the next game, Roger had warned me that he might not make the game because of a business trip. So I had prepared a little pre-game talk for the boys, in case I had to run the squad. I wanted them to pass the puck more, for we rely too much on our talented defence to embark on solo rushes—a tactic that works against slower teams, but the better ones simply swarm our rusher. End of story. Hockey is a passing game.

Head-man the puck, I would tell the defence, pass always to the man ahead. Wingers, dish the puck off to the rushing defenceman. The old give-and-go. I would tell them to slow the game down in their heads, à la Wayne Gretzky, who had this enormously high panic threshold when he possessed the puck. Take a second to lift the head and find the open man. Be calm out there, like Phil Esposito, who, as a junior player, used to sing on the ice. Pass like Wayne, I would say. Sing like Phil.

There would be no inspirational speech from me, no citing of Espo and the Great One. Just as I got set to deliver, in walked Roger in his suit.

December 6, 2000. Five of our guys play on rep teams as well as on our house-league team, so they're on the ice four to six times a week. But they seem never to tire of open ice. They line up along the sides before the Zamboni guy finishes his rounds. In the dressing room they are loud and animated, as gleeful as pups. Their great hope is that the game before ours is cancelled, in which case they dress frantically and take to the open ice. It also sometimes happens that the game after ours requires extra players—snowstorms, school dances, exams, all cut into rosters—and our guys are mad-keen to volunteer. Their parents, who seem to live at the rink all winter long, invariably groan, then acquiesce. The ice forever beckons.

I am reminded of what George Plimpton observed in *Open Net*, based on his time spent as a spare goalie during the Boston Bruins training camp of 1977. He expected that, after exhausting practices, the players would trudge wearily off to the dressing room. But, no, they lingered to practise shots and passing or to bear-wrestle each other—though "often they seemed to skate about haphazardly as if just for the pleasure of it. . . ."

Plimpton had spent similar time in the trenches with football and basketball players; when practice ended, they were gone. The writer was convinced that few athletes *enjoyed* their sport as much as hockey players did. "It's like a big kindergarten out here, isn't it?" Don Cherry—then the Bruins coach—told Plimpton.

My job as bench coach is simple: Work the doors, decide when to "change 'em up," call off players when they've been on too long. But I cannot *not* watch the game, or vent my emotions when the referee misses infractions or the linesmen blow offsides, cannot help but notice the little things a player does right, or wrong. I value my two cents' worth and offer it. I want the players to do what I myself find hard to do: slow down the game unfolding furiously in my head, lift my head, see the ice, make the smart pass, not the blind or panic one.

But sometimes I lose track of how long a line has been on the ice, and I get grief from the next line. The pups want out. "Change 'em up," one will say, knowing it's my call but trying to impose it, aware from past experience that I sometimes do lose track of time. But then I feel the need to establish some authority. And even when I know the pups are right, that I should change 'em up, I don't, to make a point.

One player, a physically imposing but gentle forward called Alex, sometimes relays his own line's time on the ice—the moment he arrives back at the bench—if he deems it unfairly slim. This irks me. But Alex has a point. I do get caught up in the game. A player who dumps the puck down the ice, without looking to pass and with no opposing player within twenty feet of him, sends me up the wall. Some nights after a game I cannot sleep. I'm still at that bench, watching, instructing, my hand on the metal bar at the bench door, my heart beating fast.

December 8, 2000. For an exhibition game, Josh (our best player) and Sandy (our goalie) have decided to swap positions. In the dressing room there is giddiness in the air, as if they've all been in hyperbaric chambers sucking on oxygen. The decibel level, alarming most times, hits some new pitch, for the boys must talk over the rap music now issuing from the boom-box someone has brought. Even their equipment has added olfactory bite.

In the warm-up, Sandy looks at sea in Josh's uniform. Wobbly as a toddler, Sandy moves in on Josh in the warm-up, then roofs one right side. This does not go unnoticed. Small cheer from Roger and Ken and me. Ken—who works the other door at the bench—is an emergency-department physician, father of Andrew, our ropey and gifted defenceman. Later in the season, Ken would almost die of cardiac arrest, likely occasioned by stress at work; in my get-well card to him I blamed the boys in baby blue.

We are at a decided disadvantage against this team, Kurt's rep team from last year. All of them, you see, can skate. Half our guys are skate-challenged. Matt has never played ice hockey before; it shows. Min, Korean-born, is in only his second year of hockey. Ian is a somewhat flappy and rugged forward who complains whenever he's touched—"What was *that?*" he will complain to the ref—but he has, to everyone's surprise, a sniper's gift around the net. Hamish moves like a wounded stork (but a very cheerful wounded stork). Mark has fair speed but is inclined to panic with the puck, especially when he finds himself the last man back, whereupon the puck becomes a live grenade. Jeff skates straight up and is so light on his feet that a breeze would drop him. Some games I look out from my spot at the gate and three of our forwards are turning slow circles like leaves in the fall. I am astonished that Canadian kids could be so at sea on blades.

I've been skating since I was four. A few years ago I started playing occasionally with teachers in Toronto, and my friend David replayed a conversation he heard before that first game.

"Who's the new guy in the green Cooperalls?" one player enquired during the warm-up. I was skating past them, my features hidden by my full-face visor and helmet.

"He's a young guy, right?" another asked.

"Well, no . . ." David replied.

Skating to me is as natural as breathing. Some of the boys in blue have trouble breathing. Aside from our defence, the heart of the team, only Kurt and Josh on the forward line skate with balance and ease. Kurt has Mahovlich strides, and I encourage him to do that little Doug Gilmour dance, that one-two-three skip that can generate speed while inviting lightness and lateral movement. And he does, but some days he has his dad's puck skills and leaves the black thing behind.

January 20, 2001. Skated on the huge pond at the Little Cataraqui Creek Conservation Centre just north of the city, drawn by the deep blue sky and the promise of skating in the open air. The ice is tapioca in places, and the cracks are wide enough to make speed dangerous. Thankfully, speed at my age is short-lived and muted in any case.

It feels strange to be on blades without a stick in my hand. There are lots of fathers and sons out there tossing a puck around, the dads torn between soft passes and look-at-me flourishes. I am always struck by how passionate kids are for the game, no matter how well or badly they play it. At Victoria Park, a minute from our house, there seems to be no correlation between the temperature outside and numbers at the several outdoor rinks. Boys play in their hockey sweaters in minus-thirty-degree cold.

That night I take up my usual spot working the doors. We are playing a minor bantam PD (player development) team, one that has soundly beaten us in the past. They're a tad younger, but much more talented.

To my surprise, we lead 2–0 in the third—but after two defensive lapses, it's tied. By now I am so caught up in the game that I let slide my duties as doorman. Again. One boy, Oscar, tries to shock me into action when he arrives breathless at the bench and finds the door closed. "Coach, coach!" he shouts, staring at me. It works, for a time.

Josh gets the go-ahead goal with five minutes to go. Earlier I had wondered if silliness was overtaking him. He had borrowed a pair of sunglasses from his buddy in the timekeeper's hut and worn them for several shifts.

"We are *not* going to lose this game," I tell the forwards, with just over a minute left. I am now totally swept up. Behind me Roger is saying, "Let's leave Kurt's line on a little longer." But I do not hear his discreet dictum, which is clearly meant for me—since I am working the forwards' door and Ken the defence. Whatever part of my brain is still functioning can only take in this refrain: *Short shifts. Short shifts.* I call off Kurt's line. They have been on for a grand total of ten seconds. I put on the next line due up, our weakest. Now the faceoff is in our zone and the other team has pulled their goalie in favour of the extra attacker.

What have I done? Why didn't Roger overrule me? Too late. "I tried to give you a hint," he tells me as the puck drops. The whole bench had groaned, Kurt's line louder than any, as our muckers cheerily trooped out. If this game ends in a tie—or worse, a loss—it'll be my doing. Our defence, thankfully, saves the day.

Kurt lectures me on the way home: tells me, rightly, that my first task is to change 'em up and work the doors. Next comes coaching, passing on tips, compliments, reminders after bad plays. But in close games, this doorman loses all sense of duty, and some hybrid form— more avid spectator than hot-blooded coach—takes over.

January 22, 2001. Walking our dog, Dusty, with Ulrike, who has returned from an aesthetics class at Queen's University's Faculty of Education and is talking animatedly about beauty—about finding it, seeing it through the fog. She tells me she had a little epiphany while walking to school that morning, a walk she has taken almost daily since September. For the first time, she saw how the red fire hydrants lined up when you let your eye take the long view up the street. An otherwise drab scene of soot-encrusted snow and bare trees had taken on a little glory.

Cut now to Harold Harvey Arena, minutes from the Faculty of Education. As Ulrike was walking to school, bound for her epiphany, I was on the ice with our Monday-noon bunch. At one point, John (he owns his own construction business and plays a clever game of hockey) was preparing to pass from deep in his end and I, seeking to defend, was curling back to cover my winger. But I had guessed, correctly, it transpired, that he would send the puck across centre to the other wing, and I immediately cut hard to my left just as he made his pass, and suddenly there was the puck on my stick. The moment would have been truly complete had I scored.

Perhaps no one else realized that the intercepted pass was anything but serendipitous. I knew, and John knew, it was not. In my sixth decade, playing lowly pickup, the game was still giving me something.

On our walk that night, Ulrike talked about some tape her professor had brought to class. The students heard an exquisite syncopation, with delicate and intricate rhythms, but no one could guess how this odd music—if music it was—might have been produced. Finally, he revealed the source: the sound of postal clerks in Ghana stamping letters. They had turned a mind-numbing task into percussive jazz.

I'm wondering if hockey played at its so-called highest levels is also played in a fog. I loathe the music they play in modern arenas, for it suggests a cynicism and lack of faith in the game itself. What is played up is hockey as entertainment—the spotlights roving the ice surface for effect, the JumboTron bullying us into making noise, the team mascot using a toy bazooka to launch souvenirs into the crowd, home teams introduced onto the ice from a shark's jaw or an oil derrick. How is one to focus on the play when the circus is not only there, but in your face?

I remember a moment in a Kingston Frontenacs game a few weeks earlier, when a Sarnia Stings player attempting to negate an icing call raced into the Kingston end. This was during play, so the rock music had given way to the pure sounds of the game. You could hear his skates carving hard, like some manic saw. Only players with weight and power can make that sound, and even up in the far reaches of the Memorial Centre where Kurt and I sat, it resonated. That's the sound I want to hear at a hockey game, not "We Will We Will Rock You."

January 28, 2001. At the Memorial Centre, there are no bad seats. I am two rows up, north end, so close to the end boards that I can hear the whack of sticks on pads and clearly see the faces of forwards as they are flattened into the glass by defencemen.

My focus is on Mike Zigomanis, the classy centreman for Kingston. Light on his feet, he has a wide-legged skating style, a kind of furious churning, with one shoulder lifting as the other drops. He's like a gyroscope, with his forward motion matched by sideways energy. The style works, for he has extraordinary lateral speed.

The warm-up skate for the refs has the loudspeaker playing the haunting Moody Blues song "Knights in White Satin" (the London Knights were in town) and it seems to lend new dignity to the otherwise drab sight of three men circling the ice in black-and-white striped shirts.

Ziggy's own pre-game skate is lively, with lots of rocking, as if he were on skis and riding over moguls. During the national anthem, he shifts weight constantly, kicking out this foot then the next, as if each big toe had a fly on the end he was anxious to dislodge.

Zigomanis is the go-to guy; he plays a regular shift, kills penalties, captains the power play (and the team, for that matter). He played on Canada's junior team at the world championship in December 2000 (inexplicably, he saw little ice time, and when they finally put him on in the final two games, he caught fire). Ziggy would rack up forty goals and thirty-seven assists in his final year with the Frontenacs, before being drafted in the second round by Carolina. His manner on the ice is poised and smart, the perfect complement to his wingers—a tough,

lanky mucker with soft hands named Brett Cloutier, and Derek
Campbell, the team's top scorer, who plays bold, clever hockey.

There is only one fight this game: Cloutier versus his counterpart
with the Knights. Words are exchanged first, then glances; helmets are
ritually doffed and they begin to circle. Each mocks the other as the
dance continues, Cloutier beckoning his opponent in with his fingers,
the other bobbing cartoonishly, until finally they lock arms and
grapple. The bout continues for about forty seconds, and the linesmen
look to be coming to separate the combatants, but no, I can clearly see
the Knight saying *no* to them, that he's not quite finished, thank you
very much. Then, with his free hand he points to something in the
crowd, Cloutier falls for the ruse and takes one in the chops, then
responds with a roundhouse swing and decks the other guy. The decision goes to the hometown boy.

To show heart, to show no fear, the other player, later in the game,
shoves Cloutier as the latter exits the ice for a line change. The Knight
gets two minutes for roughing.

You can plot the emotional course of a hockey game, much like a
stock-market graph. This game began as a clean, fast affair, with the
hitting honest but devoid of any menace. Then everything changed.
During one shift, someone clotheslined someone else and, seconds
later, a defenceman cut sharply across the ice, radaring in on someone's
knees. Though the victim swerved at the last second, like a destroyer
dodging a torpedo, everyone on the ice and on the bench took note.
Manners thereafter went out the window.

The consequential fight with Cloutier does appear to settle things
down. Those who oppose a ban on fighting in hockey would point to
this alchemy as proof, not that violence begets violence but that it
serves as an outlet. Still, I had the feeling that the fight bore the whiff
of old animosity, so that the sudden shift in the game's flavour did not
cause the fight but provided an occasion for these two to renew
acquaintances. But maybe not. If hockey players *believe* that fighting
restores peace, perhaps it does. Centuries ago, horse trainers were
convinced that ritually preparing frog bones and burying them in an

anthill magically bestowed on horsemen a mastery over horses; trainers were bolstered by that confidence, and the horses responded to the trainers' self-assurance. Mind over matter.

Peter McNab, a centreman who played with the Bruins in the late 1970s and early 1980s, once said that one team can sense when another team is sagging under pressure. He likened it to an animal in flight, a gazelle, say, weakening on the African veldt, and the predators knowing this and closing in for the kill.

Every game at the Memorial Centre is watched by scouts. Travel the corridors between periods, past the popcorn stands, and you will come to the room set aside for media and scouts. They look an unhealthy lot, perhaps from all the hot dogs and bad coffee they've consumed here and at rinks like it province-wide. The players know they are being watched, graded. How much of combat in junior hockey is simply a demonstration of prowess and fearlessness for the benefit of note-takers in the crowd? Think of pro hockey as a job pool. The average NHL career lasts a mere five years. Those below the elite players pulling in million-dollar wages must impress team management somehow. Skill is hard to manufacture; abandon is more easily conjured.

I am slowly becoming an admirer of this Frontenacs team. I like Braff, the calm defenceman. I like Campbell for his ebullience. Cloutier, a clunky skater who has this habit of snapping his head down to lower his visor, corralled the puck along the boards late in the game, when Kingston held onto a fragile lead, and he defied any Knight to take it.

The game, it occurrs to me, belongs as much to Cloutier as it does to Zigomanis. The one owns the boards, the other open ice. I know where my own heart lies.

February 9, 2000. We used to hold the odd union meeting at the RCHA (Royal Canadian Horse Artillery) clubhouse on Ontario Street, when I worked at the *Whig-Standard.* Swords on the wall, portrait of the queen, friendly old veterans at the bar, with brush cuts and Perry

Como sweaters, cigarettes dangling on the lower lips of grey men and grey women as they talked.

It's the evening before the thirty-third annual historic hockey series, commemorating a game played in 1886 between Queen's University and Royal Military College. Team captains this evening introduce their players, each one given a monicker—"Mad Dog," "Latin Lover," "Killer," "Half-Pint"—that rhymes with, or somehow suits, their actual names.

Later, there is a Hot Stove League question-and-answer session, with three former NHLers—all Kingston lads—sitting at a table up at the front, beneath the crossed silver swords. Fred O'Donnell played with the Bruins and the WHA's New England Whalers in the 1970s. Rick Smith was on that 1970 Stanley Cup–winning Bruins team with Bobby Orr. Jim Dorey, the ex-Leaf, was among the first to leap to the WHA back in 1972.

The three make for striking contrasts. O'Donnell, a real-estate agent, is conservatively dressed in sports jacket and tie, and seems the most refined of the three. Smith is casually dressed, as rumpled as an unmade bed. Jim Dorey is dapper in his black leather jacket. He looks and sounds the party-guy, and though his face is nicked from his hockey days, there is an astonishing boyishness about him.

Irreverent and funny, Dorey is a little like Dennis Hull, the master of the one-liner you want at your hockey banquet. Dorey says he got his start playing in the Church Athletic League (Kurt's league) and insists he developed his skating by making marathon trips back and forth across the lake to the American side, packing smokes and booze—"three runs a day," he says into the microphone, his face straight, the audience roaring. Dorey has probably delivered these lines many times before, yet his comic timing makes them seem fresh.

In the room, growing thicker now with cigarette smoke and the beer flowing freely, someone wants to know how these three think the game—and they mean, of course, the NHL game—has changed.

Rick Smith tells us that players in his day were smarter. "More than anything," he says, "we had more fun. Don Cherry would have gone ballistic at the idea of us getting on exercise bikes after a game the way they do now. It's not a game today but a very serious business."

Fred O'Donnell, a five-ten, 175-pounder as a player, remarks on the huge increase in the size of players and marvels at their quickness and mobility. O'Donnell believes that players in his day were not as "over-coached" or systems-oriented as they are now and that games then were more exciting to watch. No murmurs of disagreement at that notion.

But it is the clown prince, Jim Dorey, who commands the most laughs and offers the greatest insight. "What players don't have now," he says, "is individual skills. The weather in Canada has changed and we don't have the winters we used to have or the outdoor rinks where we would handle the puck for four hours a day. There are so few players, like Mario Lemieux, who have the creativity, the ingenuity to make things happen out there."

Later on, Dorey talks about the surging interest in hockey among girls and women, and he wonders if one day soon he will look out on the RCHA Club before another historic hockey series and see the room half full of women. The next day, a Queen's player they call "Half-Pint" scores a goal, the first time in the series that a woman has done that. Half-Pint is also named her team's most valuable player.

I take in the games, which were to have been friendly games involving three teams—Royal Military College (RMC), Queen's University, and the Second Regiment, Royal Canadian Horse Artillery (RCHA), Canadian Forces Base, Petawawa. The latter are there to salute the games of shinny played by Kingston garrison soldiers in the 1880s.

This event is meant to be a quaint re-creation of an historic game. But several factors combine to give the three 20-minute matches a little edge. There is a trophy to be won, putting pride on the line and inviting intensity. And after a night of rain that has destabilized the ice in Kingston harbour—traditional locale for the game—the matches have shifted to the indoor rink at RMC. In the harbour, the rink would have been defined by snowbanks, with pauses to search for buried pucks (in this case a yellow square made of sponge plastic, not wood, like pucks of yore). Inside, there are fewer pauses and momentum is allowed to build.

Teams wear traditional sweaters, the RCHA "Gunners" and RMC in toques, Queen's players in tams. They carry light, short sticks, almost half-sticks, wear no equipment, and abide by nineteenth-century rules: seven players to a team, including goal, point, cover point, left and right wing, centre and rover. "Faces" (what we call faceoffs) have players set up facing the sides, not the ends, the puck on the ice. It is only then that the referee—in a white lab coat—shouts "Play." No forward passes are allowed, and when such occur, the ref shakes his handbell, like some irate schoolmaster signalling the end of recess.

Another rule forbids "charging from behind, tripping, collaring, kicking, shinning, cross-checking, or pushing," as well as profane language.

These commemorative games may look like costume parties, but the little flares of enmity remind me of hockey's tribal origins. One gunner downs a Queen's player with a cross-check; another grabs a Queen's player around the neck from behind, after a whistle, and appears to threaten him with grievous personal harm.

Geoff Smith, who teaches both history and sports sociology at Queen's, later told me he had his team deploy a tactic from basketball, a game this California-born academic knows well. "I told our guys to give those RCHA guys—who were big and threatening to run over our players, even our women—a brush every chance they got, a little elbow, a little shoulder. Let them know we were there and not about to be overrun." His perception was that RCHA had outmuscled RMC in their 5–1 victory. Friendly game? Perhaps, had it been baseball or soccer. But this was hockey. Smith wonders if the game is unique in the "alchemic" response it stirs.

In the final game, between RMC and Queen's, one of the military men—distinguished by a long, black wig pouring out from under his toque—roughs up one of Queen's better players, number nine. I happen to be sitting in the stands near a coterie of black wig's RMC friends, who delight in the exchange. "Old-time hockey," one yells. "Old-time hockey."

Later, back at the RCHA club where trophies and crests are presented, I find myself sitting across from number 9. Geoff Smith has confided that the player is in his history class; Geoff calls him a thoughtful student.

"Why do we fight in hockey and so rarely in other sports?" I ask number 9.

"It's part of the game," he says, and insists he was not at all bothered by the trash talk or minor eruptions. He also told me that RMC-versus-Queen's varsity games—where fighting is banned—feature an unconscionable amount of stickwork. The Don Cherry school of hockey coming from an articulate university student. But has number 9 come to his own conclusions? Or is he mouthing Cherry? (A postscript: the 2002 commemorative game featured a fight involving an RMC and an RCHA player following a cross-check.)

February 11, 2001. Watching the sports roundup at the end of the day. Global TV carries a clip from Marty McSorley's first game back in the pros since the Brashear incident. He's getting in shape with an International Hockey League team in Grand Rapids, Michigan. His stint here is a preamble either to re-entry into the NHL or perhaps a job in Europe. My hope is that McSorley will be on his best behaviour, that he will take the high road. I should be more detached but I genuinely like the man and seem to have acquired a stake in his future.

The European league has blocked the Knights option and will meet March 9 to consider McSorley's appeal, which, I fear, will not be helped by his IHL debut.

The charming man I had breakfast with not six days ago is seen back out on the ice, the number 33 on his old white helmet, in a brawl. I catch his broad back amid a tumble of players, most of them on the ice and crawling over one another. The camera has eyes for McSorley, who is now standing again. He reaches over a linesman's grasp and decks another player with an overhead right. I cannot fathom this.

During our talk, McSorley had told me about enjoying a supper near Camden East at the home of Brian and Trina Kelly; Marty once played with Brian's brother. I've been to the Kelly farmhouse many times. Kurt went to school with the Kelly boys, Sean and Chad, both of whom I coached in hockey and baseball. I could imagine Marty McSorley wrestling with the boys somewhere in that farmhouse. The man on the screen, he's someone else. But who?

A letter would later appear in the *Hockey News*. Jeff Stockreef, of Walker, Michigan, says he was there at the game in Grand Rapids when McSorley made his return to pro hockey. The fan argued that all those snide comments in the media about the incident—"once a goon always a goon"—were off the mark. What this fan saw was an altercation at the end of the game, with McSorley by no means the instigator but the fourth or fifth one in. His involvement, Stockreef wrote, was a response to a teammate being ganged up on by two opposing players. "What he did," the fan wrote, "was commendable, not shameful."

February 14, 2001. Valentine's Day. Only days after speaking with local hockey historian Ed Grenda—who says he quit playing the game because it aroused certain passions in him—some of the players on Kurt's team experience the same alchemy. The boys in blue are playing a bump-and-grind team. Some of our players don't much like that brand of hockey and they turn to mockery to mask their fear.

A large defenceman for the other team, number 22, hears (as he skates backwards past our bench) the unmistakable sound that a heavy truck makes when it backs up. It's that safety clarion: *beep-beep-beep-beep*. And every time number 22 drifts past, he hears beeping. Worse, he has no sense of humour about it.

More displays of faux bravado follow. One of our players clotheslines an opposing forward late in the game and wrestles him to the ground. Two minutes in the box. Later, the same player takes umbrage at another guy's bump and begins to tail the tall, sleek forward all over the ice, at one point running him from behind but falling flat on his back as a result. Imagine a Gypsy Moth pursuing a Spitfire.

February 16, 2001. Belleville Bulls in town. First place at stake. Mike "Ziggy" Zigomanis takes a perfect pass from Cloutier, streaks in on the left wing and finds another gear to drive past the defenceman, dekes the goalie, and slips the puck in on the right side. A thing of beauty.

Later, some ugliness. A Bulls defenceman gets a mere two minutes for a hit from behind. These two teams almost came to blows in the pre-game skate, so I'm surprised there isn't more of this. Junior players are often so big, so strong, and sometimes so edgy, that a hit from behind can be career-ending.

At one point, a small Kingston forward is checked to his knees by a burly Bulls defenceman, and the whistle blows. Play stops, but another sort of play ensues. As the defenceman gets to his feet, he finds the forward's face with his glove and gently pushes. The face-wash. One of those provocative little insults Marty McSorley talks about.

The forward has no recourse but to object. Rise in anger, go at him. Simply to accept it, under current codes of behaviour, is to invite more of the same. But the inevitable consequence is much milling about, delays in the game, and sometimes fights. All from a little insult, the hockey equivalent of an older version: man takes off glove, places the wrist-end between his fingers, and uses it to slap another man's face.

February 28, 2001. A teeth-gritting game in house-league hockey. The other team's captain—and it says a lot that his type was made captain—plays with a dark ferocity. To win, yes, but also to hurt and intimidate. On the first shift, he quite savagely hooks Josh from behind as the latter breaks away at centre ice; Josh replies with an elbow to the other's head. Both go down. No penalty.

On the bench, Josh shakes his head. "That guy plays on my rep team," he tells me. "I don't go after guys I play with. But that guy, he would run you." Every shift, their captain menaces, but he also scores, and I wish our guys were less awestruck and more inclined to be in his face. As he is in ours.

Adrenaline begins to course in my body. The game turns on a play in the third period when Mr. Menace, in hiding at our blue line and unseen by our defence, takes a pass, dashes in, and scores. Anybody but him, I think, my eyes skyward. A tie game is now 3–2 for them and then comes an empty-netter.

By the time I get home, my shoulders are tight and my brain hurts from thinking vengeful thoughts.

My mood lightens when I think of a story another coach told me. One of his players was banished from a game, and the one to follow, for hitting from behind. In a league with several poor skaters, this kid is in a class of his own. The coach tried to explain to the ref the reason for the hit: The kid has no brakes. On their bench, news spreads of "Bobskate" Bill's banishment, and some of his teammates, somewhat unkindly, apparently uttered that latter-day phrase of delight, the one that comes with a clenched fist: *"Yessssss."*

February 27, 2001. An old Glendon teammate faxes me something from the *Vancouver Sun* that neatly captures how emotional hockey is, how it can bring out the worst of human nature in coaches and fans.

Columnist Gary Mason is describing a game he happened to catch in Niagara Falls, while visiting family. "The entire crowd," he nicely puts it, "got a game misconduct." With two minutes left, someone tossed a plastic water bottle onto the ice, followed by a broom, coins, batteries—all aimed at the ref. The 200 fans were ordered to clear the arena. The same thing had occurred in Toronto earlier that winter. And in Nanaimo, meanwhile, on-ice officials staged a one-day boycott of atom house-league games to protest abuse by fans and coaches. This followed several raucous incidents in which teenage referees literally came under siege from angry coaches and parents. In one case, a young official was confronted in a parking lot. In another, a teenage referee and his linesmen were locked in the officials' room for ten minutes by frustrated parents.

Mason, a bench coach for the past six years, writes that "the verbal taunts, forms of physical intimidation and general hostility that I've seen directed at refs has been enough to make me sick at times." He's seen coaches spit at refs not much older than his fourteen-year-old son (whom he would never allow to referee). One veteran referee described coming onto the ice before the third period of a midget game and being jumped by one player, who then held the official while the player's father pummelled him. The referee suffered a broken nose, dislocated shoulder, and back injuries. The same man has asked for police escorts to and from games and had police rescue his wife when she was surrounded by fans angry at the way her husband called the game.

All this abuse forced the league to react. In 2000, Pacific Coast hockey empowered its officials to banish unruly parents and coaches.

I relate some of this to my old-timer bunch, and one of the younger players (an engineering student) tells me he once went to a kids' league game with his girlfriend, whose father was a coach. When one goalie made a nice save, my friend shouted his appreciation. The woman beside him slapped him in the face.

March 22, 2001. The baby-blue team plays its last game of the season tonight. We have swooned, Maple Leafs style, since the New Year. The gulf between our rushers and sloggers is simply too great.

The opposition, a good team we have beaten in the past, defeat us 4-to-1 in a game that could have been 12-to-1 had it not been for Sandy's heroics in goal. The other captain, Mr. Menace, was wearing a shiner under his helmet. Seems he was at a tournament in Toronto, something was said off the ice, and another player landed three solid punches. He is always in the centre of things. Clever and nasty, he will barge the net, dive to draw a penalty, do what it takes to win.

He also owns enviable breakaway speed. One of our defencemen, the normally placid Rob, muscled him in front of our net last night. This is how you have to play this guy, whose arrogance on the ice goes right to me, like an errant dart.

I take his nose-in-the-air manner very, very personally. It's what I remember most about playing hockey in my late teens, being so aware of who was on the ice, and how the game, for all its collective nature, still comes down to moments. One guy with the puck, another guy daring him—eye-to-eye—to get past. Even old-timer hockey retains that flavour: You carry the puck, look up, see who is there, and decide one of two courses. This guy is too quick, too smart, I'd better pass. Or, he's slow, easily duped, I'm going round him. One move shows respect, the other a casual disrespect.

March 29, 2001. I am listening, for the first time this year, to an AM-radio broadcast of a Kingston Frontenacs game. It's been a long time since I've followed a hockey game this way, and it's quite electric. Having gone to a dozen games, I've come to know the players, or I think I do, based on how they play the game. So every time the announcer names a name, I can put a face, and even some character, to the mention.

Losers of game two, 3–2, and victims of a 10–2 pasting in game one, the Frontenacs are playing in Belleville in game three of the play-offs. In this one they are down 4–1 but storm back in the third period to tie it. With two minutes left to play, the Bulls—they have three players who rank in the top ten in league scoring—take the lead. Coach Mavety then takes a gamble: He claims that one of the Bulls is using an illegal stick. If the ploy works, the Frontenacs go on the power play. If not, Belleville does. The stick is indeed suspect and the Frontenacs score. The team is without Ziggy, its injured captain and the best puck handler on the team, but the lads are showing heart.

And speaking of heart, the announcers seem on the verge of myocardial infarction. Their enthusiasm is helping me to see and feel this astonishing game. But once the game goes into overtime, here as in the NHL, the referees put their whistles away. Hockey is the only game where refereeing in overtime disappears almost entirely. Listen as the sometimes rough-and-tumble announcers on Kingston radio see the game as it goes into one and then two periods of overtime.

> What a hockey game! Oh, it just doesn't get any better than this!
> . . . I can't take it! We're tied at 5. The fans are seeing a gem of a game tonight . . . Bodies are flying. The referees are lettin' em go.

They've put the whistle away. Ya gotta love it! . . . I'm gonna have a heart attack. Ridler another great save! Can you believe it? . . . That just sickens me. The guy was grabbing Ianero's throat. It's dog eat dog out there tonight . . . I'm so impressed by the effort I'm seeing out there tonight, I'm speechless . . . Nate Robinson, the Port Hope flash, is all over the ice. Jeez that kid can go! . . . Coughlin has him in a headlock . . . He's *still* got him in a headlock . . . It's 46–30 in shots in favour of Belleville, but that means absolute dick. The kids are givin' 110 per cent . . . Who's got gas in the tank now? It's so intense . . . Fronts are on the ropes. They're mugging, they're grabbing, they're holding

. . . It's eye for an eye . . . They had Robinson handcuffed. I don't think Houdini could have got out of that one . . . There's a war out there. Sticks are up in the faces. They're carvin' em up. They're not calling anything . . . Do or die. They're just killing each other. MacIvor almost took Robinson's head off. . . .

Finally, late in the second overtime period, Belleville breaks out on a two-on-one and scores. Thus ends almost 100 minutes of hockey on an Olympic-sized surface, and close to 40 minutes of guerrilla hockey. Only two penalties were called in overtime, coincidental minors.

The Frontenacs would lose the fourth and final game at home after a gutsy effort. There is one play that sticks in my mind from that last game. Late in the third period, I look on as Nate Robinson dashes past a Frontenacs defenceman and finds himself alone in front of the net, where he does a pirouette before passing the puck back to himself—a move, I can only guess, to confound the goalie. He does not score but he makes the move as if he has done it 100 times before in practice. Maybe he has. With that pirouette, there is an audible gasp from everyone around me.

April 15, 2001. Watching hockey on TV. With ten seconds left in a game, the Devils would win by a 2–0 margin, and Scott Stevens hits an opposing player. The victim is cut for five stitches. Don Cherry's comment: "When a pit bull smells meat, he goes for it."

May 28, 2001. I see an ad on television, pitching the Stanley Cup finals, which are mercifully nearing the end. I have watched hockey pretty much every night since April 26, and the last game will be played on June 7. The ad moves from one cut-up hockey player to another. We are meant to admire the courage of these wounded warriors.

For Don Cherry, the stitches are evidence that, in the absence of fisticuffs in the playoffs, stickwork flourishes. I wonder if something simpler is at work here. The stakes are so high in players' minds, the quest for Lord Stanley's Cup so fever-pitched, that the players compete with an abandon seldom seen in the regular season. Players dive in front of shots, take chances, sacrifice themselves. Caution is thrown to the winds.

Summer 2001. Kurt and many of his hockey buddies compete for the first time in a lacrosse league. They wear shoulder pads, gloves, and helmets, as they do in hockey. They carry sticks as they do in hockey. Indeed, they whack each other with those sticks far more than they do in hockey. And yet there is none of the pushing and shoving around the crease, no mouthing off to referees when, say, a player goes off for slashing, no cursing, no threats. Players actually chat each other up at faceoffs. Why the difference between the two games?

I have to believe it's because lacrosse is so new and fresh in the players' minds. The boys are likely unaware of the game's savage past. There is none of the claustrophobia of rinks; the field is wide and long and airy, defined only by orange plastic cones. Fans—read: parents— are relatively quiet, certainly calm, as they sit in lawn chairs along the side. They, too, have no history with this game. We are thus spared the parental war cry, "Hit him! Hit him!"

Was there no chippiness because so few boys had been exposed to the nastiness of pro lacrosse? Or does the speed of hockey—and the drama of high-speed collisions—explain the difference? Does speed alone change everything? For whatever reason, lacrosse—or at least the version I saw played this summer—is what amateur hockey should be: fun.

September 15, 2001. Dave Ellett, a two-time NHL all-star defenceman with Winnipeg and Toronto, has a smile on his face as he enters the Memorial Centre arena—on horseback.

The Kingston fall fair is featuring, as part of its Wild West show, a shooting competition. Where the ice would be, six inches of loose turf has been set down and about a dozen riders—dressed as cowboys with six-shooters or as U.S. cavalrymen, several of the women in flat black hats and looking like a cross between Black Bart and Annie Oakley—gallop several circuits of the arena, shooting and whooping to animate the crowd.

The shooting competition puts the riders on a slalom course of balloons set on three-foot-high sticks. The aim is to shoot the balloons and quick-step the course, the last half in a straight, flat-out gallop. Ellett, who only took up the sport a year ago, doesn't win but fares well against world champions. Even the moustache, which he never wore on left defence, seems to suit cowboy Ellett. And every time I see him, he's smiling. After sixteen years in the NHL, it must be nice to be in a hockey rink, riding high and fast, hitting a target that never moves, and never getting hit yourself.

November 17, 2001. Six games into a new season and the boys in blue are undefeated. Some of the older boys have moved on to midget. Three who took their place—the so-called Kid Line: Kevin, Jon-Paul, and Mitchell—are, game-in, game-out, our best. On the puck, heads up, circling and passing as if they've played together since peewee. Three mid-sized boys, they skate well and play tall, sometimes too tall. Steve, our robust defenceman, plays the same way. There is a fine line between playing with edge and going over the edge; the latter sometimes lands us in the box.

A year has made a difference to the team. Some of our boys were fourteen last year, playing against many fifteen-year-olds. Now it's reversed, and the confidence shows. Nick, Roger's son, was always steady on defence, but this year he's bulked up. Hamish is more solid on his feet and spent time in the summer working on his shot. Now he shows little flourishes: a deft little back pass, a desire to hold onto the puck longer, even a touch around the net. Min is still at sea out there, but he will occasionally unleash Wendell Clark wristers that bulge the twine, as they say. After a summer of canoeing and portaging, Mark is stronger; he shows imagination and grit along the boards and has even filled in capably on defence. No more puck as live ammunition. Jeff and Alex are more involved. Kurt gets breakaways every game and now owns a high, hard, wrist shot that puts mine to shame. Andrew's solo rushes are working now that he's gone to a shorter stick, or maybe he's just finally at home now in his lofty frame.

Meanwhile, at the bench, nothing has changed. The pups always want out.

11

WOMEN'S HOCKEY:

BETWIXT AND BETWEEN "BALLET AND MURDER"

A PRIL 9, 2001. Perched on a stool in the Split Rock Bar and Grill at the Minneapolis Airport. I am nursing a Summit Lager and going over my notes from the women's world hockey championship, when a third of the Canadian team breezes past me and occupies two tables at the back. For the past half hour, a woman four stools away has been silently downing beers while maintaining a dark, vacant, straight-ahead stare. With the players' entry, the mood of the place has suddenly lifted.

A day after the gold-medal game, I am still supping vicariously on their bliss. I was five feet away from a beaming Jennifer Botterill, when the Team Canada forward told a TSN interviewer near the dressing-room door, "There is no place in the world I would rather be than right here." Is there anything finer than rocking the eagle on eagle turf? The little beaver had nipped her neighbour. This called for a gesture.

I would buy them all a beer. The Canadian thing. But I would do it anonymously to avoid any awkwardness. If it is unseemly for an athlete to buy a scribe a beer, so, surely, is the reverse. From my seat at the bar, I beckon to their waiter and explain my proposal. Drinks on me. The bill comes soon enough and I pore over it: I'm guessing the lone team staff member with them opted for a beer, the rest had sodas, one had coffee. It dawns on me the sacrifice that Olympic athletes make: These women are going back to their league teams and playoff games; there will be no quaffing of ales. My gesture is suddenly feeling hollow, feeble—you buy pop for peewees, not world champions. The $20 tab is embarrassing. My father has

234

always had a weakness for the grand gesture in restaurants, and I have inherited that gene. So I buy the players lunch. This is more like it: $159.58 U.S.

As I board the plane, I file past André Brin, the team's ever-cheerful media-relations manager, sitting in business class. He commends me, says the players were all pleasantly surprised. I dissemble, neither confirming nor denying. "I heard *a fan* bought them lunch," I say. "But yes, it was a nice gesture, and I'd say they earned their lunch."

"They Earned Their Lunch," says André. "There's the title of your book."

Two hours later in Toronto, I watch the players line up for Canada Customs and Immigration, and I imagine the dialogue.

"You were in Minnesota. Doing what?"

"Winning a gold medal for Canada in hockey," the player in the ponytail would respond. Who would not wish to make such a declaration at the border?

Beside me on the plane was Elizabeth Etue, a writer working with a film crew preparing a documentary on women's international hockey—*Chasing the Dream*—to be aired on CBC-TV just before the Salt Lake City Olympics in February 2002. Etue co-authored a book on women's hockey, has played the game, and knows the players.

"What did you come away with?" she asked me.

"A Holiday Inn pen," I replied, trolling for a laugh.

"No, what were your impressions?" Etue persisted.

"The skill of the players," I said.

"Everyone," she told me, "has the same response."

Etue said that women's hockey—even in Scandinavian countries—has struggled for acceptance. In Russia, there may be a pool of only 100 players to choose from. Still, huge strides are being made, and the world, she said, is slowly waking up to women's hockey.

On the plane home I read the *Toronto Star,* one of its columnists reminding readers that fighting disappears in the playoffs, when NHL players suddenly discover discipline, laying off foolish penalties for fear of jeopardizing their teams' chances of a run at the Stanley Cup.

Early in the tournament, after Canada had pasted the Swedes, I spoke with Geraldine Heaney, a string-bean defender on the team, who has alternately been called "the Ray Bourque of women's hockey" and "the Paul Henderson of women's hockey"—after she scored a memorable goal at the world championship in 1990. Now thirty-four, she has played 100 games of international hockey and returned from all seven world championships with a gold medal around her neck. I am told she has the Olympic rings tattooed on one hip. Calling on her experience, I presented her with a scenario: One of your teammates has been hit by an opposing player from behind, has been hurt on the play, and the referee has failed to make the call. How do you respond?

Heaney gave a careful, considered response. "I may want to even it up," she said, "but it depends on the score. Sometimes you just have to suck it up."

During four days of hockey, watching the Finns, the Swedes, the Americans, and the Canadians play a game that was often rugged, increasingly emotional as the medal rounds approached, and always uptempo, that phrase—inelegant as it was precise—haunted me. Lots of players in the NHL "suck it up." Hammer them into the boards and they exact revenge—by scoring. Players like Detroit's Steve Yzerman and Nicklas Lidstrom, Dallas's Mike Modano, Ottawa's Marian Hossa, and Toronto's Mats Sundin. Why, I wonder, do we not honour players who *do* suck it up? Why do so many fans admire toughs who know so little of that virtue?

I had come to Minneapolis to see how the best female players in the world play the game, for I had never seen elite women's hockey save for snippets on TV. The great Canadian poet Al Purdy once called hockey a mix of ballet and murder. I anticipated that women's hockey would be purely about ballet, that women were somehow above the murderous turns that men's hockey can take.

All very noble, to be sure. But was I too steeped in that other vision of hockey? I wondered whether a steady diet of hockey as dance would come to bore me; maybe something approaching homicide was somehow—for me, anyway—central to the mix. Hearing, on the

Mariucci Arena sound system in downtown Minneapolis, "Two minutes for bodychecking" still sounded to me like "Two minutes for breathing." I left the Twin Cities convinced, more than ever, that Purdy was absolutely correct in his assessment, but the women's game, I would learn, offered its own unique blend of grace and fire.

I am leaning on the upper railing at Mariucci Arena, a splendid modern facility named in memory of a rugged defenceman who played for the University of Minnesota and then the Chicago Blackhawks in the 1940s. They call him "the godfather of hockey in Minnesota" for the many ways he encouraged Americans to play the game. Today, junior hockey players anywhere in Canada would thrill to play in this Olympic-sized venue. On either side of the arena, yellow seats have been strategically set amidst a sea of otherwise wine-coloured seats, to spell *M* for Minnesota. The state where *G* is for Gophers, *L* is for Land o' Lakes, *H* is for Hockey.

In 1989, the state passed a law requiring municipalities to offer equal ice-time to both sexes. As more and more arenas were built, girls' and women's hockey took off in Minnesota, where 10,000 females now play the game—far more than in any other state. On the American national team, six players hail from Minnesota. Here, the words "hockey" and "hotbed" pair easily.

Down below me, the Canadians are shellacking the Swedes. With seven minutes left in the first period, shots are seventeen to one in Team Canada's favour, and the 3–0 score actually flatters the Swedes. The Canadians play a true run-and-gun offence. They circle at both ends and even at centre ice, deliver daring blue-line to blue-line passes (condoned in international hockey) and set subtle little picks to stymie checkers, all the while resorting occasionally to NHL-style tactics—dump-and-chase, crash the net, plain old belligerence. Power plays are often pretty, the passing tic-tac-toe. The open "man" is a woman, and odds are she can roof the puck like nobody's business. This game prizes agility and quickness, not strength and power as the men's game does. Yet power there is.

Correne Bredin, a five-eleven, 190-pound defender playing here on the wing, is a true power forward in the NHL mould. Therese Brisson, the team captain and a stalwart on defence, reminds me of Al MacInnis, with her searing slapshots from the point. Tammy Lee Shewchuk calls to mind Lanny McDonald, with her high, hard wrist-shots. Nancy Drolet is Beliveau-like in her uncanny ability to win face-offs: She would win seventy-six per cent of them throughout the tournament. At one point in the Sweden game, Jennifer Botterill, an elegant left winger who would win the tournament's most valuable player trophy, delivered a crisp, pinpoint pass to a teammate hell-bent for the front of the net. Botterill did this while being severely harassed by a Swedish defender, while skating flat out, and from deep in the offensive zone. The pass was right on the money and was converted for yet another goal. I just wrote in my notebook: "Wow Wow Wow."

There was just as much I did *not* see that day. Penalized players did not jaw at the referee but went directly to the box. Post-whistle scrums were few and quickly dissipated. Players went boldly to the corners intent on the puck, and not, as in men's hockey, on devastation—one player seeking to deliver it, the other, cagily and by applying brakes and fakes, to avoid it.

As Brisson would later point out to me, some of these women have played ringette—"which is a lateral game. You develop agility and skating skills." It seemed to me, too, that the options available to players were greater than they are in the NHL. The virtual absence of fear and intimidation had opened up possibilities. Defencemen, especially, would seek the open man and, when that option was closed off, they would circle and seek some new pattern. Similarly pressed, many defencemen in pro hockey are more inclined to rifle the puck off the glass and hope for the best. Danielle Goyette would tell me that she came to hockey fairly late in life and was thus spared "systems coaches." If she is a freewheeling, creative offensive player, this is because she was allowed to be.

"If you're too intense out there," Brisson told me, "your perception narrows—it's a well-observed physiological response to intensity." In

Open Net, George Plimpton described the same phenomenon, how stress narrows the field of vision, "as if one were looking at the field of play down the length of a pipe." Brisson would know all this: She is a former professor of kinesiology at the University of New Brunswick. We had been talking about seeing the ice, and here she was citing science to show that too much intensity can literally blinker a player.

What edge there exists in the women's game, and at times there's plenty, is tempered by something. But what? Cassie Campbell, a veteran of the team and sometime colour commentator for the TSN sports channel, believes "It's an issue of respect. There's an unwritten rule in women's hockey. People have to go to work the next day. Male hockey players, though, are bred. It's almost cultish. At a young age, they're taught that hockey is do or die." She said that fighting in women's hockey is rare, and, given the full-face cages and masks they wear, quite senseless. (Young men in junior hockey, on the other hand, happily flail away at each other's half-visors and plastic-encased heads.) In any case, a player who drops her gloves risks banishment for a quarter of a season.

"There is stickwork in the women's game, I don't deny that, and some pushing and shoving and trash-talking," said Campbell, "but it's kept to a respectable limit. Our game is all skill and finesse and angling skills. I do roll my eyes at some of the stuff that goes on in the NHL." And even in boys' atom hockey: She had called me before the championship from Toronto, where the team had played some tune-up exhibition games. At the rink, Campbell looked on in despair as men coaching small boys uttered hockey's clarion call, "Hit him!"

Yet the women's game is not quite, as Campbell put it, *all* finesse, or a "pure" game, as Team Canada coach Danièle Sauvageau described it to me. I watched in the Canada–Finland game as Danielle Goyette, who has perhaps the softest hands in women's hockey (sixty-nine goals, 116 points in eighty-five games with the national team) engaged in a little stick-swiping before a faceoff. This was a grumpy, edgy display, more typical of men's hockey. I asked her about it later, outside her dressing room, and she dismissed the other player: "I wasn't even close to her and she was complaining." Then I asked the Finnish coach, Jouko Lukkarila, about the same incident, just as the Finnish player involved chanced by. By the look on her face, she seemed both mystified and appalled by Goyette's action. Lukkarila translated her comment, a Finnish adage: "A small tease is still a tease."

Canada's game against Sweden took on some edge, especially as the goals mounted. Perhaps the Swedes felt the Canadians were rolling up the score, for at the end of the second period, there was a good old-fashioned scrum, with both teams gathered for a little glaring, pushing, and shoving. But again, tempered. The game against Finland was even more robust, with the Finns trying to outmuscle the Canadians and failing. It was the Finns who landed in the penalty box.

Earlier in the day I had to practically step over the Finnish players in the hallway of the hotel where we were both staying. Blondes in blue sweatsuits were camped out, some curled like cats in sleeping bags, some flat on their backs, all with their eyes closed. A small speaker was emitting a soundscape of new-age music, with water softly falling and a Finnish man's voice assuring them, or so I imagined, of their unique athletic gifts. It did not work: The Finns finished, to everyone's surprise, out of the medals.

But the real eye-opener for me was the game between Canada and the U.S., for the gold. This game had edge and tempo and flare the others had not. The Kingston-born Jayna Hefford, a sniper around the net and soldily built at five-five, 140, got two minutes for working over an American forward along the boards with her stick. The American goalie was penalized for a head-snapping elbow delivered behind her net. Cassie Campbell engaged in some glove-swiping after the whistle. When an American was called for slashing the shins of Therese Brisson, I could hear the *whump* up in the press gallery. Later, Brisson roughed up an American player who dared to enter that forbidden land in front of the net. *Hockey News MVP* ranked international women players in 2000 and had this to say of the on-ice intensity of Brisson, who was deemed the most physical player: "Punishing force in front of the net . . . principal of the school of hard knocks . . . particularly effective in USA–Canada games when referees swallow their whistles and the games turn into free-for-alls. 'People don't even want to go against her in practice,' says [Team Canada coach] Danièle Sauvageau."

The last comment was surely an exaggeration, as was the commentary of the Minnesota *Star Tribune* reporter who called the gold-medal game "extremely physical, at times even violent." He should get out more. And I was puzzled by his assessment that "neither team had a clear edge." The Americans outshot Canada 35–18 and outchanced Canada; American forward Carisa Zaban had undressed a Canadian defenceman, gone in alone, and deked the goalie for what was perhaps the prettiest goal of the tournament. The difference, and the game's unquestionable MVP, was goaltender Kim St. Pierre. She was brilliant, and especially in stopping the American captain, Cammi Granato, on a breakaway.

But perhaps no one showed more courage on the ice that day than the referee who made the call she did at 59:01 of the third period. The Americans had scored only seconds earlier and had pulled their goalie. All was set for a tumultuous last minute of play, when Karyn Bye, two-time winner of USA Hockey Women's Player of the Year, was called for tripping. Hers was a flagrant trip all right, but few NHL referees have the gumption to call an infraction so late in a close game, let alone a championship game. Linesmen and refs, incidentally, are all female in women's hockey. And the game, though free-flowing and marked by several resounding checks that were not called, was by no means the "free-for-all" that *Hockey News MVP* described.

Still, it was a feisty affair. In its drive to acquire both legitimacy and a wider audience ("The hardest part," Cassie Campbell admits, "is getting people out"), women's hockey might ratchet up the intensity level, with predictable results. Everyone I talked to at the 2001 world championships—coaches, players, parents of athletes, other reporters—agreed that the speed, skill, and size of players increase every year.

After the Canada–Sweden game, I walked down to the so-called "mix zone" outside the Canadian dressing room, where reporters and athletes are paired for brief interviews. The players wore shorts, and their powerful thighs and calves spoke of long hours on exercise and weight machines. These are world-class athletes. They run, adhere to strict diets (even shrug off free beer), and are monitored by team officials throughout the year. They do not lack for strength and power. The only question is how it will be used.

"I am fearful for the direction of women's hockey," Therese Brisson told me. "In our league [she plays for the Mississauga Ice Bears in Ontario], we're hearing about concussion injuries for the first time. We're going the same way as the NHL." Brisson would herself endure a severe concussion and miss three months of play later in the year.

Cassie Campbell missed the final two games of the Four Nations Cup in 2000 because of a concussion; another player was knocked out. "Hockey," she told me, though it's pretty well what they do most days, "is not our living. If it should become our living, that may change. It may become rougher. I do fear that women's hockey could go crazy, too."

As I write this, no woman is paid to play hockey, though some, such as Campbell, have corporate sponsors. The makers of Cheerios breakfast cereal help pay her bills and support her work with children and in promoting the women's game. It's inevitable that female players will one day be salaried, and one has to wonder if their game will take the same bloody turn that the men's game did when amateurs were suddenly paid to play.

Whatever the future, I sense among these elite women athletes not just a love for the game, but a love for the game as they now play it. Their allegiance is to an original vision of the game—the one played on ponds in the nineteenth century—that's been all but forgotten.

Brisson played for a while on a women's team against a men's team at the University of New Brunswick. "It was a good experience for us," she said. "But the things men say, awful and mean things to each other. It was unbelievable. Is it a male bonding thing? I don't know." Brisson remembers, as a child of six, watching Team Canada players in Russia during the 1972 series. Again, she was appalled by the stickwork, the menacing gestures, the violence. "One of the criteria for selection to the women's team," Brisson says, "is poise." Like many on the Canadian team, she draws a huge distinction between men's hockey, especially the NHL variety, and women's hockey.

And yet the same code that rules men's hockey applies to women's hockey, though in more modest form. Campbell remembers a Swedish player blindsiding the Canadian captain in a tournament, and how quickly one of the Canadian players "stepped up," as she put it. She talks about "payback" and "taking her number." Brisson thinks the same way: "The only response to aggression that counts is to put the puck in the net. But if a certain player ran one of our players, the next time she comes in on me, I would show no mercy."

And then there's Canada's Hayley Wickenheiser, who was unable to play in Minnesota due to a knee injury. She was ranked by *Hockey News MVP* as the best female player in the world and "the game's most intimidating presence." *Intimidating*. Does intimidation have a place in women's hockey? My sense is that intimidation lurks in every hockey game, men's and women's, and it only requires a certain set of circumstances to entice it from its lair.

Someone once observed that 1992, with the announcement that female hockey players would compete in the 1998 Olympics, marked "the end of innocence" for women's hockey. Those who attended the Nagano Olympics—my brother Wayne, for example, a columnist with the *Ottawa Citizen*—remember all too well an early-round game between the U.S. and Canada, one that meant nothing, since both teams had already assured themselves a place in the medal round. In that game, the Americans came back from a 4–1 deficit to post a 7–4 victory. Here is how my brother remembers it.

"The Canada–USA women's hockey rivalry has sunk to new depths," he wrote in his column. "Of course, that just has more people antici-pating Tuesday's gold medal final—which is now taking on all the mark-ings of a bloody war." In that 7–4 game, an American player had allegedly taunted Danielle Goyette about her father, who had died of Alzheimer's disease the day before the opening ceremonies. Goyette, then Canada's leading scorer at the tournament, burst into tears at the comment.

If the unspeakable remark (officially denied by the Americans) was uncharacteristic of the women's game, so was the violence. Canadian head coach Shannon Miller said afterwards that the Americans were bent on intimidation and that some of them were "out of control." American coach Ben Smith denied such a game plan but did concede, "There's a turf war on out there." The Americans were assessed ten minor penalties and one major; the Canadians had nine minors. Wickenheiser didn't much mind the rough play. "That's the way the game should be played," she said later. "It comes down to who's got the guts."

Turns out the Americans did. The gold-medal game pitted Canadian speed against American brawn, and on that day, at least—the most important day in the history of women's hockey, for it marked the first time female players competed for Olympic medals—brawn won. It was clear to my brother, clear to Shannon Miller, that the Canadian team had been "playing scared," as Wayne put it. Coach Miller, he wrote, used the *F*-word to describe what happened to her team on the ice. "*F* for fear." A team that normally chattered in lively fashion on the bench had gone quiet—"They were very tentative, very uptight," said Miller. "I think they were a bit overwhelmed. And a bit scared."

Other players can smell that fear, as can discerning fans. Fear like that makes you ham-handed in front of the net, wary of going into corners, less quick to jump into the play. Your game turns conservative, peripheral, and such tentativeness only emboldens the enemy.

The lesson of Nagano was clear: When glory or money are on the line, all that nice talk about women's hockey being a finesse game, a purer game, rings hollow and gives way to older, harder hockey truths. Hockey played at the highest level is inevitably a game of courage.

In Minneapolis, the Canadian team still had its share of small, quick players. But the team also had size—six players weighed between 170 and 190 pounds. If push came to shove, the Canucks would push back.

After that first Canada–Sweden game, early in the tournament, I waited outside the Mariucci Arena for a cab. None came. Cabs, I would learn, are reluctant to pick up fares on Minneapolis streets. Called from a bar or restaurant, though, they come pretty quickly. And so I discovered Herb and Stubbs, a nearby bar-cum-eatery festooned with old hockey photos. Here I met Nancy and Steve, a couple from Guelph, Ontario. Nancy had "dragged" (her word) Steve to the previous women's world hockey championship in Mississauga, Ontario, and both were so impressed that they had come to the Twin Cities to watch more.

Like most fans I spoke to inside the Mariucci, Steve and Nancy were fed up with fighting and stickwork in the NHL, with huge players who make pro rinks seem small, with referees disinclined to call flagrant fouls. International women's hockey seemed to them an appealing alternative.

But here's the thing. Watching Canada paste Sweden or Finland gets to be boring after a while. When I made that complaint to Elizabeth Etue outside the Mariucci Arena one day, she asked, "What do you want, blood and guts?"

"No," I replied. "Something in the middle." I had ridden that day with an Ethiopian cab driver named Gazell, whose yellow taxi bore a significant spiderweb fracture on its front window. It seems that a drunken passenger, distraught over the fate of his basketball team during so-called March Madness, had hammered the window with his fist. Meanwhile, the week of the women's hockey tournament, ex-wrestler and Minnesota governor Jesse Ventura was making head-lines with this comment on his Vietnam tour of duty: "You haven't hunted until you've hunted man." Here was male testosterone run amuck, and men's hockey is often governed by something similar. I didn't want that.

Nor did I want stifling "trap" hockey, which clogs the middle of the ice and puts fans to sleep. The week I was in Minneapolis, Jacques Lemaire, coach of the NHL's then fledgling team, the Minnesota Wild, was quoted in an end-of-season feature, defending such tactics to an Edmonton reporter who had complained it was boring. "We could go up and down, lose 6–4 and you'll have a good time and I'll be out of a job in a year," he told the scribe. "My job is to win. If you want offence and excitement, go watch basketball." If stifle-dee and stifle-dum is the future of men's hockey, maybe I will watch basketball.

As for the women's game, I'm not sure where it's headed. Murray Costello, an NHLer in the 1950s with Chicago, Boston, and Detroit and longtime president of the Canadian Amateur Hockey Association, wrote the foreword to a book on women's hockey, in which he argued that the women's game could become the role model for men's hockey. He offered that opinion in 1990, just three years after the very first women's world championship.

Ironically, the women's game has historically been marked by the same shenanigans as the men's game. Women first played organized hockey in the 1890s, when outdoor rinks were lit at night by lanterns. Some women would recall playing in outdoor rinks in Winnipeg, and weeping from the cold, as jam jars filled with hot water were rolled over their feet after games.

One of the first female hockey clubs, the Love-Me-Littles, was formed at Queen's University in defiance of the local archbishop. Rough play and bodychecking, though frowned upon, did occur. In 1916 Albertine Lapansée, Cornwall's so-called "Miracle Maid," scored fifteen goals in one game, and when a player from Montreal tried checking her into submission, Lapansée dropped her gloves. To which the Montreal player replied, "I'll be glad to meet you after the game and we'll settle this the way men do." One reporter wrote of that match, "The war in Europe has nothing on these ladies' hockey games."

The Preston Rivulettes, a women's team from the 1930s, compiled an astonishing 348–2 record. Gladys Pitcher played for that team and told a CBC-Radio interviewer in 1991, "There was bodychecking, too, don't kid yourself . . . if somebody hooked you, you turned around and let them have it . . . somebody might have had three stitches here and three stitches there, but what's three stitches?"

Here's a *Toronto Star* reporter commenting on a game between Preston and the Winnipeg Eatons that featured seventeen penalties and two majors for fighting. "Hockey," Alexandrine Gibb wrote, "with a war club in your hands, is dangerous any time a player of either sex loses his [sic] head. . . . This isn't the first time there has been trouble on the feminine ice." Gibb was referring to a previous game in which there was so much hair-pulling and the players were so disgusted by their own actions that they made a pact to keep that particular game a secret.

There's a wonderful photo in *Proud Past, Bright Future: One Hundred Years of Canadian Women's Hockey.* It shows a young boy of nine or so in full gear with a Montreal Canadiens hockey sweater. He's leaning over his stick, on which his name, Ab Hoffman, has been inked. A slightly older figure skater, looking like a young Barbara Ann Scott, looks on, with her hands on her hips while sporting a pleasing smile. The "boy" is Abigail Hoffman, and she starred on defence in the elite Toronto Hockey League in 1955—until found out. Her coach sure liked the Hoffman kid. "I want Ab on defence," he reportedly said, "because he hands out solid checks and plays a rough game." Hoffman would later become a world-class, middle-distance runner, breaking the Olympic record in 1972 for the 800 metres and finishing one second behind the winner.

By 1990, though still excluded and still fighting for ice-time with boys' and men's leagues, women's hockey was a force in Canada. Where other competitors in world hockey could draw on 300 or 400 players, Canada had 7,500 registered female players and up to 15,000 women in total, playing the game. That year Canada outscored its competition in round-robin games 50 to 1. In the U.S., a similar revolution was marking female hockey: Four years after the 1990 world championship, registration of female players soared from 5,533 to 17,537.

In the meantime, women's hockey would go through a period of soul-searching. Was the game about speed and finesse? Or could you win by intimidation and crunching bodychecks? In 1990, international women's hockey lifted a ban on bodychecking. Administrators were convinced that if the women's game was to win recognition, it had to feature the real thing: body contact. But there was a huge disparity in ability between, say, Canadian or American players and the rest. Some players landed in hospital and bodychecking was once again banned in 1992.

There is contact in women's hockey. Lots of it. And yet ambivalence abounds. Some women like the rush that comes with a solid hit, but there is widespread fear that their brand of hockey could go the way of men's hockey, with bigger and stronger players forcing smaller players from the game. It all sounds hauntingly familiar.

As does this. On June 22, 1988, a player from Harrow, Ontario, named Trudy Banwell was convicted for assaulting an official during the Ontario championship held in Mississauga. Banwell slammed referee Angela James to the ice and separated the shoulder of a female linesman. In court, she was given a conditional discharge and ordered to serve 200 hours of community work. The Ontario Women's Hockey Association banned her for life.

In their post-mortem at Minneapolis, organizers of elite women's hockey had to be alarmed that the Swedes finished well back, and the Finns lost the bronze they had once had a lock on. Only the upstart Russians, led by the twenty-eight-year-old Ekaterina Pashkevich, a dangerous swooping forward who plays senior hockey in the Boston area, offered any cause for optimism. What is true of women's hockey has been true for a long time: Only a Canada–U.S. game gets the pot to boiling.

"Canada *Is* Hockey" read the T-shirt of one Canadian fan, one of many girls and women who had bussed down from Winnipeg for the tournament. What kind of hockey? What blend of ballet and murder? This is the conundrum facing elite women's hockey.

In February 2002, the Canadian women's team recaptured the gold medal from the Americans at the Salt Lake City Olympics (this after a Canada–Finland game that *did* get the pot to boiling). The Canadians were penalized eleven times in that final game, the Americans only four, and had the Canadians lost, I have no doubt the referee's inclination to blame Canada would have become the focus. As it was, the American referee became only a footnote. What I took from that shimmering game was the heart and vigour of those Canadian women.

12
RESTORING
THE GAME

I N SUMMER 2001, as is our custom, my brothers and I went on a baseball trip and ticked off one more major-league park. I was keen to see historic Wrigley Field in Chicago, with its ivy-covered walls and legendary bleachers. Like Fenway in Boston, Wrigley is a cathedral for baseball, but Wrigley wears its age better. There is a quiet dignity about the place, and hockey could learn something from it.

The quiet, you see, abets the dignity, and it goes the other way, too. Wrigley stands apart from just about every other ballpark in the big leagues. There are no corporate billboards anywhere in the stadium, no logos or signs of any kind. No Jumbotron blares rock music or assails your eye with video replays and neon splashes. When a player comes to bat, he is simply announced and a discreet posting beneath the scoreboard in right field lists his batting average. So the sounds I heard at Wrigley are traditional sounds: the *crack* of the wooden bat, a guy hawking peanuts, a young girl rising from her seat to cheer Sammy Sosa as he settles in at the plate and double-hammers his fist to his heart.

Baseball was played at this park before the National Hockey League came into existence. (Wrigley was built in 1914; the NHL was launched in 1917.) Fitting, then, that a place so bound up in tradition has rituals all its own—such as the one that sees a home-run ball hit by the opposition not kept as a souvenir but tossed in disdain back onto the field.

Here is another tradition. Hours before the game, patrons throng to the sidewalk patio bars and restaurants that fan out from Wrigley in every direction. Couples, friends, entire families will retreat to these same places after the game, as well, often staying for dinner. These ball fans dedicate the day to the game and Wrigley. The result is a party atmosphere that engulfs the stadium and environs and, especially, the bleachers. It's been that way for decades. Win or lose, Cubs fans are loyal. If they can't always admire the artistry of the home team, then that of the visitors will do. Wrigley Field, then, is a lesson in pure allegiance to a game. Winning isn't everything.

Tell that to Harry Neale. The colour man on *Hockey Night in Canada* broadcasts has a frank and learned take on the game that I often enjoy. But as the Scanlan boys were packing their bags for Chicago, and the playoffs were finally winding down, someone was complaining in a Toronto newspaper that hockey was no longer sport but warfare and boring to watch. Neale bristled in response. "If you don't like physical hockey," he was quoted, "and you don't like guys hating each other and you don't like guys doing almost anything to win, then you should turn to bowling." Never mind the resignation, as if hockey is how it is and cannot change. Never mind the like-it-or-lump-it manners. It's the comment about "doing almost anything to win" that set me to thinking.

Obsession with winning derails appreciation of the game's natural beauty and even of its most ingenious practitioners. How do you explain Leafs fans in 1993 chanting after a playoff game, "Gretzky sucks!!" and tossing programs, plastic cups, and miniature sticks at him and his fellow Kings as they left the ice? He did nothing to merit that treatment—only played inspired hockey that helped his team win and the home-team lose.

Look at Montreal. A grand old franchise has fallen on hard times and Canadien fans—spoiled by all those years of winning—no longer fill the Molson Centre as they once did the Forum. But what if Montreal were to emulate, say, Edmonton? The Oilers play the kind of fire-wagon hockey Les Glorieux used to play. The Oilers prize youth and speed and enthusiasm; the best match-up of the 2001 playoffs—as it was the previous year—pitted Dallas against Edmonton.

Small-market teams such as Edmonton may be hard-pressed to win another Stanley Cup, for they cannot afford to acquire or keep dominant players. Doug Weight, the Oilers captain, for example, left for the sake of a few million more in St. Louis. But Edmonton features both the best ice in the NHL and fans who appreciate the game. There's a little of that old Wrigley allegiance in Edmonton, and I hope it spreads.

For all the woes afflicting pro hockey, the wider game still exerts an astonishing grip on this country: When you tally the boys and girls, men and women, parents, coaches, and volunteers involved in amateur hockey, the figure exceeds 4 million. Enrolment in boys' hockey has dropped, but old-timer hockey is surging, as is girls' and women's hockey, organized road hockey and in-line skate hockey. *Hockey Night in Canada* remains the longest running show in the history of Canadian television. The game continues to flourish.

But if hockey is to shed its reputation as a blood sport, some new version of the game will have to be poured into the heads of boys and girls. The game children play can be modified, but what of the game those same kids watch on TV? The pros exert a powerful influence, so the game needs restoring at both ends. Can NHL hockey be fine-tuned without ripping out the heart and soul of it? What follows are some paths for the amateur and pro games to ponder.

Play hard, play fair. Soccer passed hockey as the most popular partici- pation sport in Canada back in 1990, no doubt due to many factors: changing demographics, immigrant kids bringing soccer with them, the cost of hockey equipment and registration fees versus the compar- atively minor costs associated with soccer, fear of injury in hockey— and the violence. In Quebec, hockey's decline amounted to a hemorrhage: In 1974 hockey enrolment hit an all-time high of 111,960. In 1990 the figure had reached a new low of 57,340—an incredible forty-seven per cent drop. (In girls' and women's hockey, meanwhile, sign-up quadrupled, from less than 10,000 in 1989 to almost 40,000 in 1999.)

Nation-wide, the figures were similar. Boys were playing less, girls were playing more. From 1983 to 1989, boys' minor hockey saw a

17.4 per cent drop in registration while registration among females rose 68.6 per cent.

In Quebec, hockey authorities sought to restore hockey's place in amateur sport by a simple tactic: Reward sportsmanship, punish aggression. And it appears to be working. The Quebec City region was the first to use the so-called fair-play system on a large scale during the 1988–89 season after the now-defunct Quebec Nordiques offered grant money to get the ball rolling. Today, more than 15,000 players throughout Quebec compete under the formula.

Gaston Marcotte, a professor in the Department of Physical Education at Laval University in Quebec City, is unaware of any league that has abandoned the fair-play system once they've tried it. He calls fair play "the best system available to protect our youth and the future of hockey."

The system owes a great deal to a sociologist named Edmond Vaz, who studied some 2,000 hockey players aged seven to eighteen in 1979. He concluded that boys were being systematically taught aggressive and violent behaviour, which had become an inherent part of the sport. Vaz, who would write *The Professionalization of Young Hockey Players*, wondered if intimidation, violence, and cheating could be curbed and even eliminated if sportsmanship were incorporated into the game.

An early version of what would come to be called "fair play" was tried at Laval University, where some ninety teams play in intramural leagues. If a team, for example, recorded fewer than four penalties in a game, it earned a point for sportsmanship; meanwhile, a team that incurred more than a certain number of penalties during the season was banished from the playoffs. The system worked to curb the rough stuff, and other universities followed suit.

Still, this radical departure from traditional hockey struck many observers as complicated. A simplified version was tried in Quebec City in 1987 and was also shown to reduce penalties; dramatically so in the case of major penalties. Peewees and bantams playing traditional hockey had five times more major penalties and twice the number of game suspensions as leagues deploying fair play.

Key to the system is consensus on what constitutes unsportsmanlike conduct. In bantam and peewee hockey, six penalties per team might be chosen as a dividing line. Teams respecting that limit earn one point; teams exceeding it lose a point. After research at the bantam level revealed that typically three players on each team account for fifty per cent of the penalties, leagues instituted bans—one- to five-game suspensions when players reached agreed-upon penalty plateaus. Coaches of much-penalized teams similarly faced suspensions.

The whole approach is described in a book called *Safety in Ice Hockey*, which includes a survey of seventy-eight Canadian university hockey players. The poll delved deeply into hockey's emotional physics. The players were asked how often they experienced the desire in a game to injure an opponent. Only 6.4 per cent said they never experience that desire; the corollary is that 93.6 per cent do (though, thankfully, most do not act on that desire).

Safety in Ice Hockey was published in 1993. Since then, fair play has been tried across the country. Invariably, it works. In Dartmouth, Nova Scotia, for example, the system was introduced in 1994 amid grave doubts. Parents worried that their local association was no longer interested in competitive hockey, that players were being taught to shy away from confrontation when that was "just part of the game." Five years later, fair play had clearly made its mark. In that time span, Dartmouth teams won four provincial championships, as many as they had won in the decade before fair play was introduced. More telling was this statistic: In 1999, player suspensions fell from seventy-eight, the season before, to thirty-eight—a drop of more than fifty per cent. The injury rate also fell, and players and parents said they enjoyed the game more. Referees stopped quitting in disgust: The dropout rate among officials in Dartmouth is one-third the national average.

Bill Schipilow, an official with the Dartmouth Whalers Minor Hockey Association, brought the fair-play message to the Halifax hockey symposium early in October 2001. A hockey father—he allowed as how the punky smell of hockey gear occasionally wafts through his house—recalled going to the local rink in the pre–fair-play days and hearing a coach ranting at kids behind closed doors, and every child coming out crying. Schipilow remembered two fathers in a nose-to-nose confrontation after a game, the raised voices an inch away from raised fists. All of it, he said, occasioned by a win-at-all-costs approach to hockey.

Schipilow and others cast about for a solution and, in 1994, chanced across the European fair-play model, one that fosters respect, safety, sportsmanship, honesty, and integrity.

Schipilow came to realize that how coaches, officials, players, and spectators interact shapes the game. "If you go to the grocery store and the clerk makes a mistake," he said, "it's no problem. But go to the rink and everything changes. People don't approach the game as they do life." The repercussions can be dramatic: In Massachusetts in July 2000, a fistfight between a 160-pound coach and a 270-pound parent following a peewee scrimmage left the coach dead and the father later found guilty of involuntary manslaughter. In Canada, some 10,000 hockey officials quit every year—one-third the total.

The fair-play system requires that each parent sign a contract outlining his or her rights and responsibilities. Referees fill out post-game assessment forms, and abusive coaches are quickly identified and turfed. It all sounded straightforward, but at one point Schipilow looked at his audience with a steady gaze and said, "None of this is a smooth road, OK? You have to keep running up the hill with the ball." Translation: The old guard in minor hockey is not easily overthrown.

Schipilow was followed by Rod Bossy, brother of Mike, who showed a "Chevrolet Safe & Fun Hockey" video, featuring Bobby Orr. The greatest defenceman who ever played is heard to decry the hit from behind—"That's so dangerous and it happens all the time." Rod Bossy, who played pro hockey in Europe (where, he told me, only the Canadian players fought), suggested that parents ask their kids after a game, not, Did you score? or Did you win? but Did you have fun?

There are victories in the battle to restore peace to kids' hockey. The Minor Hockey Association of Calgary oversees some 12,000 players, making it one of the largest of its kind in North America. In 1997 the association implemented what it calls the turning-point program—one that emphasizes values, fun, respect, and positive development.

All players now wear a "STOP" (Safety Towards Other Players) logo on the backs of their sweaters. Players are reminded that "if you can see the 'STOP' sign on the back of a player you are going to check, you must hold up from checking him/her, as serious injury could occur." Players, parents, coaches, and officials also sign a fair-play pledge, acknowledging their commitment to the "STOP" and turning-point programs.

British Columbia has a system called "team first," which sounds much like fair play. "Fun team Alberta" offers kids the chance to play pickup hockey free of pressure. Other provinces have "speak-out" programs designed to boost sportsmanship. The "respect" program is aimed at curbing abuse of officials. After the Canadian Amateur Hockey Association (now called the CHA) introduced programs encouraging fair play and fun in the mid-1990s, male registration rose thirty per cent from what it was in 1989.

What finally occurred to many hockey organizers across Canada is that it makes more sense to operate their leagues in the best interests of the clear majority of boys, who will never play pro, and not for the minuscule number who will. In 2001, some 500,000 boys and girls were playing hockey in Canada. Of the boys, one-sixth of one per cent will get drafted, and most of them will be contemplating life after pro hockey at the age of thirty. They would join the estimated 1.2 million boys and men, girls and women who play hockey for fun in North America.

Educate fans. If the game is to survive with dignity at the professional level, fans must bring to the sport a certain level of sophistication and understanding. It's much simpler to debate who won or lost a hockey fight than it is to analyze the breakdown in defence that led to a goal—or to grasp the many subtleties of an impossibly quick game. The watchful eye is rewarded.

Professional hockey may have painted itself into a corner, peddling a watered-down product to a great many fans who do not understand the subtleties of the game. Ted Leonsis, owner of the Washington Capitals, calls professional sport a "fundamentally broken" industry. "Ratings are down, the love of the product is down, attendance is down, and yet, prices for ads and tickets go up." Leonsis calls his hockey team a "new-media" company, one that will live and die by its marketing and sales team. "You can't have your head in the sand," he says. Leonsis knew he had a loyal group of 10,000 or 15,000 people who would come to games. But to fill the rink, he would have to reach what he called "the non-hockey aficionados."

I'm not sure one can be a non-hockey aficionado, but never mind. I understand what he's saying. To get to those fans and educate them, Leonsis has revamped the Caps' Web site. It features post-game interviews with coaches and players and receives more than 1 million "hits" a month from Internet surfers.

But those of us old enough to remember the failed experiments— "Peter Puck" cartoons and the phosphorescent trail meant to help uninformed hockey fans follow the puck—know how annoying it is to be patronized. Like teachers who must decide whether to pitch to the brightest or the slowest, television producers have an unenviable task—especially south of the border. Do you take the viewer by the hand and explain the offside rule? Or do you presume and celebrate Mario's nifty little move at the blue line?

Marty McSorley told me that some fans are keen students of the game and appreciate, say, the penalty killer who shuts off a portion of the ice by his knowledge of angles and selective pressure tactics. Other fans have asked him after a game, "How come you leave the ice after forty seconds?"

Perhaps the key is for each of us to continue developing a deeper understanding of the game. Case in point: Nicklas Lidstrom, with Detroit, won the Norris trophy as best defenceman in the NHL during the 2000–01 season. Joe Sakic, who won the Lady Byng trophy as most gentlemanly player, had almost twice as many penalties as Lidstrom— while playing forward. This caused some to wonder why Lidstrom didn't win both trophies.

Here's slick St. Louis centre Doug Weight, on Lidstrom:

> You can't get the red line on him. You get the puck at your own
> blue line and he's two feet from you and he's matching your
> speed defensively. He's such a great skater that you have no room.
> I want room when I have the puck. That's everyone's game as a
> forward. Getting room, drawing people, changing speeds. You
> can do none of that with Nicklas because he's so explosive back-
> wards he's not afraid of you. I think it's a tremendous asset, his
> skating ability—which I don't think people notice as much as his
> great hands and his vision.

As he was the two years previously, Lidstrom was runner-up for the
Lady Byng in 2000–01. Sakic likely won the trophy because he's a
flashier player, with his bursts of speed and deadly accuracy around the
net. The cool efficiency of Lidstrom is harder to appreciate; not
enough sports writers who cast votes and decide the trophy winners
notice how much harder it is for a defenceman to play a clean game.
It's been almost half a century since a defenceman won both trophies
in the same year: Red Kelly did it in 1954 with the Wings. Like
Lidstrom, he recorded a mere eighteen minutes in the box. If the
scribes—and broadcasters—who chronicle the game were to value
quiet artistry, their audience might begin to, as well.

Loosen history's grip on the game. Dallas Stars instigator Grant Marshall
(traded since to Columbus) commenting on fighting in the spring of
2001: "There's a hundred reasons for fighting. And for some of the
things that happen on the ice, a fight is the only answer." Another
hockey man striking a note of finality and fatalism.

If hockey seems a closed book to many players, maybe it's because
so few players have actually turned to books. Football, baseball, basketball—their players come through colleges and some actually get an
education. Hockey players, including many born in Canada and
Europe, still come through the puppy mills of the Canadian junior

leagues. Teenagers struggle with high-school homework while living virtually the life of a professional hockey player. The few chosen by pro teams seldom continue their education. Small wonder that pro hockey players are prisoners of hockey's violent past: The only real school they know is that famous one of hard knocks.

For half the twentieth century, goalies' mugs were sacrificed, until Jacques Plante defied tradition and donned a mask. Hockey does change. But working against change are coaches who are incapable of change, and worse, who will not quit. The old men—who played in an atmosphere of barely controlled mayhem—still live, still shape the game.

John Brophy, the former Leafs coach who turned sixty-eight in 2001, is still coaching, in the East Coast Hockey League, with the Wheeling Nailers. Brophy is a send-in-the-goons kind of coach, or so he was when he guided the Leafs. His record of wins in pro hockey is second only to that of Scotty Bowman's NHL record—proof, perhaps, that goonery in hockey (as currently played) can work.

Don Cherry, meanwhile, went behind the bench in fall 2001 to coach the woeful team he then co-owned—the Mississauga Ice Dogs of the Ontario Hockey League. Cherry is sixty-seven. He helped fill rinks in the league that year; he also ensures that an old vision of the game endures. We skate in the path of our hockey ancestors, and though the equipment has changed, along with the rules and much else, the mindset remains locked in place. Sometimes I have to stop and remind myself how young hockey is: Pro hockey is only about eighty-five years old—call it one enduring man's lifespan.

But surely some holy tenets of hockey no longer apply, such as the one that says unless you respond to violence, you're branded a coward. John Ziegler, the former NHL president, once countered critics of fighting in the NHL by noting that basketball, baseball, and football have not managed to eliminate fighting (though the scale of fighting bears no comparison). In those sports, fighters are automatically elim-inated and often suspended. Ziegler worried that were that rule to apply in hockey, it would be an easy matter for a lesser player to bait a star player with a swing. The star would have no choice: Respond or be embarrassed.

But what if fans applauded the star for turning the other cheek? Hockey players now take dives and feign injury, hoping to coax the referee into calling a penalty. So, in a very real way, World Wrestling Federation antics have already crept into the game. Visualize this scene: one player daring another to fight or provoking him, and the other responding with a mocking no-thanks gesture—hands up, palms out in front of his face, head turned to the side.

Remember what Bobby Smith said, how football and basketball players help each other up, how first base is a friendly chat zone. Hockey frowns on such behaviour. As a junior, John Ferguson once aimed a puck at a fellow player's head during the pre-game warm-up, when the player was spotted shooting the breeze with the enemy. Would a kind word or a respectful tap on the shins be so out of place on an NHL rink?

Maybe it will take someone with his own mind to break with tradition. What if Gretzky, before he retired, had rubbed his glove over Patrick Roy's head after an exceptional save? What if more had done as Bobby Orr once did, offering a "Nice play" compliment when Dennis Hull made a nifty move to assist on his brother Bobby's 600th goal? If hockey is a test of courage, so is defying tradition.

Here's another revolutionary thought. What if one team simply let it be known that no one on that team was prepared to drop his gloves and fight? That heresy was at least discussed in 1998 by Father Thomas Mohan, principal of St. Michael's College School in Toronto and head official behind the junior team, the St. Michael's Majors. "It's a very beautiful game and I feel fighting detracts from the game," he said then. "I'd rather resurrect the sport of boxing than promote fighting in hockey."

If fans and players alike knew that one team was simply not going to fight, what might happen? Mark Napier, the St. Mike's coach, offered barely cautious approval of the idea. The former sniper with Montreal is an interesting study: As a junior player he put up some hefty penalty numbers, but as a pro he was a Lady Byng type. Something, or someone, had changed him.

Still, Napier was not sure that flashing the peace sign on the ice would have the desired effect. He cited as an example an incident during the last game of the 1998–99 season, when an Oshawa player butt-ended one of his smaller opponents and no penalty was called. The only recourse, Napier said, was for one of his players to challenge the Oshawa player to a fight.

Modern NHL players can choose not to fight, leaving the task to designated tough guys. But should toughs have that freedom, as well? What if the bruisers formed their own union? The anecdotal history of the NHL is full of privately struck arrangements in which two players essentially agreed to stay out of each other's hair. Shack and Howe had such an informal arrangement, and Semenko had one with goalie John Garrett.

Oiler coach Glen Sather wanted Semenko in the goalie's face, and Nordique coach Michel Bergeron had instructed Garrett to whack Semenko if he parked himself in the crease. From the bench it appeared that Garrett was indeed hitting Semenko on the ankles with his heavy goalie stick. But those love taps, Semenko said, wouldn't have broken a pane of glass.

"Sammy, don't get mad," the goalie whispered through his mask, explaining that the coach expected him to respond. Semenko co-operated and moved out about six inches so as not to rile Bergeron or arouse Sather's suspicions.

Gordie Howe would sometimes issue warnings to players as he moved in to check them hard. "Unknown to a lot of people," says Howe, "many times I have gone into the boards behind somebody I liked or with whom I had an understanding, and I would yell, 'Look out!' *Then* I would drill him. That was my job, to take him out, but I'd warn him first. So when you holler at a guy and he knows he's going to get hit, he'll protect himself, put both hands on the boards to brace himself and ignore the puck. You get the puck, but you don't hurt the guy. That's really doing your job."

Howe had been taught that courtesy by Harry Watson, a Leafs winger in the '40s who met Howe when the latter was a teenager playing in Saskatchewan. "Look out, Gordie!" he yelled one time in Howe's first year in the league. Later in the game, Howe returned the favour and yelled, "Look out, Mr. Watson!" The Leaf looked over his shoulder and told Howe, "We're going to get along just fine!"—proof that private arrangements can counter the heavy hand of hockey tradition.

I wish I had seen this moment in hockey: two tough guys settling their differences with their hands, but in a creative, playful way. In March 2001, two players in the Quebec Major Junior Hockey League—centre Bobby Naylor of the Moncton Wildcats and defenceman Richard Paul of the Quebec Remparts—had finished their pre-game skate and were the last players to exit the ice. Both, though, wanted to be last off—perhaps superstition, perhaps ad hoc notion. The Zamboni had already done a few circuits of the ice but neither player was budging.

Finally, Paul invited Naylor to centre, where both dropped their gloves and a buzz of anticipation ran through the arena. No punch was thrown, though. The boys engaged in three rounds of rock-paper-scissors, a game they had likely played as boys. Naylor won the series and thus the right to leave the ice last.

Get serious about penalties. There might be less retribution in hockey if players had more confidence that fouls would be caught—and injurious fouls severely punished. The less faith there is in referees and league officials, the more players are inclined to mete out their own justice.

In their book *The Death of Hockey,* Bruce Kidd and John Macfarlane wondered why teams are allowed to ice the puck during a penalty. It's still a good question. And should a penalized team not serve the entire two minutes, as once was the case? The great Montreal teams of the 1950s would sometimes score several goals during a two-minute time span, and so the mercy rule was introduced. Maybe the old way is worth reinstating. (In 1998, Jeff Klein and Karl-Eric Rief would write a book bemoaning the state of hockey. Its title? *The Death of Hockey.*)

Hockey is a stickler for retaliation. One slash merits two in return, the gloves get dropped, and, like a boulder heaved into a pond, the energy ripples from there. Scott Young, the longtime *Globe and Mail* columnist, wrote of the night in the 1950s when Jack Evans hammered Bronco Horvath with his stick, leaving him unconscious in a pool of blood on the ice. Evans claimed he was only responding to Horvath's awful spear, and Young believed him.

Young lamented in 1959 that the NHL calls too few spearing infractions and penalizes them too lightly. "Some provisions of the league's rulebook are enforced," he wrote, "others sometimes are enforced, others never are enforced. If one took the Ten Commandments and decided to ignore the ones on theft, murder, and adultery on the grounds that they are extremely popular, and too hard to stop anyway, one would have an exact definition of the way the NHL regards its rulebook."

The spearing controversy had reached a flashpoint that year, after Andy Bathgate—the 1959 Hart trophy winner as the most valuable player in the league—had co-authored an article in *True* magazine, decrying spearing and warning that "someone is going to get killed" unless it were curtailed. In a piece called "Atrocities on Ice," Bathgate quoted Carl Voss, then the NHL's referee-in-chief, who called spearing "a vicious thing" and "a deliberate attempt to injure." The outspoken Bathgate went further: He named names. He listed Boston's Fernie Flaman, Montreal's Doug Harvey and Tom Johnson, Chicago's Ted Lindsay and even his own teammate Lou Fontinato as accomplished spearers. He likened the NHL to "jungle warfare" and branded Gordie Howe the meanest player in hockey.

What had moved Bathgate to write the piece was a vicious spear in a game against Montreal that had felled his teammate Red Sullivan. The players thought he was just winded, but when he passed out he was rushed to hospital, where the distraught Bathgate, along with his wife and Sullivan's wife, were all told by a doctor, "We've lost him." The spear had ruptured Sullivan's spleen. Another physician then miraculously revived the player by inserting a needle into his heart. A mild uproar followed Bathgate's article. Some NHLers conceded that, of course, they speared—but only in response to illegal interference. Boston coach Milt Schmidt excused spearing as accidental in ninety per cent of cases. King Clancy, the Leafs assistant manager, had heard it all before. "One of these days," he said, "somebody might even find out that hockey is a mighty rough game. But I don't know of any new tricks they weren't using twenty-five years ago." Official response was more stern. Clarence Campbell reminded Bathgate of his "responsibilities to the league" and fined him $500, then a sizable sum. That zipped up Andy Bathgate.

He was a goal scorer, someone the other team keyed on and tried to stop, by any means necessary. Maurice Richard got the same treatment. He was not a big man, at five-ten and 170 pounds, but he was ferocious when attacked. And he was always being attacked, which explains why one year, 1952–53, he led the league in penalty minutes, with 112. It all seems, in hindsight, a waste. For years, my brother Tommy had a colour poster on his bedroom wall of his favourite player, Bobby Hull, with blood streaming down his face after a fight.

When Peter Forsberg—who plays the game for Colorado with much the same fire as Richard did for Montreal—left hockey in the fall of 2001 (he did return in spring 2002 for the playoffs), perhaps he did the sport a favour. As an elite player with a rugged style, Forsberg has paid a mighty price: three concussions; surgery on his knees, shoulder, and ankle; and, in spring 2001, he ruptured his spleen during a playoff game. He's twenty-nine and already the game has ravaged him. Suddenly, the $11 million in annual salary and the chance to play for Sweden in the Olympics don't matter. Hockey would do well to ponder why a marquee player, and a courageous one, is weary of the war after just seven years in the NHL.

His father saw it coming. In summer 2000, Kent Forsberg—coach of the gold-medal–winning Swedish hockey team at the 1994 Olympics—warned that "The NHL has to do something. You put your life in danger to play in the NHL. This has to stop. It's not just about Peter. It's about everybody."

"No one complains about the violence of the game," Roch Carrier wrote of Richard-era Quebec. "That's hockey. For the priests in our seminary who preach love thy neighbour on Sunday, it's a real treat when the Rocket sends his fist into the face of another Christian. That violence isn't shameful; it's noble."

Times have changed, and our tolerance for violence is not what it was. Many players are reporting near-catastrophic injuries: During the 2000 season, Montreal's Brian Savage suffered a broken neck, Edmonton's Frank Musil and Calgary's Steve Smith came perilously close to spending the rest of their lives in wheelchairs, Montreal's Trent McCleary almost died from a slapshot to the neck. The game's most skilled players continue to be the targets of strategic violence. Mike Modano, the Dallas Stars best player, was asking in fall 2000, "Do we have to wait for someone to be killed or paralyzed?"

What if the way the game is called were to be radically changed, so that instigators of fights or the authors of stickwork were not only banished but their teams routinely made to play short-handed for five minutes or more? I am not the only one to be struck by the sudden acquisition of player discipline during the playoffs. Roy MacGregor makes a good point in *Road Games:* "If fighting is nothing but the release of frustration, then a very few players get frustrated almost every time they step on the ice and most players don't get frustrated at all. It is arrogant and narrow-minded for hockey players to presume their game is inherently more frustrating than others."

Suggestion: Get tough on all stick infractions—spearing, slashing, and high-sticking. First stick infraction in a game, two minutes in the box. A player's second merits four minutes. A third leads to ejection. And where a player has been badly hurt by a slash, let the referee use video replay to determine the appropriate penalty. If a disputed goal merits "going upstairs," as it's called, then surely a crippling injury—a hit from behind, say, or a kneeing incident that threatens a player's career—merits the same immediate scrutiny. There would be a great uproar while this was being introduced, but perhaps players would grow weary of the slash and find other means of retribution—like a hard, clean check or improving their play-making and goal-scoring skills.

Perhaps coaches could be given limited opportunities (once a game?) to challenge a referee's call, or non-call. If one coach is adamant that a penalty should have been called, let him make the challenge. But if the videotape supports the referee, the coach has to send someone to the box for two minutes (or more if that becomes necessary)—as happens with illegal stick calls late in games. Similarly, a coach certain that a penalty should *not* have been called can insist on seeing the video evidence, with the same risk attached.

Here's an idea from Dave Schultz and his book *The Hammer*. (It may seem rich coming from an erstwhile thug, but perhaps thugs know a thing or two.) Any illegal use of the stick, decrees Schultz, should be a five-minute, not a two-minute, penalty. Anyone who deliberately injures another player with his stick should be suspended at least one month. Any player who even carries his stick above his shoulder gets two minutes.

As for those who make a practice of the crippling hit, take away their licence as we do with bad doctors. Why, I wonder, is someone like Bryan Marchment, of the San Jose Sharks, still playing in the NHL? In 2001, the *Hockey News* called him "the game's top cheap shot artist." Between 1992 and 2001, Marchment was suspended a total of forty games for thirteen separate incidents—four for kneeing, the rest for checking from behind, spearing, headbutting, and other violations. In November 2001 he was suspended yet again for elbowing Carolina's Shane Willis in the head, resulting in a concussion.

Checks in which the hitter leads with his leg can tear ligaments and end careers. Marchment's hit on Doug Weight earlier in the 2000–01 season provoked the normally mild-mannered Weight and led to a brawl. Speaking in his own defence, Marchment refers to himself in the third person, as if the leveller on the ice were someone else. "It's a man's game," he says. "Not everybody's a saint. . . . Hey, if Bryan Marchment's not aggressive, I might be in the league, but does Bryan Marchment make the money he's making?"

From my old-timer hockey bunch came this idea to deal with a player found guilty of intent to injure. If his action puts a player out for three months, let the perpetrator also sit out for three months. To which I would add, a second such offence doubles the period out of hockey and a third offence merits banishment. A three-strikes rule would have put Bryan Marchment out of the game long ago.

Maybe hits from behind should be recorded throughout the season, so that perpetrators have their penalties increased by two minutes with every new infraction. By incident number eight, that player would sit for sixteen minutes and there would be no need to banish him: His team would see that playing him constituted too great a risk. The player would either reform or retire.

A friend—he and his wife Kathie run a horse-and-dairy farm north of Kingston—read *Grace Under Fire* in manuscript form. Francis Groenewegen would read a portion, go out to the cow barn, and cogitate. Here is what came to Francis as he sat beside the milking machines and took in the sweet smell of fresh milk: Let hockey punishment reflect both the sin and the sinner.

The system might work like this. Have the players, or their reps, decide on a sliding scale at year's end, with each player assigned a rating according to his penalty minutes the previous season. A Level I player might have been lightly penalized; Level II players more so; Level III players were habitual fighters; Level IV players were guilty of attempt to injure. A Level III player who instigates a fight with a Level I star player might be suspended, and one of his own team's elite players would sit in the box for five minutes. The system sounds complicated, but it's not, and it might be worth a try.

Scott Young was urging, back in 1974, that hockey emulate basketball's "foul-out" system. Basketball players foul out of the game after a certain number of infractions; players "in foul trouble" must be used judiciously, and the more trouble they're in, the more likely they are to sit on the bench. Young's idea was to clean up amateur hockey, so that boys don't emulate the pros. Give, for example, game misconducts for fighting; hand out multiple-game suspensions for stick-swinging.

Minor players who amass more than twenty minutes in a season for slashing, spearing, roughing, boarding, or fighting would enjoy the rest of the season from the stands.

Some observers have suggested that pro hockey emulate baseball, football, and basketball—and have referees and linesmen travel in teams.

And if a simple ban on fighting has worked in American-college and Canadian-university hockey, might it not also work in the NHL? William R. McMurtry is convinced it's worth a try. Author of the one-man task force into hockey violence in 1974 (the forty-page document was called *Investigation and Inquiry Into Violence in Amateur Hockey*), McMurtry was no academic, eyeing hockey from some great height. He won an intercollegiate middleweight boxing title and played both hockey and rugby at Royal Military College in Kingston. He sustained some twenty fractures, separations, and ligament tears while playing twenty-five years of contact sports.

McMurtry's report, a distillation of 1,256 pages of evidence, followed extensive interviews—with executives at the amateur and professional levels, professional and junior coaches, and, significantly, numerous professional players, some then still active, some retired, including Bobby Hull, Bob Baun, and the now-deceased Carl Brewer and Billy Harris.

McMurtry was, and is, convinced that hockey players can switch off the testosterone when forced to. "We played hockey in a local league in Kingston when I was at RMC," he says, "and in one game against the Kingston police team I was in three fights. I was in fights all the time. But playing in intercollegiate games in a league where fighting was banned, against Queen's and McGill and so on, I was never in a fight. Nobody was. You'd have been suspended."

A game seemingly beyond policing can perhaps be policed after all. And that old hockey saw—take away fighting and the stickwork begins—also merits scrutiny. A *Hockey News* survey in 1989 polled twenty all-stars, and nine disagreed that a ban on fighting would lead to more stick infractions. Some players, at least, were convinced that when rules are enforced and teams are hurt by penalties, players learn to control their sticks. And their tempers—as they do in football and basketball. Mario Lemieux opined that "If the right people care enough about it, it will happen."

Some hockey purists remain convinced that a ban on fighting leads to more stickwork. In college hockey, fighting merits ejection from the game; a second fight in the season means a three-game suspension and a third fight ends that player's year. Mike Keenan, the veteran NHL coach now with the Florida Panthers, formerly worked at the university level. "I was appalled," he once said, "at the amount of stickwork I saw at the University of Toronto, where fighting was removed from the game and players were wearing face masks. In the near future, most players in the NHL are going to be wearing face masks and the possibility of removing fighting from the game—I'm really fearful of the stickwork."

Donny McClean, mentioned earlier, has a vivid memory of Mike Keenan, when the latter was coaching the U of T varsity team in the early 1980s. Donny was playing for Waterloo and was third in the league in scoring. During one game he got a goal, and at a subsequent faceoff, Keenan leaned over the boards and said to Donny lining up at right wing, "You're a dead man. I'm sending out somebody to get you." Donny did a double-take. "It was clearly a mental tactic," he says now, "meant to throw me off my game."

Yet Keenan may have been prescient in his remark about face masks and stickwork. Donny remembers that one year—after a Laurier player lost an eye—the league made full-face cages mandatory. "I never got whacked so much in my life," says Donny, "by suddenly brave and anonymous little guys." But whether players are little or large, visored or bare-faced, they should all keep their sticks down, or pay a hefty price when they don't.

Perhaps the cure for childish behaviour in hockey is the one long practised by many kindergarten teachers and parents. William C. Carey of Nutley, N.J. (home to Sandy Vigilante, collector of hockey-fight videos), suggested this in a letter to the editor of the *New York*

Times in 1986: To diminish fighting, deploy the countdown. Linesmen faced with two brawling hockey players should simply approach them and say, "Gentlemen, you have seven seconds." If the two fail to separate in the allotted time, they get an automatic suspension—"a time out," as the parenting books call it—which is redoubled if the linesmen must pry them apart.

How about pepper spray if the fighters really lose it? Maybe a net could be dropped from the rafters?

Don't be afraid to tinker with the game. Hockey was once a seven-on-seven sport, played without substitutions on pre-Zamboni ice that turned to corn snow by the third period. The game has been, and can still be, reinvented. Why not drop one player, so all hockey is four-on-four (five-on-five if you count the goalie)? Four-on-four hockey—as one sees in overtime—fuels offence, frees up space, and immediately involves the defence in the attack.

Glen Sather, now general manager of the Rangers, once said that new possibilities for hockey were awakened in him in 1978, when he and the Oilers made an exhibition swing through Scandinavia and he watched peewees playing in Turku, Finland. "It was the movement, the skills, the push of the puck that excited me. Those little kids had the right idea." Wingers switched sides, defence moved into the attack.

Twenty-three years later, we still have the trap, systems hockey, wingers patrolling their wings like dull beat cops. Where is the innovation, the creativity? Where are the hockey visionaries?

I wonder if the NHL could both curb fighting *and* introduce more imaginative hockey by achieving a better balance between NHL teams. Do as the NBA does: Share the revenue. Stop the pattern of small-market teams being forced to play defensive hockey (for grinders and pluggers come cheaply) and the big-market teams rolling out the offence (and all those pricey stars). Share the finances, share the finesse.

"As for the game itself, its decline is painfully obvious," Bruce Kidd and John Macfarlane wrote in *The Death of Hockey.* "Sportsmanship, skill and beauty have been sacrificed for profit. Professional hockey has abandoned the grace and style so natural in a skating-passing game because, as everyone knows, winning teams sell more tickets than losing teams, and if you cannot win the way you are supposed to, win any way you can." Those words were penned thirty years ago.

Roy MacGregor, in *Road Games,* nicely summed up the overwhelming influence of the hockey status quo: "Most owners merely wanted their teams to keep up the only way they knew how. Most referees merely wanted to get along with most players. Most players merely needed the edge illegal tactics could give them."

Glen Sather was proposing, in 1985, a kind of Banff School of Fine Arts for hockey players. In addition to hockey, young players would be exposed to dance, gymnastics, cross-country skiing, off-ice training, and a far more rigorous academic training than junior hockey players currently receive. No one went for it, possibly because someone would have to put up the money, and the current apprenticeship method—as flawed as it is—enriches the owners of junior teams. But I love the idea of at least some Canadian boys emerging from such a program with both hockey skills *and* an education.

In 1999, a select committee of hockey brains took a hard look at the Canadian amateur system and urged major reforms. One of the keys, the Open Ice Summit concluded, was to reduce the number of games kids play and to work on skill development in practice. In many Canadian house leagues, we're stalled in the old way. One game a week, a practice every two weeks. Europeans insist on a ratio of five practices to one game.

League play, with its focus on winning, will not teach boys hockey skills or creativity. Bruce Dowbiggin offers an amazing statistic in his book *Of Ice and Men.* A Swedish study clocked how much time players spent handling the puck in games: The centre, the game's dominant player, touched the puck for a total of forty-seven seconds. The defenceman and the right winger clocked in at five to ten seconds.

The design of rinks might also need rethinking. Bobby Clarke cared little for the well-being of the enemy when he was a player, but the Flyers' hard-nosed GM has taken a sudden interest in player safety, now that he pays their wages. He makes a good point about the glass around rinks. The higher panes have spared the fans from injury but heightened the risk for players. Because the glass has to be more solidly braced, the boards don't give as they used to. In the case of taller players, their hips no longer hit the boards but, rather, rigid glass. Engineers can resolve this one, as they already have in some rinks.

Here is an idea from Phil Jones, the ex-Argonaut. "The crux of the issue [fighting] is that the regular season has to be made more urgent." Jones's suggestion? Make hockey more like baseball, so that winning your division really counts for something, and a sixteenth-place team can't sneak into the playoffs and possibly win the Stanley Cup.

Owners, though, crave those playoff revenues and would balk at this suggestion. What about a variation on this theme: A team that finishes first in its division only has to win two games in the first playoff round, while a team at the bottom has to win four? This approach might shorten that impossibly long playoff round that now ends in June.

Scotty Bowman's idea: Make more room in the attacking zone by removing the red line at centre ice. In other words, set the blue lines further out and make the defensive zones bigger, so attacking players have room to manoeuvre.

Finally, bigger rinks. Many like this idea. The 200-by-85-foot size, standard in the NHL, pales beside the European model, which is three stick-lengths wider and far roomier behind the net. Bigger rinks would let the little guys back into the league and even give them an advantage over the behemoths, who have less trouble tracking down small darting players in today's rinks.

Watch local hockey, not just NHL fare. This idea harkens back to the beginning of this chapter, back to Wrigley Field and expressing faith in the game—and not just the brand pitched on TV. Watch good hockey wherever you find it, including amateur hockey, collegiate hockey, junior hockey, or pro hockey one or two levels down.

Canadian Business magazine of April 2, 2001, tallied the cost of four prized seats in the Air Canada Centre in Toronto, plus a pizza, soft drinks, and parking: $1,360. Earlier that year, I happened to be north of Quebec City on a family holiday and ventured into town for a game (a blizzard afterwards added a Canadian touch to the experience). My centre-ice ticket to watch the Rochester Americans and Quebec Citadelles play elegant hockey in the rink that once housed the Nordiques: $16.

Pat Quinn was asked, when the Air Canada Centre opened, if he feared losing the blue-collar fan. "We've already lost the blue-collar fan," he replied. "I'm worried about the white-collar fan."

Fans who balk at the cost of live hockey—or the prospect of pay-per-view hockey on TV—might consider following the game on radio, much as we do baseball. Peter Gzowski reminded us that radio is the most visual medium, but the images the listener conjures are more refined than the real thing. "No one spits on the radio," he once wrote. "No one grabs his crotch and rearranges his privates"—or discharges the contents of his nose, one nostril at a time.

Austin Willis, the Canadian actor, was an entertaining after-dinner speaker at the aforementioned Halifax hockey conference, where he remembered his days talking hockey on wartime radio's *Hot Stove League*. He and Baldy Cotton, Elmer Ferguson, and Milt Dunnell would sit around a table at Maple Leaf Gardens and chat between periods about the game that night. Foster Hewitt, of course, called the play-by-play. Willis and the other three commentators would watch the game live *and* listen to Hewitt, and the discordance between what they saw and what they heard was sometimes striking. Hewitt transformed every game, even the dull ones, into a dramatic struggle for supremacy. "One night," said Willis, "Baldy Cotton whispered to me, 'I wonder what rink *he's* at!'"

Let kids be kids. Vancouver Sun sports columnist Gary Mason stirred the hockey pot in fall 2001, when he identified the reason that Europe, not Canada, is producing the most skilled hockey players in the world. It's because we toss a few kids into the pressure-cooker at the age of nine and ignore all the rest.

Mason spoke with the director of hockey development for the Canadian Hockey Association, Johnny Misley, whom he called "one of the smartest thinkers on hockey in the country. He has seen more research, been in more of Europe's rinks, been part of more summits and inquiries into the game than almost anyone around. He knows what he's talking about."

Misley decried the Canadian system that essentially makes binding, and often flawed, decisions about a player's ability when the child is still in atom hockey. Supposedly separating wheat from chaff, coaches hold tryouts and tell one boy he's got the right stuff (join my rep team) and "cuts" the rest (go play house league). The system is not only hurtful but fuels the high dropout rate that plagues minor hockey. House-league players suffer from less ice-time, less instruction, and often fail to develop; rep kids, meanwhile, learn that hockey is about pressure and travel and practices at dawn. Hockey most certainly is not about fun.

The Swedes, said Misley, "prepare their kids to peak athletically in their early twenties. In Canada, we do it by peewee." Unfortunately, the real power in minor hockey lies not with Misley and the CHA but with provincial associations—who seem determined to go on separating nine-year-old wheat from nine-year-old chaff, with the nod always going to the biggest kernels.

Murray Costello played in the NHL in the 1950s and was for many years president of the Canadian Hockey Association. Costello, then, understands hockey at both the amateur and professional levels. His suggestion? Stop the NHL from drafting eighteen-year-olds. Costello argues that by offering million-dollar contracts to teenagers, the NHL exerts pressure on amateur hockey that reaches down into the peewee level. A twelve-year-old who catches the eye of a scout or agent suddenly becomes a hot property, and the atmosphere around that boy becomes charged.

Mark Recchi, the slick right winger with the Flyers, was twenty-nine in 1997 and still with Montreal when he was quoted in a magazine article entitled "Can the Game We Love Survive?" The big change that

Recchi observed in hockey concerned the impact of money on players, owners, coaches, parents, and fans. Lost, he noted, is respect.

That erosion of respect, Recchi is convinced, begins in junior hockey, when a first-round draft pick suddenly sees enough money in his bank account to put a sports car in his driveway and Armani suits in his closet. An attitude develops in that boy's mind, says Recchi. "It's a 'me' mentality, and it wasn't there just a few years ago."

Consider the example of Ilya Kovalchuk, chosen first in the 2001 NHL draft pick by Atlanta. Igor Tuzik, general manager of Russia's team at the 2001 world championship in Germany, described him thus: "He's very strong and aggressive and he's focussed when he plays, but he's a typical modern hockey player. He thinks of himself more than the team. That's what we call a modern player." At the World Under-17 Tournament in Timmins, Ontario in 2000, Kovalchuk notched ten goals and four assists in six games. Afterwards, the Hockey Hall of Fame meekly asked for one of his sticks. Imagine what all this adulation does to one who is still more boy than man.

We take our hockey seriously in this country, so much so that the seriousness of the pro game filters down, tainting a kids' game meant to be fun. I love the story that follows. In *A Wilderness Called Home*, the author, Charles Wilkins, recounts the experience of Jari Sarkka, who taught at the Summer Beaver Reserve in northern Ontario. Sarkka describes the community's historic tradition of playing a game of shinny each year in late November, after the lake freezes. Every villager capable of playing gets out there, with sometimes fifty players a side. There are no goalies; the game is simply one of puck possession. At times, said Sarkka, "a single player would break free and skate a kilometre or more up the lake, swooping and teasing as the others followed in a scattered parade."

Sarkka now coaches minor hockey in Thunder Bay. "If you could somehow bottle the spirit of the way they played the game at Summer Beaver," he told Wilkins, "you could use it to cure almost anything that's wrong with contemporary organized hockey."

Red Storey, who refereed in the NHL in the 1950s, has a cure of his own: Ban parents from arenas. Hockey parents, he is convinced, pressure their kids, who are "over-dressed, over-coached, over-supervised, and they're not having any fun, so they quit." Storey tells parents, "Supply the equipment, supply everything, and drive your kid to the arena. But then go home and leave him be."

One day in January 2002, I did just that. On a weekday holiday from school, one of Kurt's pals organized an impromptu game of shinny at Harold Harvey Arena. The boys wore light equipment—only helmets, gloves, and skates—and, free of coaches and referees and parents, played their own game. I dropped Kurt off and he made his own way home, the skates hanging on his stick and set on one shoulder as they walked in a group through the snow. For days afterwards, he talked about that hour in the arena, what pleasure it gave, how free and easy it was. How they laughed. The score, he said, was a million to a million.

EPILOGUE

WELL. WHY *IS* HOCKEY SOMETIMES SO VIOLENT?

The question is much more complex than I had imagined. Each act of hockey violence has its own genesis. Some violence, or at least the threat of it, even makes a kind of sense—given how the NHL rulebook is so loosely interpreted. Otherwise an easy target, Gretzky needed Semenko for his talent to bloom. And in many ways, the modern game is safer, the fighting—though more common—is more predictable and largely confined to specialists; no more donnybrooks. (Though gang warfare might return: Two games in December 2001— Calgary–Anaheim and Los Angeles–Ottawa—had moments when every player on the ice was brawling. Goalies fought each other; goons stalked stars; one player even left the bench to join the brouhaha. This was either an aberration or a return to old values.)

What is incontestable is that some rough stuff is petty and staged: a player who has been a healthy scratch for six games will often, once back in the lineup, fight (on little pretext) to show desire and impress the coach. There is yet another kind of violence rooted in loss of control or a wish—a casual, malicious desire—to put the other guy out of action. A rock-hard elbow to the head. Butt-end in the eye. Knee on knee. The common refrain heard in pro dressing rooms is that respect has gone out the window—as if this was new. It is not. What is true in hockey has been true for more than a century: Violence occurs because the penalties are so light.

The violence is condoned.

No one element fuels hockey hysteria. It requires synchronicity— tacit agreement among those who watch, those who play, and those who govern play. Owners and players, coaches, fans, and referees are all complicit in creating an atmosphere in rinks that paves the way for hockey violence in its myriad forms.

For all its brief history, hockey has gathered vested interests, many of them opposed. Star players and their agents want free and open ice. Fill those nets. Owners and advertisers want packed houses and continental television contracts. Fill those seats. Coaches and fans both want wins. Fill those victory-parade fire trucks. Referees want some measure of control but no controversy, and thus swallow their whistles—for who wants striped-shirts deciding things? What striped-shirt wants the job?

It's a tricky business accommodating all those interests. And the power is shared badly, with owners and players most empowered, fans much less, coaches and referees least. But when the bargain tilts towards murder and cares too little for ballet, the bargain becomes a Faustian one, unworthy of a great game. Even were only one of the major stakeholders to rethink, hockey could curb the unseemly violence.

Belligerence is good box office, and owners have known it a long time. "The late Tex Rickard brought hockey to Madison Square Garden. . . ." wrote Robert Lewis Taylor in the *New Yorker* in 1947.

> Rickard saw in hockey a heartier version of his favourite sports—boxing and wrestling—and worked hard to capitalize on its bone-crushing aspects. He believed that a fight between two men was interesting but that it was more interesting if they were provided with clubs. With his experienced promoter's eye, he saw, too, that group exercises of this sort could be highly entertaining. As the crowds filed into the Garden for a game, he would send fleets of ambulances, their sirens wide open, screeching up the nearby curbs to await the outbreak of hostilities inside. He encouraged the players to fill those vehicles as rapidly as possible.

NHL owners and league brass today piously deny what Rickard and Frank Selke and Conn Smythe freely admitted decades ago. Listen to

John Ziegler, the former NHL president, as he addressed a U.S. Congressional hearing in November 1980. An Ohio Democrat had introduced the *Sports Violence Act,* legislation that would have penalized any athlete in any sport who engaged in "unreasonably violent" activity. Offenders would have been liable to a $5,000 fine, one year in jail, or both. Spokesmen from North America's major sports— football, baseball, basketball, and hockey—were invited to address the Subcommittee on Crime.

Ziegler rightly complained that "unreasonably violent" makes for a slippery definition, which is probably why the legislation faded into oblivion. But Ziegler's remarks suggest that he either knew little of hockey history or accepted a whitewashed version. "There have been so few prosecutions [in hockey]," he testified, "because there have been so few instances in hockey which would warrant assault or aggravated assault prosecutions. The facts just do not support the fictitious allegation that hockey is engulfed in some sort of epidemic of criminal violence." He's technically correct: A century of violence saw one player spend a few hours in jail. Yet no sport sheds blood the way hockey does, so Ziegler's claim for hockey innocence rings hollow.

Many current owners spout platitudes about how fighting, though regrettable, must be allowed lest players resort to spearing and high-sticking. Implicit is that beating a man with your hands is nobler and safer than clubbing him with your stick. Better the fist than the spear, as if the fist could banish the spear. Yet stickwork and fisticuffs have coexisted for all of hockey history.

Some owners may personally find the violence abhorrent. But that doesn't mean they're about to ban fighting and risk losing the fans who like it—even when the players themselves request a ban.

In 1975 the National Hockey League Players' Association (NHLPA) urged the league to consider a trial year of a ban on hockey fighting. Each player who threw a punch would be banished from that game and the one to follow, with more suspensions for repeat offenders. The NHLPA reps voted twenty to four in favour of the plan and presented it to a June meeting of the owners. The proposal was flatly rejected.

Three years later, the NHL commissioned a major study of injuries and found that forwards were at lower risk than defencemen, with goalies most vulnerable of all. Players on a team leading in score were also more vulnerable. The report's major recommendation was for a larger ice surface. Since that time, the vast majority of teams have built new rinks. Not one is bigger.

Belligerence pays, and players know that, too. In the 2000–01 season, Leafs winger Gary Valk notched eight goals and seventeen assists. His teammate Tie Domi recorded thirteen goals and seven assists—hefty numbers for him. Both are capable defensive players, but Valk is the more reliable. Valk earned $600,000; Domi pulled in $1.4 million. Only Domi's prowess with his fists explains the huge discrepancy.

Enforcers would have us believe that justice is meted out on the ice—not by referees, who cannot catch every slight—but by each team's town marshal and his deputies. If that system ever worked to control the mayhem (and history tells me it did not, though not for lack of trying), it does no longer. NHL teams—now a bloated thirty in number—can typically ice at least two boxers each. So pretty well the same sixty men demean themselves over and over again, with fewer than ten per cent of players responsible for ninety per cent of the fights. The boxing is highly predictable, coming to a virtual stop in the playoffs.

Malice in hockey is grotesque, in part because it's so ubiquitous. After the hockey conference in Halifax, I boarded a stiff, old airport bus at dawn. Beside me was a woman with Mr. Magoo eyes—a New England librarian who was hooked on hockey research and who played in a coed league. I gathered that she is wobbly on skates, yet she had repeatedly been cross-checked from behind; a certain man on an opposing team found her an easy target. Ms. Magoo tried confronting him verbally, warning him that such hits are both reckless and unseemly. And when shame did not work, she countered in classic fashion. She saw him coming out of the corner of her eye, dropped low to the ice in a kind of splits, and her tormentor tumbled headfirst into the boards. "He never bothered me again," she said, sounding in her parable like every warrior who ever played the game.

And while certain NHL players never fight (they would be foolish to risk their million-dollar hands punching a helmet), they do push and trash-talk and thereby invite enforcers to fight for them. Most players, like most owners, do not challenge the status quo. Even former players long opposed to fighting (Gretzky, Dryden) must find it too lonely in opposition, for they seem to have softened their stand. I am told that of the men and women who sit in arena press boxes, two-thirds see a place for fighting in the game. "Hockey intellectuals" who think otherwise take a constant ribbing. Photographers record hockey bouts, and the battlers get their pictures in the paper; bedtime television offers news, weather, and sports—with hockey scraps invariably part of the highlight package.

Like a Canadian river in spring, the hockey current is cold and fast and deep. Few players dare swim against it.

Few coaches know how to. In fall 2001, York University was the scene of a day-long seminar on violence in hockey—and sports in general. Among the speakers that day: a criminologist with a keen interest in hockey violence; a conflict resolution specialist who described his experiences mediating coach–player–parent squabbles in little-league hockey; and two experts on hazing rituals. We also heard from Bob Bain, coach of the York University men's basketball team. I was intrigued by what he had to say.

For Bain, the key question is, "What constitutes violence? What happens if the other team takes advantage of your star, a skilled and passive player? How do you even the playing field?" Bain's instinct is to respond early in the game: Let the other team know you won't be pushed around. Bain called this "instrumental aggression." It sounds almost clinical. But one man's meat is another man's poison: One coach may perceive his team's aggressive play as purely "instrumental," while the other coach may see a message of intimidation and respond in kind. The violence escalates.

Hockey history is replete with examples of coaches either telegraphing or overtly commanding their players to commit violent acts. But, as Bain noted, there is no punishment for coaches who put their tough guy on the ice in the dying minutes of a 5–1 game, inviting the other coach to reply. Why, for example, did Bruins coach Pat Burns put out McSorley near the end of that game in Vancouver? And why did Vancouver coach Marc Crawford have Donald Brashear out there?

Nothing will change, Bain declared, until violence stops selling or tragedy intervenes. "When a player the calibre of Orr or Gretzky dies," he said, "then you'll see a change." Until then (and such a death in pro hockey seems inevitable), the coach in minor hockey will think like his counterpart on TV. That's because both the peewee coach and the NHL coach face the same terrific pressure—win, or lose your job. No NHL coach wants to be the first to blink, to be without his tough guys on the bench. Like owners, like players, coaches are loath to break with hockey tradition.

And too few fans really want to. Remember Conn Smythe's line. We're going to have to do something about all this violence, he said, "or people are going to keep on buying tickets." Smythe had a point. If the game is so brutal, why do the fans keep coming?

"You can't score from a stretcher," says Sandy Vigilante, the New Jersey collector of hockey-fight video. The sentiment seems almost light and cheery, as if hockey violence were a video game.

Is it possible to be an astute observer of the game *and* enjoy the fisticuffs? I doubt it. Many fans deplore the violence, as do many players. In any critique, two valid questions are always, Who benefits? and Who pays? Allowing the fighting to continue clearly benefits three groups: rich team-owners (especially in the United States, where fights are seen as part of the entertainment package), well-paid enforcers, and hockey-fight fanatics. Who pays? I would argue the game itself pays a terrible price for condoning violence.

When the lid comes off hockey, when the game is just about mayhem, I feel only revulsion. I remember a third-period brawl between Chicago and Toronto on December 7, 1963, when I was fourteen years old. The whole sordid affair—launched by Reggie Fleming pitch-forking Eddie Shack in response to an earlier spear—was shown on national television. We watched as every Leaf and every Blackhawk fought, on and on, and the worst was seeing Carl Brewer down, Murray Balfour on top of him at the door to the penalty box, so that only Brewer's legs poked out. Balfour had chased Brewer all over the ice and now he was laying on a beating, his victim either out or senseless, and Punch Imlach, the Leafs' coach, was trying desperately to haul Balfour off. Bill Fitsell has seen footage of the donnybrook, and he says that as the fighting continued a brass band at the Gardens played marching music. What a bizarre choice: martial music to restore peace.

Brewer would die in 2001, and they would say at his funeral that no one had fought harder to break Alan Eagleson's grip on the players' pension fund, no one had been braver or more resolute in his long and lonely battle to improve the often-precarious lot of NHL old-timers. But on that night in 1963, for whatever reason, Brewer fled, and for that he would be labelled a coward.

Worse, in a way, than that awful night of '63 were the playoffs of '68, when the Leafs—one year after winning the Stanley Cup and trying to muster some scrappiness against the big bruising Bruins—brought in Forbes Kennedy, a five-eight, 150-pound pepper-pot. The Bruins took turns beating up their former teammate, they bloodied him and taunted him and he eventually made a fool of himself. He looked like the knight in *Monty Python and the Holy Grail* who is still issuing challenges after his arms and legs have been lopped off. The film is funny; Forbes was not. He head-butted his opponents, punched a referee, and never played another game in the NHL. That night, hockey—as hockey can be—was pitiless.

In the '70s, it was Borje Salming—among the gutsiest men ever to don a Leafs sweater—who took horrific abuse from the Philadelphia Flyers in playoff games. Salming was the heart of the defence and, some nights, of the offence, so he was a target. It didn't matter that the rangy Swede could not fight. The Flyers cut and swarmed him, and he flailed away as best he could.

I can call up better Leafs memories. Darryl Sittler potting six goals and four assists that night against Boston in '76, when the puck had eyes. Davey Keon streaking in on breakaways (and not scoring, but never mind). The aging Bower–Sawchuk tandem sparkling in net in the '67 hurrah—and which Leafs faithful pray is not the last. The Entertainer, Eddie Shack, picked as a game star and tearing around the ice in a black cowboy hat. Gilmour the gnat, Wendel the leveller, swooping Mats.

But these other, darker memories are powerful, and I cannot excise them.

Referees in hockey are like judges in autocracies: Real power lies elsewhere. Referees' striped shirts feature such defined edges, black bars against white bars, but their job is all about shades of grey. They are mere courtesans who must be ever-alert to subtle shifts in the mood and thinking of royalty.

A trip is a trip in the first period, but not necessarily in the third. In overtime, and especially during the playoffs, a trip is almost never a trip. A defenceman running interference on a forechecker may be penalized one year, not another. The rules are written in sand.

Have you ever wondered why a referee who has just called a penalty skates *backwards* to the penalty box, once play is stopped? Former NHL referee Vern Buffey explained in his book *Black and White and Never Right* that an official who turns his back on a player may miss the player's "uncomplimentary gesture" and "show of disrespect" that "undercuts your authority." What authority? So tenuous is that authority that a referee takes care never to look a penalized player in the eye while skating backwards to the box; he looks to the player's left and right, so as not to rub salt in the athlete's wound. And the referee never points a finger at the guilty player, but the entire hand—so as not to belittle or aggravate the athlete.

I can't think of another sport where the referee is so abused and vilified. Buffey reports being assailed by garbage and all manner of verbal abuse, being punched and kicked by fans. One telephoned him and said he planned to throw acid in Buffey's face. During one game in the 1950s, when screens—not glass—protected fans at the end-boards, referee Red Storey called down the police after a fan brandished a gun and threatened to blow Storey's head off. But the worst abuse of all is abuse from on high.

Red Storey quit, famously, in 1959 after Clarence Campbell second-guessed him loudly in the press following an important game in Chicago. Campbell insisted that Bobby Hull was tripped by a Montreal player; Storey saw the Golden Jet take a dive, and after the season Hull admitted as much. Storey would join other referees who quit when the league hung them out to dry: Jack Mehlenbacher, Eddie Powers, George Hayes.

In his book *Red's Story*, published in 1994, Storey remembers an owner standing up at a meeting, pounding his fist on the table, and setting him straight about where the real power lies in the NHL: "We own this league," he proclaimed, "and by God you'll run it the way we tell you to." Clarence Campbell once told Storey, "I'm not the president of the league. I'm the manager for six owners and I do what I'm told."

Storey is convinced, as I am, that if referees were given the power to call the game by the book—starting in the pre-season exhibition games—players would quickly adjust. But Storey doubts that will happen. Too many NHL owners, he laments, have never donned skates in their lives. If owners are worried, they don't seem worried enough to consider reforming the game.

Michael Barnett is one who is worried. The erstwhile agent for several current and former stars (including, ironically, both Wayne Gretzky and Marty McSorley) and now general manager of the Phoenix Coyotes once warned that "One of these days, a guy's going to get the upper hand in a fight and he's going to land a bomb in the wrong place . . . and someone could die. And then all hell will break loose because everyone will stand back and say, 'How did we ever let this happen?'"

A few things, at least, are clearer in my mind now. One, there are as many opinions in this country on violence in hockey as there are citizens. Two, some degree of edge in hockey may be central to the mix. And three, the game can be played with all kinds of edge and still be a game about athletic skill, team chemistry, and individual creativity and courage.

The best hockey is world-champion and Olympic hockey—fast, intense games devoid of fighting and played on a wide surface with the pride of nations at stake. That alone offers hope for the future of the game.

And hockey—regular season, NHL hockey—can still be a beautiful game. I was at the Corel Centre on November 22, 2001, when Calgary came back in the third period from a 4–2 deficit to even up the game and almost win it in overtime. The game was exceedingly fast and rugged, yet cleanly played; Jarome Iginla of the Flames and Daniel Afredsson of the Senators (then first and third in league scoring) were the two dominant players, conspicuous by their acceleration, their imaginative play-making, their grit and leadership.

Then there was the 2002 Olympics in Salt Lake City that ended with hockey gold for the Canadian men's team. If we had all forgotten just how elegant, how tension-filled and compelling hockey could be, here was a vivid and lasting reminder. No scrums, no face-washing, not one fight. Just the best players from all over the world wearing their hearts and flags on their sleeves. And with the 15-second hurry-up faceoffs and the virtual absence of commercials during play, the game itself was bestowed a supremacy it hadn't enjoyed in decades.

I've aired all the arguments for and against fighting in hockey and I'm convinced that the game will never eliminate fighting, any more than baseball and basketball can. But if there is to be a fight in hockey, let the consequence also be meaningful.

The lesson of world-champion and Olympic hockey, of Canadian and American college hockey is clear: Where hockey's decision makers ban fighting, the bans work. The National Hockey League should *try* a ban—starting with exhibition games in the pre-season. And if sticks flare as a result, get stern with those who wield them.

May the version of hockey that this generation passes on to the next look a lot like the one I saw that cool clear night in the capital, and not like the one in which Shack and Fleming exchange breath-stopping spears to the gut. On any given night, the NHL offers both versions of the game.

"The game is better than the carny-spectacle fighting can make of it," my brother Wayne wrote me after the Ottawa game, which he called one of the best he had seen in years. My brother had it right.

And Ken Dryden was right, too, when he said that this book is ultimately *my* take on the game, that without some sort of answer to the critical question—Why is hockey sometimes so violent?—all I had was "a bunch of stuff." Maybe the critical question needs reframing. Perhaps we should ask ourselves: "Should violence have *any* place in hockey?"

I am convinced that were the NHL to ban fighting in hockey, with stiff penalties for those who defy the ban or who wield their sticks recklessly, there would be an immediate result. Terrific pressure would come to bear on referees, but in time they would find their way. The fighting would not stop completely, but there would be far less of it. That change, coupled with a European-sized ice surface, would free up space for the small, quick player, and elite athletes would no longer require thugs to ride shotgun alongside them; room to manoeuvre and enforced civility would liberate them and the game itself. Grace and fire would complement each other, not be at each other's throats.

In the meantime, it lies with fathers and mothers to choose what octane of Al Purdy's blend to pass on to their sons and daughters. Maybe the kids themselves will find the answers they need at the local pond or outdoor rink.

Donny McClean told me that what he remembers fondly of playing hockey outdoors as a kid was the shock of light when he came out of the dark, warm hut to rejoin the pickup game on the pond. How the best part of shinny was that older kids schooled the younger ones, passed to them and involved them, laid down the law about "no raisers."

The sense of smell provokes memory, and Donny recalled the peculiar tang that comes off wet woollen mittens drying on a rad. For him that smell conjures hockey, much as mulled wine and cinnamon sticks simmering on a stove can conjure Christmases past.

I thought of coming in from night games on the old outdoor rink at MacGregor when I was a boy, my feet purple and numb, my father rolling them in his large hands, just as I would later warm my own son's feet by the kitchen stove after a day at the Newburgh pond. Hockey has many faces, some warm and familiar and soft, others fierce and hard and terrible, and we choose the ones we like. We should choose wisely.

For many reasons, some of which I do not fully understand, I aim to keep playing and skating until physics rules it out—or the green Cooperalls disintegrate. Until then, like Nesterenko, I'll keep my aging frame open to chance and circumstance—a sheet of clear ice on a windswept lake, a blue sky and a cold pale sun, a small voice that says, "Get your skates on." Stick in hand, I'll lean into the wind, put on a burst of speed, and chase some unseen puck, sure that somewhere on the horizon an open net beckons: my own private, almost perfect, breakaway.

BIBLIOGRAPHY

Batten, Jack. *The Leafs: An Anecdotal History of the Toronto Maple Leafs.* Toronto: Key Porter, 1994.

Beardsley, Doug. *Our Game: An All-Star Collection of Hockey Fiction.* Victoria, B.C.: Polestar, 1997.

Beddoes, Dick. *Greatest Hockey Stories.* Toronto: Macmillan Canada, 1990.

Benedict, Michael and Jenish, D'Arcy, editors. *Canada on Ice: 50 Years of Great Hockey.* Toronto: Penguin, 1998.

Bidini, Dave. *Tropic of Hockey: My Search for the Game in Unlikely Places.* Toronto: McClelland & Stewart, 2000.

Bossy, Mike with Meisel, Barry. *Boss!: The Mike Bossy Story.* New York: McGraw-Hill, 1988.

Boyd, Bill. *Hockey Towns: Stories of Smalltown Hockey in Canada.* Toronto: Doubleday, 1998.

Buffey, Vern, as told to Soucie, Robert and Monty, Michael. *Black and White and Never Right.* Toronto: John Wiley, 1980.

Carrier, Roch. Translated from the French by Sheila Fischman. *Our Life With the Rocket: The Maurice Richard Story.* Toronto: Penguin, 2001.

Castaldi, C.R., Bishop, P.J. and Hoerner, E.F., editors. *Safety in Ice Hockey.* Philadelphia, PA: American Society for Testing and Materials, 1993.

Cohen, Jason. *Zamboni Rodeo: Chasing Hockey Dreams from Austin to Albuquerque.* Vancouver: Greystone, 2001.

Connor, Ralph. *Glengarry School Days.* Toronto: McClelland & Stewart, 1929.

Cruise, David and Griffiths, Alison. *Net Worth: Exploding the Myths of Pro Hockey.* Toronto: Viking, 1991.

Cuthbert, Chris and Russell, Scott. *The Rink: Stories from Hockey's Home Towns.* Toronto: Penguin, 1997.

Diamond, Dan, ed. *The Official National Hockey League 75th Anniversary Commemorative Book.* Toronto: McClelland & Stewart, 1991.

Diamond, Dan, ed. *Total Hockey: The Official Encyclopedia of the National Hockey League.* New York: Total Sports, 1998.

Diamond, Dan, ed. *Total Hockey: The Official Encyclopedia of the National Hockey League.* Kingston, New York: Total Sports Publishing, 2000.

Dowbiggin, Bruce. *Of Ice and Men: Steve Yzerman, Chris Chelios, Glen Sather, Dominik Hasek: The Craft of Hockey.* Toronto: Macfarlane Walter & Ross, 1998.

Dowbiggin, Bruce. *The Stick: A History, A Celebration, An Elegy.* Toronto: Macfarlane Walter & Ross, 2001.

Dryden, Ken. *The Game: A Thoughtful and Provocative Look at a Life in Hockey.* Toronto: Macmillan Canada, 1983.

Dryden, Ken. *Evaluation of Aigles Bleus' Hockey Program.* Moncton, N.B.: Université de Moncton, 1996.

Etue, Elizabeth and Williams, Megan K. *On the Edge: Women Making Hockey History.* Toronto: Second Story Press, 1996.

Fawcett, Brian. *My Career with the Leafs & Other Stories.* Vancouver: Talonbooks, 1982.

Fischler, Stan. *Bad Boys: The Legends of Hockey's Toughest, Meanest, Most-Feared Players.* Toronto: McGraw-Hill Ryerson, 1991.

Fischler, Stan. *Bad Boys Two: More Legends of Hockey's Toughest, Meanest, Most-Feared Players.* Toronto: McGraw-Hill Ryerson, 1995.

Fitsell, J.W. *Hockey's Captains, Colonels & Kings.* Erin, Ont.: Boston Mills, 1987.

Gaston, Bill. *The Good Body.* Dunvegan, Ont.: Cormorant/Stoddart, 2000.

Gitler, Ira. *Blood on the Ice: Hockey's Most Violent Moments.* Chicago: Henry Regnery Co., 1974.

Goldstein, Jeffrey H., ed. *Sports Violence.* New York: Springer-Verlag, 1983.

Gruneau, Richard and Whitson, David. *Hockey Night in Canada: Sport, Identities and Cultural Politics.* Toronto: Garamond Press, 1993.

Gzowski, Peter. *The Game of Our Lives.* Toronto: McClelland & Stewart, 1981.

Harris, Billy. *The Glory Years: Memoirs of a Decade, 1955–1965.* Scarborough, Ont.: Prentice-Hall, 1989.

Harrison, Richard. *Hero of the Play.* Toronto: Wolsak and Wynn, 1994.

Hull, Dennis with Thompson, Robert. *The Third Best Hull: I Should Have Been Fourth But They Wouldn't Let My Sister Maxine Play.* Toronto: ECW Press, 1998.

Hunter, Douglas. *Open Ice: The Tim Horton Story.* Toronto: Penguin, 1994.

Imlach, Punch with Young, Scott. *Hockey Is a Battle.* Toronto: Macmillan Canada, 1969.

Irvin, Dick. *In the Crease: Goaltenders Look at Life in the NHL.* Toronto: McClelland & Stewart, 1995.

Kendall, Brian. *Shutout: The Legend of Terry Sawchuk.* Toronto: Penguin, 1996.

Kidd, Bruce and Macfarlane, John. *The Death of Hockey.* Toronto: New Press, 1972.

Klein, Jeff Z. and Reif, Karl-Eric. *The Death of Hockey: Or, How a Bunch of Guys with Too Much Money and Too Little Sense Are Killing the Greatest Game on Earth.* Toronto: Macmillan Canada, 1998.

Lasch, Christopher. *The Culture of Narcissism: American Life in an Age of Diminishing Expectations.* New York: Norton, 1978.

MacGregor, Roy. *The Home Team: Fathers, Sons and Hockey.* Toronto: Penguin, 1995.

MacGregor, Roy. *The Last Season.* Toronto, Macmillan Canada, 1983.

MacGregor, Roy. *Road Games: A Year in the Life of the NHL.* Toronto: Macfarlane Walter & Ross, 1993.

MacSkimming, Roy. *Cold War: The Amazing Canada–Soviet Hockey Series of 1972.* Vancouver: Greystone, 1996.

McDonell, Chris. *Hockey's Greatest Stars: Legends and Young Lions.* Willowdale, Ont.: Firefly, 1999.

McDonell, Chris. *For the Love of Hockey: Hockey Stars' Personal Stories.* Willowdale, Ont.: Firefly, 1997.

McFarlane, Brian. *One Hundred Years of Hockey.* Toronto: Deneau, 1989.

McFarlane, Brian. *Proud Past, Bright Future: One Hundred Years of Canadian Women's Hockey.* Toronto: Stoddart, 1994.

McKinley, Michael. *Putting a Roof on Winter: Hockey's Rise from Sport to Spectacle.* Vancouver: Greystone, 2000.

McMurtry, William. *Investigation and Inquiry into Violence in Amateur Hockey.* Toronto: Ontario Government Bookstore, 1974.

O'Brien, Andy. *Headline Hockey.* Toronto: Ryerson Press, 1963.

O'Brien, Andy. *Rocket Richard.* Toronto: Ryerson Press, 1961.

Ondaatje, Michael. *Anil's Ghost.* Toronto: McClelland & Stewart, 2000.

Plimpton, George. *Open Net.* New York: W.W. Norton & Co., 1985.

Podnieks, Andrew. *Portraits of the Game.* Toronto: Doubleday, 1997.

Quarrington, Paul. *Original Six: True Stories from Hockey's Classic Era.* Toronto: Reed Books, 1996.

Richards, David Adams. *Hockey Dreams: Memories of a Man Who Couldn't Play.* Toronto: Doubleday, 1997.

Richler, Mordecai. *On Snooker: The Game and the Characters Who Play It.* Toronto: Knopf, 2001.

Robidoux, Michael A. *Men at Play: A Working Understanding of Professional Hockey.* Kingston, Ont.: McGill-Queen's, 2001.

Robinson, Dean. *Howie Morenz: Hockey's First Superstar.* Erin, Ont.: Boston Mills Press, 1982.

Robinson, Laura. *Crossing the Line: Violence and Sexual Assault in Canada's National Sport.* Toronto: McClelland & Stewart, 1998.

Ronberg, Gary. *The Violent Game: A Close Look at Pro Hockey and its Bad Guys.* Englewood Cliffs, N.J.: Rutledge Books, 1975.

Russell, Scott. *Ice Time: A Canadian Hockey Journal.* Toronto: Penguin, 2000.

Salutin, Rick with an assist by Dryden, Ken. *Les Canadiens.* Vancouver: Talonbooks, 1977.

Schultz, Dave with Fischler, Stan. *The Hammer: Confessions of a Hockey Enforcer.* Toronto: Collins, 1981.

Semenko, Dave with Tucker, Larry. *Looking Out for Number One.* Toronto: Stoddart, 1989.

Smith, Michael D. *Violence and Sport.* Toronto: Canadian Scholars' Press Inc., 1983.

Stein, Gil. *Power Plays: An Inside Look at the Big Business of the National Hockey League.* Secaucus, N.J.: Birch Lane Press, 1997.

Storey, Red with Snyder, Brodie. *Red's Story.* Toronto: Macmillan Canada, 1994.

Terkel, Studs. *Working.* Toronto: Avon, 1975.

Updike, John. *Golf Dreams: Writings on Golf.* New York: Alfred A. Knopf, 1996.

Vaughan, Garth. *The Puck Starts Here: The Origin of Canada's Great Winter Game.* Fredericton, N.B.: Goose Lane Editions, 1996.

Weir, Glenn, Chapman, Jeff, and Weir, Travis. *Ultimate Hockey.* Toronto: Stoddart, 1999.

Whitehead, Eric. *The Patricks: Hockey's Royal Family.* Toronto: Goodread, 1983.

Wilkins, Charles. *A Wilderness Called Home.* Toronto: Penguin, 2001.

Wilkins, Charles. *Breakaway: Hockey and the Years Beyond.* Toronto: McClelland & Stewart, 1995.

Worsley, Lorne "Gump" with Moriarty, Tim. *They Call Me Gump.* New York: Dodd Mead & Co., 1975.

IMAGE CREDITS

ACKNOWLEDGEMENTS

M Y THANKS TO THOSE WHO READ THIS BOOK in earlier forms and who helped shape it. Family: my partner Ulrike Bender (who, bless her, read it twice), my son Kurt Scanlan, my father Bern Scanlan, my brothers Tom Scanlan, Wayne Scanlan, my sister Rosemarie McClean and her husband Donny McClean. My old team-mates: Andy Raven and Gary Young. Fellow scribes: Tom Carpenter, Bill Fitsell, and Roy MacGregor. Friends: J.D. Carpenter and Francis Groenewegen.

Others assisted in myriad ways: David Battistella, staff at the Gorsebrook Research Institute of St. Mary's University in Halifax, staff at the LaMarsh Centre for Research on Violence and Conflict Resolution at York University in Toronto, Stephen Hardy, Queen's University professors Jean Côté, Hart Cantelon, and Les Monkman, David Adams Richards, Guy Vanderhaeghe, Lorne Flynn, Judy Spring, Brian Wilson, Jim Swan, Terry Walker, Rod Jamer, and Paul Patskou.

My thanks to Jan Whitford, erstwhile agent, now retired and still my good friend; Jackie Kaiser, erstwhile editor become agent and good friend; and Diane Turbide, good friend become my editor. If you followed all that.

Several books on hockey stand out among the many I read while researching this book: Ken Dryden's *The Game*, Peter Gzowski's *The Game of Our Lives*, and Charles Wilkins's *Breakaway*. Dan Diamond's *Total Hockey*, the hockey bible of stats, was, of course, indispensable.

I especially wish to thank Bill Fitsell, the eminent hockey historian, who gave me access to his considerable hockey library and extraordinary files and who gave this book and its author more help and encouragement than I had dared hope for.

INDEX